LIVE PICTURE™
REVEALED

LIVE PICTURE™
REVEALED

JOSH KARSON

Hayden
Books

Live Picture Revealed

Library of Congress Catalog Number: 95-81210
ISBN: 1-56830-272-X

Copyright © 1996 Hayden Books

Printed in the United States of America 1   2   3   4   5   6   7   8   9   0

Publisher	Lyn Blake
Editor-in-Chief	Michael Nolan
Managing Editor	Lisa Wilson
Developmental Editor	Beverly Scherf
Acquisitions Editor	Robin Graham
Technical Editor	Stuart Torzewski
Technical Assistance	Newsware S.A.
Publishing Coordinator	Rosemary Lewis
Production	STELLARViSIONs
Indexer	Tom Dinse

This book was produced digitally by Macmillan Computer Publishing and manufactured using 100% computer-to-plate technology (filmless process), by Shepard Poorman Communications Corporation, Indianapolis, Indiana.

ACKNOWLEDGMENTS

I'd like to sincerely thank the following people. From the Live Picture team, engineers Eric Santarelli, Philippe Bossut, and Adolfo Vide, who took the time to explain some of the more technical and hidden facets of Live Picture. Robert Blumberg at LPI, who gave everyone involved in this book a warm reception and provided me with a steady flow of LP-related information. TJWolf, Eric Petillot, and the other digital artists who helped illustrate this book and spent a good deal of time assembling FITS and IVUEs. Anders Rönnblom, whose music made long hours of batch conversions more bearable. Bernadette Jaulin, for being enthusiastic about the book and occasionally boiling water. Beverly Scherf, whose professional approach and highly supportive backing helped me through the rough early days. Michael Nolan at Hayden, who believed in this book before I knew I would write it and guided it all the way home. Eric Petit, whose great generosity made the whole process a lot simpler and more comfortable.

COMPOSITING AND PHOTO CREDITS

"Electronic Musician," "Sybex Multi-Media Textbook," "IBM Anti-Virus Package" by David Bishop, San Francisco, CA - phone (415) 566 5846 Photography by David Bishop

"Pollution," "Multimedia," "Clock" by Didier Boutet, Paris, France for the Image Bank - phone (33) (1) 4200 8844 Photography by Didier Boutet

"Retouched Building" by Atelier Fournier Schneck, Paris, France - phone (33) (1) 4314 9292 - fax (33) (1) 4314 9393 Photography by Atelier Fournier Schneck

"16.D." and "58.D." by Peter Greenaway/Andromaque, Strasbourg, France Photography by Jean-Louis Hess

"Choice Fruit 1," "Choice Fruit 2," "The Wedding of Brother Wolf" by Helen Hann, England - phone (44) (0)1 925 228 892 Photography for Choice Fruit 1 and 2 by Saul Gardiner, England - phone (44) (0)1 619 986 777 "Wolf" courtesy of The Image Bank, Manchester "Roman Floor" and "Clock Face" by Imagina (Architecture CD) "Orchid" and "Sky" by Metatools (KPT Power Photos)

"Rolex," "Poison," "Vodka" by Marc Harrold, Paris, France - phone (33) (1) 4202 0120 - fax (33) (1) 4202 4276 Photography by Marc Harrold

"Sacred Datura, Escalante, Utah 1976" by Joseph Holmes, San Francisco, CA - Web site http://www.josephholmes.com Photography by Joseph Holmes

"Welcome Fisherland," "No Box" by Ich & Kar, Paris, France - fax (33) (1) 4349 3216 - Internet Fishland@Micronet.fr

"Taxi Girl" by Bruno Juminer/Gérard Branchet, Hondo Associés Photography by Bruno Juminer, Paris, France - phone (33) (1) 4453 9703) Image processing by Gérard Branchet, Hondo Associés, Paris, France - phone (33) (1) 4262 4151 Courtesy of Marilyn Agency for models

"Tropical Darkening," "Red and Sepia" by Josh Karson, Paris, France - email jkarson@club-internet.fr Photography by Josh Karson Other photography: "Butterfly", "Cheetah Lying," "Cheetah Sitting," "Moorea," "Giraffe," "Parrot," "Red Tiles," "Turquoise Pool"

"Raychem Cable," "New Beginnings," "Radio Waves/TSI" by John Lund, San Francisco, CA - phone (415) 957 1775 Photography by John Lund Design for "Raychem Cable" by Greg Lee Concept for "New Beginnings" by Patricia Shrimpton

"Eyelid," "Nur Die," "Lips," "Julie" by François Marquet, Paris, France - phone (33) (1) 4380 6072 Photography by François Marquet Other photo: "Woman in White Bathrobe"

"Ilse on Motorcycle," "Florence," "Tefal," "Watch," "Paraboot," "Sonia," "Millesia" by Jean-Luc Michon, Ecully, France - phone (33) 78 33 02 35 - fax (33) 78 33 24 46 Photography by Jean-Luc Michon

"Balloon" by Uve Ommer, Studio 4 x 5, Paris, France - phone (33) (1) 43 44 68 71 Compositing by Josh Karson Photography by Uve Ommer

"Homage to Magritte," "Car" by Loïc Pénet, Studio Renaissance, Lomme, France - phone (33) 2092 7682 - fax (33) 2009 4295 Photography by Loïc Pénet

"Information Superhighway 1, 2, 3 and 4", "Blue Book", "Hachette", "Paris", "Young and Old" by Thierry Petillot, Paris, France - phone (33) (1) 4579 2860 - email tpetillot@pratique.fr Photography by Thierry Petillot

"Sleep", "Wind", "Dark Days" by Andreas Pfeiffer, Paris, France - fax (33) (1) 42 53 58 03 Photography from personal collection

"Sky Theatre and Metal Pizza Dreams #1 - Oh!," "Freaky Type 1," "Freaky Type 3," "999 Poster" by Anders F. Rönnblom and Mariann Eklund/Studio Matchbox, Sweden Photography by Mariann Eklund *Mac Art and Design* magazine subscriptions: fax (46) (8) 15 55 49

"Season's Greetings" by Bernard Rossi, Paris, France - phone (33) (1) 4239 8110 Photography by Bernard Rossi

"Meeting Jasiu", "Eva in Prague", "Letter to Nadja" by Jean-Luc Touillon, Paris, France - phone (33) (1) 4642 8111 Painting and direct scans by Jean-Luc Touillon Photography by Nadja Other direct scans: "Pillows", "Engraving", "Red Etching", "Old Paper"

"Stair to Heaven," "Cybergirl Dance" by Lee Varis, Varis Photomedia, Los Angeles, CA - phone (213) 937 3793 - internet varis@primenet.com - email LeeVaris@AOL.com - Web Site http://www.interverse.com/~varis/ Photography by Lee Varis

"Edith," "Optimistic?," "Debbie caught in Time" by Terri J. Wolf, San Francisco, CA - phone (415) 566 5846 - e-mail TJWOLF2@aol.com Photographs of "Debbie" and "Glass" by Jenny Gorman, NYC Photograph of "Gears" from PhotoDisc Paintings in "Edith" and "Face" by Terri J. Wolf

Contents At a Glance

HAYDEN BOOKS

The staff of Hayden Books is committed to bringing you the best computer books. What our readers think of Hayden is important to our ability to serve our customers. If you have any comments, no matter how great or how small, we'd appreciate your taking the time to send us a note.

You can reach Hayden Books at the following:

Hayden Books
201 West 103rd Street
Indianapolis, IN 46290
(800) 428-5331 voice
(800) 448-3804 fax

Email addresses:

America Online: Hayden Bks
Internet: hayden@hayden.com

Visit the Hayden Books Web site at *http://www.hayden.com*

You can reach Josh Karson at: *jkarson@club-internet.fr*

TABLE OF CONTENTS

PREFACE

My involvement with Live Picture began in August 1993, on the opening day of Mac-World, when my assistant brought me to a private suite where Bruno Delean and Robert Blumberg, co-founders of Live Picture Inc., and Kai Krause of MetaTools showed me an early version of the application. I was deeply impressed; in fact I though it was phenomenal. I sent a note to Bruno saying that I felt that his invention had the potential to change the future of photography.

While President of Apple, we were involved in the creation of desktop publishing roughly 11 years ago, first by helping Adobe get started and then by creating the LaserWriter, the first printer to use scalable font technology. Looking back, its easy to see that an idea enabled by some great technology has created an entire industry—desktop publishing. And here, with Live Picture, was something that looked like it had that kind of potential again. I believe that digital photography is soon going to be an explosive market. But this time it's not about text and graphics on laser printers. It's about true photo realistic documents being created by photographers, and graphic artists and designers as well by families in the home. It's also about publishing from servers and networks.

If you see that digital photography is going to be an important part of our lives, you will appreciate how important Live Picture and its technology are. For the first time, it is possible to design in real time with high-resolution images and do the kinds of things that people only dreamed of in the past. This is a real breakthrough. Only a few times have I seen a "light bulb turns on" type of product and this is one of them.

CD-ROM is another example of a technology that eventually turned into a market. For years people expected CD-ROM to take off. Then in 1992, Apple and a few other companies decided that we would build a CD-ROM into our computers and price that CD drive at cost. We chose to do it when the manufacturers could deliver double speed drives and when there were authoring tools to work with. This was exactly the catalyst that was required and suddenly the whole thing came together and a new market emerged.

Now in 1996, a similar set of circumstances is shaping up for digital photography. It isn't just that there is a way to digitize an image, or that digital cameras or printers that can produce photograhic quality prints are now available. It takes many companies working together, enabling technology, strategic pricing, and killer applications to stimulate a new industry. This is happening now with digital photography and as President of Live Picture Inc. I'm pleased to be in the center of it.

One of the unique aspects of Live Picture, the application, is that it contains several breakthrough technologies. The principal technologies are IVUE, which is about fast imaging off disk, CD-ROM and especially across networks and FITS, which stands for Flexible Image Transformation System, which is a resolution independent system for describing and rendering photo documents.

Last year we licensed the IVUE technology to Eastman Kodak Company. Working with Kodak and several other partner companies, we are enhancing this technology to become what a growing number of companies believe will be the next big imaging standard. The great advantage is that people will now have the ability to browse, crop, scale, rotate, and postition images in real time. Until Live Picture, that hasn't been possible with high-resolution images—at least not without spending hundreds of thousands of dollars on special purpose workstations. The technology is also ideal for sending images over networks because only the image data required to fill the display window needs to be transmitted, and it can be compressed. So, you're only sending over the network what is being displayed on the monitor rather than the entire image file. We believe that this will become a well-adopted industry standard, because Kodak has already succeeded in recruiting many other companies to join with them in supporting this new image file format.

So when you use Live Picture, you're way ahead because you're working with new technology that will soon become an adopted standard. Of course, in many ways the real magic is the FITS technology. It is this technology that lets you apply a 1 million pixel, perfect quality airbush in real time, or apply distortion with a brush and then progressively modify and even undo that distortion. Today leading photographers, graphic artists, and prepress professionals throughout the world are using Live Picture. Many of the top images for magazines, posters, album and CD-ROM covers, and even Web pages are being created in Live Picture. And while Live Picture is unique in its capability to let you work effortlessly with large files, in fact it is being used more broadly. Live Picture is being used by creative professionals to make complex or very creative images. It increases their range of visual expression and lets them create a new distinctive look. Live Picture users are doing things that that would be very hard or even impossible with any other application.

We've found that most Live Picture users already have and use Adobe Photoshop. So its important to understand that Live Picture works well with Photoshop, as well as independently from it. With our newest release, 2.5, we've made it even easier to take images from Photoshop and move them into Live Picture to do compositing and to apply special effects. It's also possible to work from scan to print entirely inside Live Picture. So Live Picture fits in with Photoshop but also stands out.

No company before us has developed resolution-independent photographic quality tools for creative professionals. This is a new domain and one that we will continue to explore. We aren't aiming Live Picture at existing products like Photoshop. We want to take imaging professionals in a new, fertile direction.

John Sculley

INTRODUCTION

Something big is happening in digital imaging—a new, powerful, and highly creative software package called Live Picture. If you are already involved in digital imaging, or if you are just getting interested in creating or manipulating photographic images on a computer, this is one piece of technology you should know about and experience first-hand.

My own contact with Live Picture goes back almost three years. I witnessed the development of the software from its beginnings and watched it grow to maturity. Writing the greater part of the software's first user guide, I worked closely with the engineers and Live Picture's French inventor, Bruno Delean.

Over these three years, I've given dozens of training courses on Live Picture. Some of the people I teach have never used an imaging program. Some have never used a Macintosh. Others are experienced users of pixel-editing programs, such as Adobe Photoshop. Yet others are Live Picture users in search of more advanced skills.

Through all this writing and teaching, two things have become apparent. First, people often have all kinds of ideas about what Live Picture can do. But once they actually start using the program, it's as if they're entering a whole new world. They may be reasonably impressed, astounded, or disappointed (rarely), but almost every time there's a realization that they're in contact with something drastically new. Second, I noticed that during the training courses, the same questions are asked, and the same areas and concepts require clarification.

And as with all software, many current Live Picture users are always in search of a new method or tip that will carry their ideas and creativity yet further. Something to help them to probe deeper into the software.

This book hopes to address these three areas. If *Live Picture Revealed* succeeds in revealing the magic of Live Picture to a larger number of people, and if it helps reveal some of its better-kept secrets to current users, then its goal will be realized.

ABOUT THIS BOOK

Live Picture Revealed covers these different levels:

- For beginners, Parts 1, 2, and 3 offer an introduction to the interface, tools, and layers used to create composite images.

- For current Live Picture users, Part 4 contains advanced skills, such as simulating movement, embossing effects, and luminance masks, which bring a combination of tools and layers into play.

- Simple step-by-step exercises using images from the CD-ROM supplied with the book walk you through a number of operations, such as silhouetting, selective color correction, and cloning.

- Key concepts such as masks and stencils are explained through the use of exercises.

- Sophisticated images created for actual jobs are used to illustrate many aspects of the software, such as distortion, gradients, and movement.

- Every chapter contains a wealth of comments and tips addressing the questions most frequently asked by users, such as the implications of resolution independence, how to distort and silhouette the same image, and so on.

- The Live Picture Gallery contains a sample of the work currently being done with Live Picture in the United States and Europe by some of the world's foremost digital artists.

- A brief introduction to digital imaging and a problem-solving chart are provided in the Appendix.

In the final analysis, by showing you the basic and the complex, this book hopes to reveal the very logic behind Live Picture. Once you've fully grasped this logic, you'll have all the tools you need to creatively solve problems not specifically addressed in this book, and to develop new, innovative ways to create images.

NOTE: When referring to operations normally performed with a mouse, this book refers to a stylus. That's because Live Picture's tools are pressure-sensitive, and using a stylus and digitizing tablet allows you to control your tools intuitively. However, the software can be used and the exercises can be performed using a standard mouse.

ABOUT THE IMAGES

When explaining an imaging program, nothing quite compares to using an image, and this book contains plenty of them. The Live Picture Gallery is a showcase for some of the most recent, beautiful, and interesting art created using Live Picture.

Within the body of the text, every effort was made to find images that eloquently illustrate the task at hand, and that are actual jobs created by imaging professionals. These images offer a glimpse into the techniques used by some of today's leading digital artists.

Additionally, simple images were specially created for the step-by-step exercises to help concentrate on a specific set of tools, such as the silhouetting or color correction tools. These simple images are also used to illustrate such key concepts as masks and stencils. The images are found on the CD-ROM provided with the book.

Many chapters combine simple images (used in the step-by-step exercises) and actual professional jobs (used as illustrations). This dual approach provides you with a straightforward, hands-on experience, while illustrating how the tools can be used to create sophisticated artwork.

ABOUT THE CD-ROM

The CD-ROM that comes with this book contains five folders:

- The Open First—LP 2.5 folder contains a demo version of Live Picture. The demo version contains all the features of a full version of Live Picture, but you cannot save, build, or print images.

- The Open Second—Instructions folder contains a quick demo of Live Picture. The demo is not self-running. Rather, it allows you to jump right into Live Picture and experience it first-hand without even picking up the book.

- The Copy me to Hard Drive folder contains FITS files. These files are used both in the quick demo and in the step-by-step exercises contained in the book. When an exercise requires that you open a FITS file, you'll find it in this folder. Copy this folder to your hard drive to work faster.

NOTE: To open a FITS file, the associated IVUE files are required. The IVUE files are on the CD-ROM. Insert the CD-ROM in your drive before you open a FITS file.

- The IVUE folder contains IVUE images. These images are used in the quick demo and in the exercises contained in the book. When an exercise requires that you open an IVUE image, you'll find it located in this folder. Also, you can use the IVUE files to create your own composites.

NOTE: All the IVUE files contained in this folder are compressed using JPEG QuickTime. This allows for faster viewing and manipulation.

- The Photographic Essay folder contains an essay by photographer Joseph Holmes entitled "Editing Photographic Tone and Color in Live Picture." This paper is an addition to the book, and its scope goes beyond Live Picture. It should prove of great interest to photographers and anyone else interested in modifying and controlling color in photographic images.

Important: All the images and composites contained on this CD-ROM can be used freely for the purpose of learning Live Picture. The images and composites cannot be redistributed, sold, or used for commercial purposes.

PART

i

WHAT'S SPECIAL ABOUT LIVE PICTURE?

Throughout this book, you'll have the opportunity to experience Live Picture first-hand. But before you actually begin to use the software, it's interesting to know the capabilities and features that make Live Picture something truly special. This chapter summarizes those features in "A Revolution in Digital Imaging."

This chapter also contains one section devoted to digital imaging newcomers, Adobe Photoshop users, and Live Picture users, respectively. In these sections, Live Picture is dealt with from each perspective.

A REVOLUTION IN DIGITAL IMAGING

In product literature, magazine articles, or trade show conversations, you may have heard the term revolutionary associated with Live Picture. Why?

Live Picture is based on two new file formats: IVUE, and more importantly, FITS. IVUE is an extremely efficient file format that lends itself to FITS in terms of file handling, and contributes to speed. FITS is the first technology capable of describing composite images in resolution-independent form. As an analogy, PostScript was the first language to describe text and line art in resolution-independent form. FITS could be considered to images what PostScript was to text and drawings—a revolution.

The following items listed are possible only because of FITS, IVUE, and resolution independence.

Unlimited image size

You can open and manipulate images of any size with 18 MB of application RAM. The image can be 5 MB or 500 MB, all it takes is 18 MB of RAM.

Speed

The speed of most operations is close to instantaneous. This is true no matter what the size of the image. Almost all effects can be applied with a brush, in real-time, no matter what the size of the brush.

Unlimited number of images

You can insert an unlimited number of images to create a composite (though it helps to have more than the minimum RAM for a large number of images).

Unlimited brush size

The brushes are resolution-independent. By adjusting the size of the image on the screen, you can brush one pixel or 500 MB in a single stroke.

Unlimited number of layers

This lends to a truly flexible editing environment. You can create and manipulate dozens of layers with ease. Some users purposely create additional layers to maintain complete control over even subtle details.

Unlimited undo

The original images are never modified. All edits are stored in separate layers. You can therefore remove any edit at any time, partially or completely. Nothing is permanent if you don't want it to be.

New networking possibilities

Several users can manipulate the same image simultaneously over a network to create different composites. Likewise, each user can work on a different part of the same composite, and then merge the parts. Compressed images can be read over a network without decompressing the entire image. Manipulating large images over a network can be as fast, or faster than working on a single Mac.

TO THE DIGITAL-IMAGING NEOPHYTE

Live Picture is a great way to break into working with images on a computer for several reasons.

First, for people used to working with brushes, paper, or film, Live Picture comes as close to direct painting or airbrushing as you can on a computer. Its real-time, pressure-sensitive brushes respond like traditional brushes. Because you can experiment and undo indefinitely, your ideas will emerge and develop as you work.

Second, the resolution-independent masks and 48-bit color allow you to produce high-quality, photorealistic composite images. If you're a designer, photographer, or artist, Live Picture on your computer means no compromises when it comes to quality.

Third, this software allows real-time image creation. Waits are rarely more than a few seconds. Like a pencil on paper, you'll see the result of your work instantly. Because the computer can keep up with your creative impulses, you will have more time to try new ideas.

TO THE PHOTOSHOP USER

Live Picture and Photoshop are complements. This is the case because Photoshop does not do everything that Live Picture does, and vice versa.

The differences in possibilities are mainly due to the differences in technology. Photoshop edits image pixels directly. Live Picture creates a mathematical description of the edits and re-creates the image afterward. Many operations are faster or easier to perform in Live Picture. However, you may sometimes find that a simple operation in Photoshop is more complex, or even impossible to do, in Live Picture. It usually all boils down to the difference in technology.

At the risk of oversimplifying things, Photoshop excels in pixel editing, while Live Picture excels in image creation and compositing. In reality, there is an area where the two applications overlap. In that area, use the software or features you feel most comfortable with.

Live Picture is a creative tool and a productivity tool. You can experiment in real time with multiple high-resolution images, because of its speed, coupled with its unlimited undo. Some of the images shown in the Live Picture Gallery illustrate its creative potential.

In Live Picture, the original images are never modified. The whole image is there all the time, even after it has been silhouetted and the background appears to be permanently gone. Furthermore, effects such as sharpening and color corrections sit in layers by themselves.

Live Picture doesn't use selections in the Photoshop sense of the term (except to apply Photoshop-compatible filter plug-ins). There are several ways to constrain an image, color correction, or effect to a specific area, but it's not a selection.

Finally, the resolution-independent brushes can be used to apply anything, from sharpening to image ghosting to distortion. These pressure-sensitive tools offer new possibilities in image creation.

To summarize, there are two leading, yet distinct, imaging tools on the Macintosh. Having both of these tools will give you unprecedented power, flexibility, and creative freedom.

TO THE LIVE PICTURE USER

This book provides clear explanations on most of the tools and concepts. It also contains numerous tips and descriptions of some of Live Picture's lesser known features. Furthermore, the Live Picture Gallery and other illustrations throughout the book demonstrate how other digital artists are using Live Picture.

To those who have just bought Live Picture, to the early adopters who began using it before it was sold in any store, and to all the other users, I wish you many hours of fast imaging and creative explorations.

CHAPTER 2

AN OVERVIEW

The information contained in this chapter is very general. You don't need to read it to start using Live Picture, so if you're just not in the mood, read it later. However, the Live Picture technology and "approach" are quite different from those used by any other existing software. A full grasp of this technology and approach will help you use Live Picture to its full potential.

You will find in this chapter:

- A description of the file formats and technology used in Live Picture

- An introduction to the user interface

- An explanation of *layer logic*, or what it means to work with layers in Live Picture

THE THREE TYPES OF FILES

You will be dealing with three types of file formats when working with Live Picture: IVUE, FITS, and a standard format for the finished output file: TIFF, EPS, DCS, Photoshop 3.0, PICT, Scitex CT, or IVUE. Figure 2.1 illustrates the Live Picture work flow.

IVUE

A *pixel* is a picture element in digital images. It is the basic building block. IVUE is a pixel-based format, much like a TIFF or a PICT. It contains a fixed number of pixels. Each pixel describes a color in the original image. While other standard pixel-based formats are of a single resolution, for example 300 dpi, IVUE contains the 300 dpi image, plus a series of subimages at lower resolutions. For that reason, IVUE is termed a "multiple-resolution" format.

    + = or or or or

Image 1   Image 2   Image 3   Composite   TIFF output   IVUE output   EPS/DCS output   Photoshop output   PICT output   Scitex output

Figure 2.1   The Live Picture work flow

How does this benefit you? Pixel-based applications, such as Adobe Photoshop, load the entire image into memory (RAM). This is time consuming. In Live Picture, however, only the amount of information needed to fill your screen is extracted from the file and loaded into memory. This is called working at *screen resolution*. Because computer monitors only display around 72 dots per inch (dpi), there's no point in loading the entire image into RAM. Because an IVUE file already contains a series of precalculated subimages, it quickly extracts the necessary data.

Questions/Answers

So am I always working on a low-resolution image?

Definitely not. If you were working on a low-res image or substitute (sometimes called a *proxy*), as soon as you zoomed, you would see pixels because the image contains such little information. This is a serious handicap for doing quality retouching. When you zoom in Live Picture, the screenful of data currently loaded into RAM is replaced by a new screenful of data extracted from the IVUE. So you are always working with *all* the data of the high-res image, except that you only load a screenful at a time instead of loading all the data into RAM at once. The advantage—speed.

What happens if I zoom and the data needed is not contained in any of the pre-calculated subimages?

Live Picture interpolates. It goes to the subimage immediately above the resolution needed and calculates a screen image based on the two closest subimages at the resolution needed.

Is the quality of the screen display as good as that obtained in pixel-based software?

As good, and in some cases better. You have access to all the information of the high-res image. For instance, when you view an image at a ratio of 1:4 in pixel-based software, the screen displays 1 pixel out of 4. This means the display is somewhat rough. By interpolating between the subimages, the Live Picture screen render is recalculated each time you zoom; so the display is much closer to the actual output, even at low viewing ratios.

Additionally, Live Picture offers an antialiasing option for the highest screen-viewing quality. This option smoothes jagged edges resulting from the relatively low resolution of the screen. No matter how far you zoom in, you never see a pixel. Screen antialiasing is useful for displaying hard edges, such as text, especially when your client wants to view the image on-screen.

If I'm always working with a 72 dpi screen representation, won't there be a quality loss in the final output?

This would be the case if you were actually modifying the full IVUE image based on the 72 dpi screen display. Though the image on the screen is dynamically linked to the original IVUE, Live Picture uses the IVUE only to extract or read data. It doesn't write or record on to the IVUE. IVUE is a read-only format.

So if Live Picture doesn't modify the original image, and doesn't work on a low-res image, how does it record what I've done on the screen?

See "FITS" in the following section.

To summarize what we've covered so far:

- An image must be in IVUE format to be used in Live Picture (with the exception of EPS files, which can be inserted directly).

- IVUE allows you to open and edit high-resolution images in near-real time.

- The original image is unaltered.

- Quality loss associated with low-resolution proxies does not occur.

To obtain IVUE images, you can do the following:

- Scan directly into IVUE using Photoshop-compatible scanner plug-ins.

- Convert other formats to IVUE using the Converter menu in Live Picture or the Image Vue application supplied with Live Picture.

For more information on scanning and converting images to the IVUE format, see Chapter 7, "Inserting Images."

FITS

FITS

The document is the workspace where you'll be compositing IVUE images, resizing and creating perspectives, making color corrections, sharpening, distorting and creating text, or just removing a wrinkle. When you save the document, or composite, you save it as a FITS file.

You do not actually modify the high-res IVUE images used when you composite in a FITS file. Nor do you modify a low-res proxy. Your work is recorded at no resolution because FITS is resolution-independent.

What does resolution independence mean? It means that changes, or edits, made to images have no resolution—they are not affected by the resolution of your original image. Masking, positioning, color corrections, distortion, and so on are expressed in purely mathematical terms in a FITS file.

The mathematical description of your edits is applied to each screenful of data. When you rotate an image you see it rotate on the screen, because the algorithm describing that rotation is applied to the current screenful of data. And when you zoom, the algorithm is reapplied to the new screenful of data. Because these modifications only go "screen-deep," a great amount of time is saved.

So when are the edits applied to the full, high-res IVUE files? That takes us to our next step: building the output file.

But first, let's summarize what we've learned so far:

- With the IVUE format, Live Picture creates a screen representation of each image used, at each level of zoom.

- With the FITS resolution-independent tools, you use that screen display to create a composite.

Output file

As you create your composite, the FITS algorithms are recalculated for each new screenful of data. This calculation is called the *screen render*, or *screen RIP*. The screen render only involves a screenful of data at a time.

When you finish the composite, you need to apply the FITS algorithms to the full IVUE file. This operation is also a render, or RIP. But because this RIP actually builds a new image, it's called the *build*.

When you build your image, you choose the resolution and format of the output file. The outcome is a standard image format such as TIFF, EPS, DCS, or Photoshop 3.0.

The build, or RIP, was the missing link between the full-resolution IVUE images and the edits that you performed on the screen. RIP stands for Raster Image Processing. Note that RIPs are nothing new. PostScript uses a RIP for text. It's called a PostScript RIP. Now Live Picture has one for composite images, and it's called a FITS RIP.

QUESTIONS/ANSWERS
When I build my output image, am I modifying the original IVUE images?

No, you never modify the original IVUEs. When you build an output, you create yet a third file (after IVUE and FITS).

What happens to the FITS file after the build?

Nothing. It remains just as it was before the build, fully editable, with all its layers intact.

Can I modify my composite, or FITS file, and build another output file?

Absolutely. You can use a single FITS file to build several output images. If you make significant changes, you can save the FITS file under another name. FITS files are very small.

Can I throw away my IVUE files and keep just the FITS file?

If you do, you won't be able to build another output file. To build, you need both the original images (IVUE) and the FITS file. If you inserted EPS files directly in a FITS file, you also need the EPS files. However, if your original images were in a format such as TIFF, and you converted them to IVUE, you don't need to keep the original TIFFs.

Does resolution independence mean that I can scan at low resolution and output my final image at a high resolution?

No. Resolution independence refers only to the edits contained in the FITS file. IVUE is a pixel-based format. If you scan at a given resolution and output at a higher resolution, interpolation occurs as it would in any pixel-based software. However, tests with Live Picture have shown that in most cases you can safely interpolate up to twice the original size of the file.

Does the FITS RIP replay all the edits performed up to that time?

No, that would be a script. In Live Picture, each time a FITS RIP occurs, whether on the screen or during the build, the composite is recalculated and expressed in its simplest form. This approach avoids cumulative errors and quality loss in the final output. For instance, if you extensively distort and undistort an image and finally leave just a bit of distortion, that bit of distortion will be applied to the image as if that's all you'd ever done.

Advantages to the IVUE/FITS approach

- You can work much faster. The time it takes to open or edit a 5 MB image is the same as for a 300 MB image. In both cases you're loading only a screenful of data into memory.

- You never alter the original IVUE images. But the edits you perform are always based on the full-resolution of the originals.

- The FITS file and all its layers remain fully editable after you build your output. You can go back and output a similar composite without having to redo the whole thing; and FITS files are small. No need to keep multiple copies of large images on your hard disk.

- Because of the resolution-independent FITS file, you can output the same composite at several different sizes and resolutions.

- The FITS RIP does not cumulate operations, it recalculates. This ensures maximum quality.

- The IVUE approach requires much less RAM: you can open and manipulate a 300 MB image with just 18 MB of application RAM. You are loading the equivalent of a 72 dpi file into memory.

For a full discussion of these advantages, see Chapter 27, "The Most Flexible Software You've Ever Seen." Other advantages are discussed in Chapter 3, "The Tools Revealed," and Chapter 30, "Compression, CD-ROMs, and Networking."

THE USER INTERFACE

The user interface is the part of the software you will be dealing with to access this sophisticated underlying technology. With Live Picture running, if you choose New in the File menu, the screen looks like figure 2.2.

The toolbars

The toolbar on the left of the screen is called the creative toolbar.

The tools in the creative toolbar allow you to bring in parts of an image, fade out others, change colors, distort with a brush, sharpen eyelashes, paint skies, and so on.

Click on the mode toggle (see figure 2.2). The toolbar changes to display the positioning toolbar.

The positioning toolbar allows you to reposition, change size, rotate, create perspective, crop, flip, and more—the "spatial" operations.

The mode toggle allows you to switch back and forth between the creative tools and the positioning tools. This can be done when you insert an image, or at a later time. The creative and positioning tools are described in Chapter 3, "The Tools Revealed."

There is a third toolbar, called the view toolbar. Use it to create or modify views. To see this toolbar, choose Add/Edit in the View menu.

Views are described in Chapter 6, "Using Views." To return to the creative toolbar, click on the mode toggle.

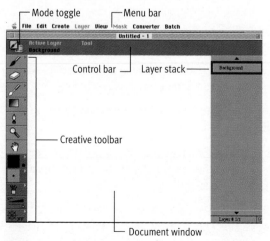

Figure 2.2 New document

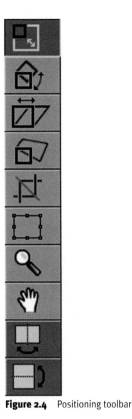

Figure 2.5   View toolbar

Figure 2.4   Positioning toolbar

Figure 2.3   Creative toolbar

The control bar

The control bar is located at the top of the document window. It displays information and can be used to enter information. The control bar changes depending on the type of layer that is active, and whether you are in creative, positioning, or view mode.

The layer stack

The layer stack is located to the right of the document window. Like the control bar, it provides feedback on the current composite and allows you to modify it. Feedback includes the name, type, order, and status of each layer. Controls include manipulating masks and stencils, and hiding and showing individual layers. The layer stack is described in Chapter 5, "Handling Layers."

File Edit Create Layer View Mask Converter Batch

Figure 2.6 Menu bar

Figure 2.7 File menu

Figure 2.8 Edit menu

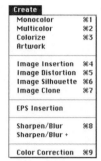

Figure 2.9 Create menu

The document window

The document window or workspace is the area framed by the toolbar, control bar, and layer stack. It is here that your composite comes to life.

The menu bar

The menu bar is the horizontal bar with a series of headings at the very top of your screen. Each heading provides access to a different menu.

THE FILE MENU

The File menu concerns FITS files, not IVUE files. It allows you to open, save, or close FITS files, to mention just the most common operations. The File menu is also used to build an output image when you've finished creating your composite and to control the separation if you are building an output in CMYK.

THE EDIT MENU

The Edit menu contains the preferences and a few other default settings. (The Cut, Copy, and Paste commands are only provided to comply with Macintosh standards. In the land of FITS, these operations are performed via other means described throughout this book.)

THE CREATE MENU

"Create" is really short for "Create a Layer." It's the key menu. You can't do anything until you create one of the 12 layer types available. For more information on the different types of layers, see Chapter 4, "The Layers Revealed."

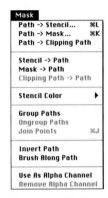

Figure 2.10   Layer menu   **Figure 2.11**   View menu   **Figure 2.12**   Mask menu

THE LAYER MENU

The Layer menu is used to handle existing layers, not to create new layers See Chapter 5, "Handling Layers." It also allows you to make global color corrections to IVUE images and use filter plug-ins.

THE VIEW MENU

The View menu is used to create and modify views. It is also used to hide and show rulers, paths, and so on, and to use Apple ColorSync 2.0. See Chapter 6, "Using Images." For ColorSync, see Chapter 29, "Quality Color Separations in Less than One Minute."

Figure 2.13
Converter menu

THE MASK MENU

The Mask menu is used for converting paths to masks, masks to paths, paths to clipping paths, and so on. It also allows you to create and remove alpha channels.

THE CONVERTER MENU

The Converter menu is used to convert images to the IVUE format, or to scan (acquire) images directly in IVUE format. See Chapter 7, "Inserting Images."

Figure 2.14
Batch menu

THE BATCH MENU

The Batch menu is used to defer one or several builds to a later time. See Chapter 28, "Building Outputs and Printing."

LAYER LOGIC

Live Picture uses layers. When you save a FITS file, you are actually saving a set of layers. Each layer describes a particular set of operations in mathematical terms. For instance, if you insert an image, scale it down, flip it vertically, and erase parts of it, all that information is contained in a layer. If you insert another image, silhouette it, and change it to black and white, all the information concerning the second image is contained in a second layer. The images are not contained in the layers, but the FITS file records a link to the image.

This layering technology has induced a particular logic within Live Picture. I call it "layer logic." When you begin to use Live Picture, you may find that you are unaccustomed to this type of logic. But once you get used to it, you'll probably find it quite intuitive. And the smoothness and power it allows is impressive. Let's examine this layer-induced mindframe.

One function/one layer

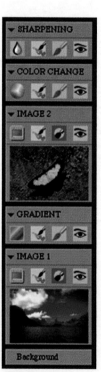

Live Picture has 12 types of layers (refer to figure 2.9). Each layer type allows you to do a specific thing or set of things. So, each time you do anything significant in Live Picture, you ask two questions and perform one action:

Question 1: "What do I want to do?"

Question 2: "What type of layer will allow me to do it?"

Action: Create the appropriate type of layer.

You are now ready to proceed.

This is what you could call the "structural" side of layer logic. However, once you've assimilated the different types of layers, creating the right type of layer will become second nature.

The different types of layers are described in Chapter 4, "The Layers Revealed."

Everything is a layer

For some of you, having images in layers is nothing new. But in Live Picture, to create a color gradient, you create a layer. When you change the color of a flower from red to orange, the color change is contained in an independent layer. And if you sharpen the petals, the sharpening is also in a separate layer. In Live Picture, everything is a layer.

Figure 2.15
Each layer has a function

Remember, one function per layer. An image layer does not allow you to change the color of an image. It allows you to insert or erase parts of an image, but not to modify image colors or image sharpness. To do that, you create the appropriate layer.

Number of layers

A composite can include anything from one to 50 layers, or more. There is no limit. Unlimited layers are available because Live Picture *is* layers. No layers, no composite. Naturally, you shouldn't create layers unnecessarily. Often, several similar operations can be contained in a single layer. But there is a great advantage to storing information in separate layers. You can edit the layers independently. So sometimes, you may want to create several layers even if technically one layer is sufficient. You can then go back and modify the actions in one layer without affecting the others.

The more layers you have, the longer it takes your Macintosh to refresh the screen and do the final build. However, the speed decrease is nothing compared to that experienced in pixel-based software where each layer actually contains all the information of a full image. A layer in Live Picture can be quite small. You may create a layer just to remove a scratch. Or a layer may describe complex image distortions. The type and complexity of each layer determine how it affects screen refresh and build times. For more information see Chapter 31, "RAM and Acceleration Tips."

Opacity and transparency

As the term "Layer Stack" indicates, layers are stacked or piled on top of each other. When you look at a composite on your screen, it is as if you are looking down through a stack of layers (or front-to-back if you prefer). This means that the top layer may hide everything beneath it.

A layer can be opaque or transparent. More specifically, each point or area in a layer can be opaque (opacity = 100%), transparent (opacity = 0%), or anywhere between these two extremes (0% to 100%). If an area in a layer is 50% opaque, then you see a blend of half that layer and half the layer beneath it.

In figure 2.16, the "Roman Floor" image was inserted at an opacity of 100%. The "Red Tiles" image (see figure 2.17) was then inserted directly above the "Roman Floor" image.

Figure 2.16   Roman Floor

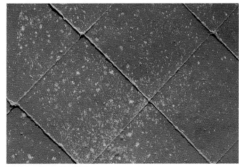

Figure 2.17   Red Tiles

Figure 2.18 shows what the composite looks like when "Red Tiles" is inserted at an opacity of 100%. "Red Tiles" is completely opaque and masks "Roman Floor."

As you lower the opacity of "Red Tiles," it begins to become transparent. The more transparent "Red Tiles" becomes, the less it masks "Roman Floor." In figure 2.19, the opacity of "Red Tiles" is 75%: you see 75% of "Red Tiles" (the top image) and 25% of "Roman Floor." In figure 2.20, the opacity is 50%, creating an equal blend of both images. In figure 2.21, at 25% opacity, "Red Tiles" is almost transparent and you mostly see "Roman Floor."

Opacity plays a key role in layer logic. In the previous example, we modified the overall opacity of an image. Also, adjustments can be made to the opacity of text, color, or any other type of effect. And they can be made locally or globally. The illustrations, exercises, and tips in this book provide concrete examples of how you can use opacity to obtain a wide variety of effects. At this point, keep in mind that in the land of Layer Logic, playing with opacity can open doors to a wealth of creative solutions.

Figure 2.18   Red Tiles at 100% opacity

Figure 2.19   Red Tiles at 75% opacity

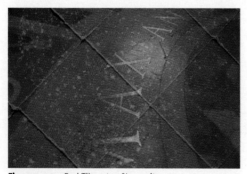

Figure 2.20   Red Tiles at 50% opacity

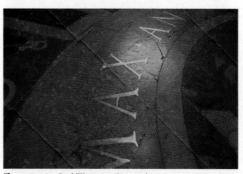

Figure 2.21   Red Tiles at 25% opacity

CHAPTER 3

THE TOOLS REVEALED

This chapter describes the creative tools, the positioning tools, and the color tools. Use the creative tools to insert images, paint backgrounds, brush in color corrections, create gradients, and so forth. Use the positioning tools to perform spatial operations such as scaling, rotating, and cropping. Use the color tools to select colors.

This chapter contains a basic description of the creative tools, as well as finer points and tips to help you gain full control over these tools. An exercise shows how to use the positioning tools. It includes a number of tips. The color tools are described at the end of the chapter.

THE MODE TOGGLE

Before describing the creative tools and the positioning tools, first, a quick word about the mode toggle. The mode toggle is located directly above the toolbars. It allows you to switch back and forth between the creative tools and the positioning tools. Click anywhere on the toggle to change toolbars.

The mode toggle also allows you to quit the view tools. See "The View Tools" later in this chapter.

A FEW CREATIVE TOOLS, MANY CREATIVE OPTIONS

One of the nice things about the Live Picture interface is its simplicity. The creative toolbar features just a few tools (see figure 3.1).

Don't let that simplicity fool you, though. Each tool offers access to many options. And the type and number of options change, depending on what type of layer you create. For instance, in a Multicolor layer, the Brush option allows you to paint.

In an Image Silhouette layer, the Brush options are used to isolate an image from its background.

Brush

Eraser

Palette
Knife

Marquee

Path
tools

Zoom
tool

Pan
tool

Color
selector

Size

Style

Pressure

Direction

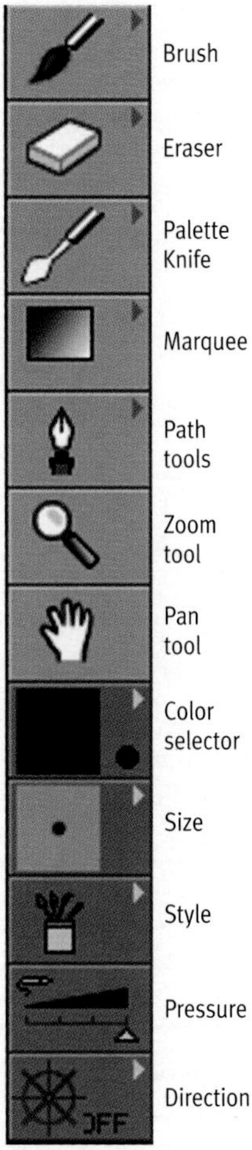

Figure 3.1
The creative toolbar

Because each tool offers several options, it's not enough to just click on a tool. You have to select an option also. To select an option, press the tool and drag to the option in the pull-out menu.

The option selected is displayed in the control bar, under the heading "Tool."

The first option in the pull-out menu is selected by default. So if you are using the first option, you can just click on the tool. However, if you select another option, the new option becomes the default option until you activate another layer.

Intuitive, sensitive, and highly flexible

The Brush, Eraser, Palette Knife, and Marquee are the four main creative tools. In the toolbar, they may resemble other tools you have seen in other programs. But using them is a unique and sometimes exhilarating experience.

First, tools are pressure-sensitive if you have a digitizing tablet. So you gain unprecedented control for inserting images and creating color and effects. Second, you can apply almost anything with the Brush: transparency, blur, color correction, sharpness, lightening, distortion, and more. Third, you can combine these tools with complete flexibility. For example, you can create a sharpening gradient for an entire image, then erase the sharpening in some areas, and apply blur in others. Fourth, the size of these tools is unlimited.

Never before has digital imaging offered such fine, responsive, and intuitive tools; to the point where some artists use Live Picture only to composite and ghost images with the Brush

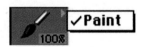

Figure 3.2 Paint option in a Multicolor layer

Figure 3.3 Auto option in an Image Silhouette layer

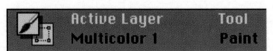

Figure 3.4 Control bar displays Paint option

Figure 3.5 Control bar displays Auto option

Using a digitizing tablet

All the exercises in this book refer to a stylus and digitizing tablet. A *stylus* is an electronic pen that you drag on a tablet, much as you drag a mouse. However, unlike a mouse pad, the tablet represents the different parts of your screen. When you click on the upper right-hand corner of your tablet with the stylus, the cursor always appears at the upper right-hand corner of your screen. You don't need to drag the stylus to get there. In that sense, it's closer to working on a real piece of paper.

Live Picture does function with a mouse, and you can perform the exercises in this book without a digitizing tablet. However, with a digitizing tablet, you'll discover the true beauty of this software. The fact that you can change pressure intuitively, and that the soft-edged tools are sensitive to your touch, makes using the simplest option an experience in itself. Without a digitizing tablet, it's difficult to use some of the tools effectively (such as the Retouch option).

I recommend a tablet no larger than an A5. A bigger tablet doesn't mean added precision, and it will just get in your way. Even the small Wacom Artpad or an equivalent allows for highly detailed work and is easy to handle.

NOTE: If you are working with a mouse, you can change the pressure using the numeric keypad: 1 is the lowest pressure, and 0 (representing 10) is the highest pressure. As an example, 5 is a medium pressure.

THE CREATIVE TOOLS

This section contains a general description and tips for each creative tool. After you read this section, the exercises in this book will allow you to experience them first-hand.

Brush

The Brush is your basic tool. Use it to "apply" or "reveal" whatever source or substance is contained in the active layer. A source or substance can be paint, image, blur, and so on.

There are different ways to visualize the Brush. The options are available in the General Preferences dialog box (Edit menu). The most useful is probably the Size Circle. (The Size Circle disappears when you apply pressure to the stylus).

Click here and drag

Figure 3.6 Brush with Opacity slider extended

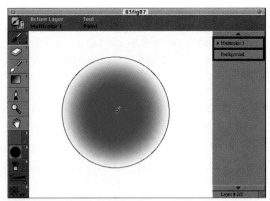

Figure 3.7 Soft-edged brush

When you use the Brush, notice that the source (paint, for instance) is not evenly applied throughout the Size Circle. It comes on strong in the center, diminishes as you move toward the edge of the circle, and is virtually non-existent at the edge. This "soft edge" allows you to do very fine work and avoids blotching and jagged edges.

The Brush Opacity slider is a wonderful tool. Each brush stroke can have a different opacity. In an image layer with the image inserted at an opacity of 100%, decrease the opacity to 70% and brush, move to another area and decrease to 50%, brush, and so on. No matter how much you brush, you'll never go below (or above) the opacity setting.

The Brush and its Opacity slider is one of the keys to your creative freedom. This real-time, unlimited-size brush is one of the tools that makes Live Picture unique. It responds each time you make the slightest change in pressure. Use it to brush in images, blur, sharpen, change colors, and distort images. In terms of intuitiveness and creative pleasure on a computer, this is the ultimate tool. As for the Opacity slider, play with it, experiment, remember it's there!

Eraser

Generally speaking, the Eraser does the opposite of the Brush. It removes or undoes whatever has been done. However, it undoes gradually.

In some layers, the options allow you to undo certain things selectively. For instance, in an Image Distortion layer, you can choose to either erase the image or remove the distortion.

In a Colorize layer, the Eraser removes paint, lightening and darkening indiscriminately.

Figure 3.8 Eraser pull-out menu in an Image Distortion layer

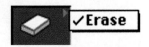

Figure 3.9 Eraser pull-out menu in a Colorize layer

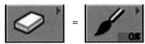

Figure 3.10   Using the Brush at 0% opacity is the same as erasing

KEYBOARD SHORTCUT: If the Brush is selected, toggle to the Eraser by holding and pressing the Command key. When you release, you go back to the Brush. You can toggle in any layer, using any Brush option.

Because you cannot toggle from the Eraser to the Brush, it's more practical to leave the Brush selected. When you toggle from Brush to Eraser, the Eraser option is automatically the opposite of the Brush option. For example, in an Image Distortion layer if you are using the Brush Insert option and press the Command key, you toggle to the Erase option. If you are using the Freehand (distortion) option, you toggle to the Undistort option.

There is no Opacity control on the Eraser, so you control it by varying stylus pressure and using the Pressure control (see "The Creative Tool Controls" later in this chapter).

Palette Knife

The Palette Knife is such a neat little tool that a separate chapter is dedicated to it (Chapter 26, "The Palette Knife: Most Underrated Tool"). The Palette Knife pushes or diffuses whatever has been applied with the Brush or Marquee.

Marquee

The Marquee is used for fills and gradients. As with the Brush, its edges are soft. With this tool, fills and gradients can be created in a matter of seconds for images of any size.

To create a fill, choose the Fill option in the pull-out menu. Then drag open a box in the composite. When you release the stylus, the area within the box is filled with paint, image, color correction, or another effect, depending on the type of layer chosen.

See Chapter 17, "Creating Gradients," to easily make all kinds of wonderful gradients.

NOTE: When you click on a creative tool, Live Picture takes a few seconds to "open" the active layer. The more complex the FITS file, the longer it takes. To avoid unnecessary waits, check that the correct layer is active before clicking on a creative tool. For information on activating layers, see Chapter 5, "Handling Layers."

TIP

Use the Brush as a controllable eraser. For example, for an image inserted at 100%, set brush opacity to 40% and brush. Image opacity will gradually fall to 40% but won't go any lower. Using the Brush at 0% opacity is the same as using the Eraser.

TIP

Use the rectangular Path tool to create a hard-edged fill.

└─ Click here and drag

Figure 3.11   Marquee with Opacity slider extended

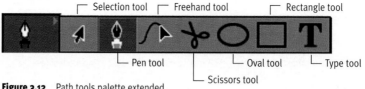

Figure 3.12 Path tools palette extended

Path tools

The Path tools allow you to draw shapes, which are then converted to masks or stencils. Learning to use the Path tools takes a bit of practice, but they are tools you'll probably need sooner or later.

An advantage of the Path tools is that you can define how soft or hard you want your edge with a great deal of precision.

You can also convert masks or stencils to paths. The paths can then be modified or exported. For a full description of the Path tools, refer to the Live Picture User Guide.

Type tool

The Type tool is a Path tool. Type is immediately vectored, or, in other words, displayed as paths. This makes it easy and flexible to use. For more information see Chapter 16, "Creating Type."

Zoom and Pan tools

The Zoom and Pan tools in the creative toolbar work the same way as the Zoom and Pan tools in the positioning toolbar. They are described in "Using the Positioning Tools" later in this chapter.

TIP

To avoid unnecessary waits, do all zooming or panning before clicking the Brush, Eraser, Palette Knife, or Marquee.

THE CREATIVE TOOL CONTROLS

With the creative tool controls, you can modify, adjust, and generally control the effect of the creative tools. The creative tool controls allow you to change the size and pressure of the creative tools. They also allow you to apply certain texture-like styles, and to constrain the direction of the tools.

The creative tool controls do not affect all the creative tools. Tools affected are indicated at the beginning of each section.

Size

Tool size affects the Brush, Eraser, and Palette Knife. There are two sets of tool sizes: the default brushes, and a smaller set of brushes called minibrushes.

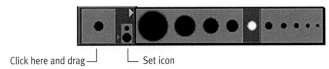

Click here and drag ⌐   ⌐ Set icon

Figure 3.13 Tool Size palette extended

The default brushes are the ones described previously in the Brush section. They are most frequently used. The minibrushes were designed for detailed work. As their name indicates, they are smaller than the default brushes.

To select a tool size, click on the Tool Size control and drag to select a size.

....

KEYBOARD SHORTCUT: Press the + (plus) key once to increase tool size by one; press the - (minus) key once to go down one size.

....

To toggle between the two sets of brushes, click on the Set icon on the Tool Size control. The sizes of the two sets of brushes overlap. The small default brush is the same size as a middle minibrush.

The minibrushes are not available in every layer, or with every option. To see if they are available, select an option. The Set icon is visible only when they're available for the option selected. Furthermore, you cannot set the opacity of a minibrush, so they are less suited for creating transparency. They are also harder edged than the default brushes. Try them to feel the difference.

Styles

Tool styles affect the Brush. Use them to brush in textured effects in any type of layer. You can brush in an image or paint with the styles.

To select a style, press the Style control and drag to a style in the pull-out menu.

To deselect a style, click and drag to the selected option.

Styles remain selected even if you change tools or layers. If a style is selected, the Style control is red and the style selected is checked (see figure 3.14).

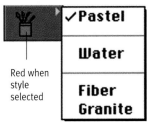

Red when style selected

Figure 3.14 Style

TIP

The Pastel and Water options can be used to soften whatever you are applying. They work well with the distortion options.

TIP

If you press hard on your digitizing tablet and almost nothing is happening, it could be that a style such as Water is selected.

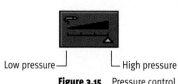

Low pressure └─ ┘ └─ High pressure

Figure 3.15 Pressure control

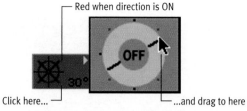

┌─ Red when direction is ON

Click here... ─┘ └─ ...and drag to here

Figure 3.16 Direction control with direction dial

Pressure

The Pressure control affects the Brush, Eraser, and Palette Knife. It works in conjunction with your digitizing tablet. A predefined range of pressures is available at each pressure setting—within this range, control the pressure by pressing more or less with your stylus.

If you don't have a stylus and digitizing tablet, please read "Using a digitizing tablet" earlier in this chapter.

Direction

TIP

If you brush and nothing happens, it could be that the Direction control is on and you are brushing in another direction.

The Direction control affects the Brush, Eraser, and Palette Knife. Use this to constrain the angle at which you brush. The Direction control works in any layer and for any option. For instance, you can constrain a blur to an 89° angle.

To use the Direction control, press the Direction control button, drag to the dial, and choose an angle. The red line shows the angle.

KEYBOARD SHORTCUT: To define the direction intuitively, press and hold the Control key, and click and drag anywhere in your composite. A direction vector appears, and all brushing is constrained to the angle of the vector.

To deactivate the Direction control, drag to OFF in the center of the dial.

When you set a direction, it remains set even if you change tools or layers. If a direction is set, the directional line on the Direction control is red (see figure 3.16).

THE POSITIONING TOOLS

The positioning toolbar contains the positioning tools (see figure 3.17). Use these to scale, rotate, skew, crop, flip, and create perspective for objects.

The most common use of these tools is to position image layers. However, you can also reposition other objects, such as paths, stencils, EPS files, and layer groups.

To reposition any object, it's important to understand these two special features: the Positioning Box and the X-point.

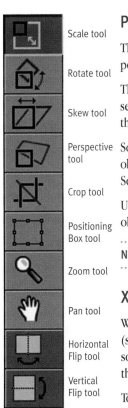

Scale tool

Rotate tool

Skew tool

Perspective tool

Crop tool

Positioning Box tool

Zoom tool

Pan tool

Horizontal Flip tool

Vertical Flip tool

Opacity tool

Figure 3.17
Positioning toolbar

Positioning Box

The object selected for positioning is framed in a Positioning Box when you switch to positioning mode. This box has eight handles and a center point (see figure 3.18).

The Positioning Box does not define the area to be repositioned. For instance, if you select a layer, the entire layer will be repositioned regardless of the size or position of the Positioning Box.

So what purpose does the Positioning Box serve? It acts as a reference for repositioning objects. By clicking and dragging the Positioning Box handles, you reposition the object. See how to use the Positioning Box in "Using the Positioning Tools" later in this chapter.

Use the Positioning Box to move, scale, rotate, skew, apply perspective, and crop an object. It is not used to zoom, pan, or flip an object.

NOTE: To reposition part of an image, see Chapter 20, "One Image, Two Layers."

X-point

When you toggle to positioning mode, an X appears in the center of the Positioning Box (see figure 3.19). This is called the X-point. The X-point is like a thumb tack. Stick it somewhere, and the image, text, or whatever you're repositioning remains stationary at the X-point. For example, if you rotate an image, the X-point is the axis of rotation.

To move the X-point, you drag it. But first make sure the cursor becomes an arrow—if it's not, that means you're not exactly on top of the X-point and you'll move the object instead of the X-point.

The X-point snaps onto the handles and center of the Positioning Box.

- To move the X-point and the selected object, position the X-point. Then enter the X-Y coordinates you want in the control bar (see figure 3.20). When you press Return, the X-Point moves to the X-Y coordinates, and the object moves with it.

TIP

You can position objects with precision by snapping the X-point onto a Positioning Box handle and entering X-Y coordinates in the control bar.

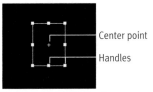

Center point

Handles

Figure 3.18   Positioning Box

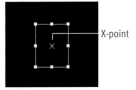

X-point

Figure 3.19   X-point at center of Positioning Box

Enter coordinates here

X Point H 20   Size W 2,736   Scale W 18,9%   Rotate ▼ 0°
Y 15   H 3,445   H 18,9%   Skew ▼ 0°

Figure 3.20   Entering X-point coordinates in the control bar

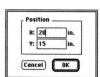

Figure 3.21
Position dialog box

- To move the X-point to precise coordinates without moving the selected object, double-click on the X-point and enter the coordinates in the Position dialog box.

Use the X-point to move, scale, rotate, skew, crop, and flip objects. The Perspective, Pan, Zoom, Opacity tools, and the Positioning Box are not affected by the X-point.

NOTE: The X-point only affects the Crop tool if you define the cropping area by entering values in the control bar.

USING THE POSITIONING TOOLS

The positioning tools can be used to reposition one or several objects. In this exercise, you'll reposition a group of layers. To reposition the group, you'll select it first. The procedure is the same for repositioning other objects, such as single layers or paths. Whatever is selected will be repositioned.

To reposition a layer group:

1. In the File menu, choose Open FITS.

2. Locate "Butterfly" in the Copy me to Hard Drive folder, and click on Open. The composite of a butterfly and orchid appears on your screen.

   There are two bars in the layer stack. The bar titled "Orchid" is the layer containing the image of the orchid. The bar titled "Butterfly & Shadow" is a group containing two layers: a silhouetted butterfly, and its shadow. In this exercise, you'll be repositioning either the orchid, or the butterfly and shadow. Grouping is discussed in Chapter 5, "Handling Layers."

   If your screen is larger than 13", you can drag the bottom right-hand corner of the document window so it fills the screen. To recenter the image, in the View menu, choose Go To and drag to Orchid & Butterfly in the pull-out menu. The image once again fills the document window.

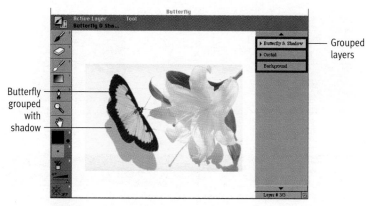

Figure 3.22 Butterfly composite

Positioning box ——— Group selected ——— Cursor ———

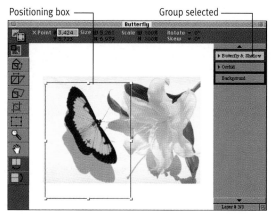
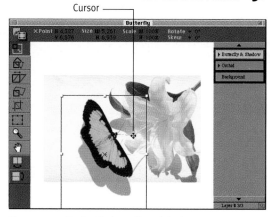

Figure 3.23 Repositioning mode with "Butterfly & Shadow" group selected

Figure 3.24 Moving the butterfly and shadow

3. In the layer stack, click on the layer group "Butterfly & Shadow." The layer group is framed in blue, which means it is selected and will be repositioned (see figure 3.23).

4. In the control bar, click on the mode toggle. The interface switches to positioning mode. The positioning toolbar appears to the left of the document window (see figure 3.23). The butterfly and shadow are framed by the Positioning Box. The X-point lies in the center of the box.

5. Position the cursor inside the Positioning Box, on the tip of the butterfly's bottom feeler, and drag as shown in figure 3.24. The butterfly and shadow move, and the orchid remains stationary.

   You can position the cursor anywhere inside the Positioning Box to move an object. However, one of the top four positioning tools must be selected (Scale, Rotate, Skew, or Perspective). The Move cursor (4 arrows) indicates that you can move the object.

6. Drag the X-point from the center of the Positioning Box to the top left handle, as shown in figure 3.25. (An arrow indicates that you can drag the X-point.) The X-point snaps onto the handle.

7. In the View menu, choose Show Rulers. The horizontal and vertical rulers appear (see figure 3.26).

8. In the control bar, click on the X-coordinate field for the X-point and enter 3. Then press the Tab key and enter 2 in the Y-coordinate field (see figure 3.26). You have defined the new position for the X-point.

9. Press Return. The X-point, Positioning Box, butterfly, and shadow move together. The X-point and top left handle are now positioned at the ruler coordinates X=3, Y=2.

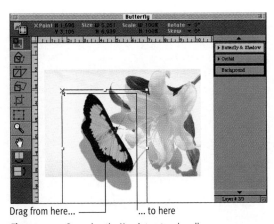

Drag from here... ———————— ...to here

Figure 3.25 Snapping the X-point onto a handle

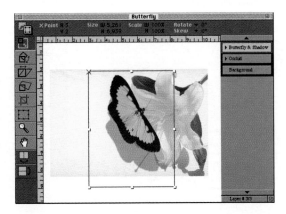

Figure 3.26 Positioning with precision using the X-point and control bar

10. Drag the bottom right handle inward toward the butterfly (see figure 3.27). The butterfly and shadow are scaled down. Notice that the X-point on the top left handle did not move—the butterfly is scaled toward that point.

11. Drag the X-point to the cross at the center of the Positioning Box (see figure 3.28). Then drag the bottom right handle away from the butterfly. This time, the image is scaled from the center, where you placed the X-point.

So far, all scaling done has been proportional. To change the proportion of the image, drag the middle handles. Changing the proportions of an image is explained in detail in Chapter 11, "Distorting Images."

NOTE: The Scale tool is selected by default when you switch to Positioning mode. To scale an object after using another positioning tool, click on the Scale tool first.

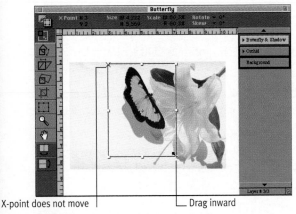

X-point does not move | ———— Drag inward

Figure 3.27 Scaling with X-point on a handle

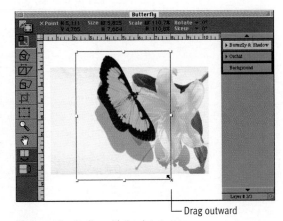

———— Drag outward

Figure 3.28 Scaling with X-point at center

Rotate tool   Rotate arrow —— ┌── Rotate field

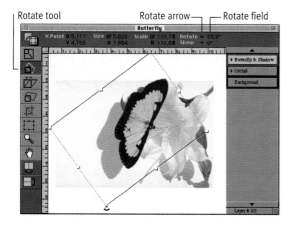
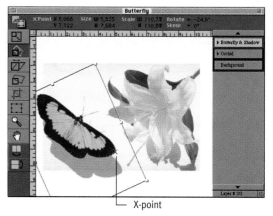

└── X-point

Figure 3.29   Rotating an object around the center point   **Figure 3.30**   Rotating an object around any point

12. In the toolbar, click on the Rotate tool. Then drag the bottom right handle clockwise (see figure 3.29). The image rotates around the X-point.

   You can also enter specific rotation values in the Rotate field in the control bar, or press the Rotate arrow to rotate by increments of 90°. A positive rotation value creates a clockwise rotation, and a negative value a counterclockwise rotation.

13. Drag the X-point to the tip of the right wing. Then drag any corner handle counterclockwise (see figure 3.30). The image rotates around the tip of the wing.

14. In the toolbar, click on the Skew tool.

15. Drag the X-point to the center of the butterfly, as shown in figure 3.31. Then drag a corner handle to skew the image.

. . . .

KEYBOARD SHORTCUTS:
- With Scale selected, press the Option key to rotate and the Command key to skew.
- With Rotate selected, press the Option key to scale and the Command key to skew.
- With Skew selected, press the Option key to scale and the Command key to rotate.

. . . .

16. To cancel all rotation and skewing, click on the Rotate and Skew arrows in the control bar and drag to 0° in the pull-down menus.

Important: One of the great advantages of the FITS technology is that you never modify the original image. If you perform several rotations or skews on an image in a pixel-based software, you are destroying and re-creating data each time. The FITS technology is non-destructive. When you cancel rotation and skewing, even long after the file has been saved, you return to the original, unmodified image. This means you can experiment with the positioning tools without fear of quality loss.

17. In the toolbar, click on the Perspective tool.

Skew tool

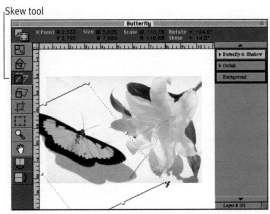

Cancel rotation and skew

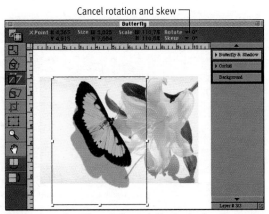

Figure 3.31   Skewing an object

Figure 3.32   Resetting rotation and skewing to 0°

18. Drag the top middle handle downward to create a perspective effect (see figure 3.33).

19. Now drag the top right handle upward, as shown in figure 3.34. This time, the Perspective tool is used to create distortion.

20. In the layer stack, click on the layer named "Orchid." The layer is framed in blue, and the Positioning Box now surrounds the background image "Orchid." The repositioning tools will now affect the "Orchid" layer.

21. In the toolbar, click on the Crop tool.

22. Drag the middle right handle inward, as shown in figure 3.36. The background image is cropped.

23. Position the cursor inside the Crop Box and drag to the left. The cropped area changes as you drag, but the size of the crop remains the same (see figure 3.37).

Perspective tool   ┌─ Drag downward

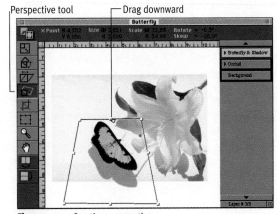

Drag upward ┐

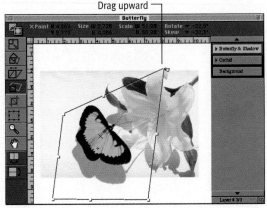

Figure 3.33   Creating perspective

Figure 3.34   Distorting with the Perspective tool

Click here ⌐   ⌐ Crop tool   ⌐ Drag to here

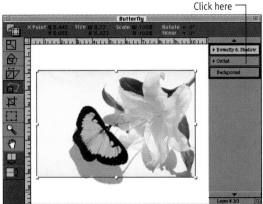

Figure 3.35 Selecting a different layer

Figure 3.36 Cropping an image

24. Position the cursor on the middle right handle and drag outward as far as you can go. Notice that a black edge appears (see figure 3.38). This occurs because that part of the image was originally cropped when the FITS file was created.

In Live Picture, you never destroy image data. The whole image is always there. Instead, by cropping, silhouetting, and so forth, you determine what parts of the image you reveal and what parts you hide. You can change your mind at any time, as shown in step 23, where a cropped area reappears.

NOTE: The Crop tool is available only in Image Insertion and Image Distortion layers.

25. In the layer stack, click on the layer group "Butterfly & Shadow."

26. In the toolbar, click on the Positioning Box tool. Then drag open a rectangle from one wing tip to the other wing tip.

⌐ Drag inside box

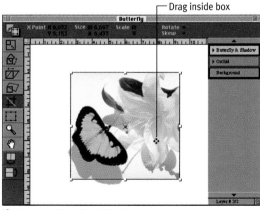

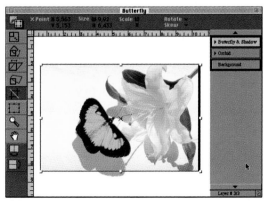

Figure 3.37 Dragging a Crop Box

Figure 3.38 Cropped areas are not destroyed

TIP

Use Option with the
Positioning Box tool to
undo perspective.

Because you can only scale, rotate, and perform other operations from a handle, redrawing a Positioning Box allows you to position the handles where you want. Also, the default Positioning Box sometimes lies outside your document window. In that case, either zoom out or draw a new Positioning Box.

The Positioning Box tool can also be used to undo all repositioning (except cropping). To undo all repositioning, press and hold the Option key and draw a new positioning box. The image or other object becomes the size of the new positioning box.

27. In the toolbar, click on the Zoom tool. Click and drag slowly from the center of the butterfly outward. Release the stylus when the zoom box resembles the one in figure 3.40.

    When you release the stylus, the area inside the zoom box fills your document window (see figure 3.41). The center of the zoom box is the center of the new window.

28. Click once lightly and briefly with your stylus on the head of the butterfly. The magnification level doubles, and the point clicked (butterfly's head) is at the center of the document window.

....

KEYBOARD SHORTCUT: Spacebar-Command keys

....

29. Press and hold the Option key. The Zoom tool icon switches from + (plus) to − (minus). Click once lightly on the head of the butterfly. The magnification level is halved. The point clicked is at the center of the window.

Positioning Box tool

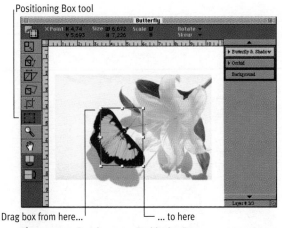

Drag box from here...   ... to here

Figure 3.39   Drawing a new Positioning Box

Drag from center to here

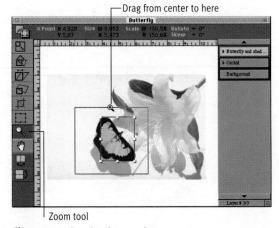

Zoom tool

Figure 3.40   Drawing the zoom box

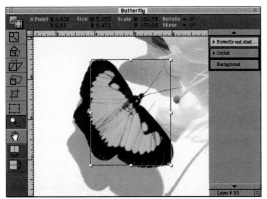

Figure 3.41 Zoom box fills document window

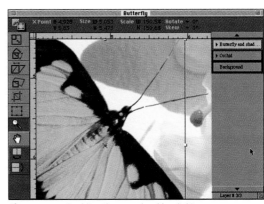

Figure 3.42 Doubling the zoom level by clicking

30. Press and hold the Option key. Then click and drag from the flower's pistil. Release the stylus when the zoom box resembles the one in figure 3.44.

   When you release the stylus, the initial document window fills the zoom box, and the new document window is filled with the rest of the image (see figure 3.41). The center of the zoom box (the pistil) is the center of the new window.

KEYBOARD SHORTCUT: Spacebar-Command-Option keys

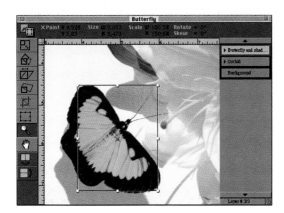

Figure 3.43 Halving the zoom level by clicking

Drag from here...

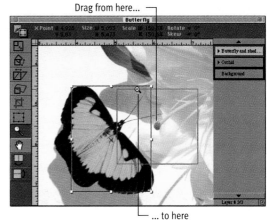

... to here

Figure 3.44 Drawing the zoom box

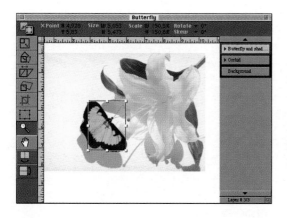

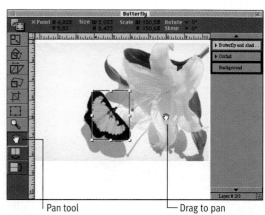

Figure 3.45 Document window fills zoom box

Figure 3.46 Panning in document window

Pan tool — Drag to pan

31. In the toolbar, click on the Pan tool. Then drag the composite as shown in figure 3.46.

    The Pan tool moves the entire composite. To move separate objects, see steps 5-9 in this exercise.

    ....

    KEYBOARD SHORTCUT: Spacebar.
    ....

32. In the layer stack, click on the layer called "Orchid." The layer is selected (framed in blue). The "Orchid" image will be repositioned.

    We are now going to flip the "Orchid" image.

33. In the toolbar, click on the Scale tool. Then position the X-point as shown in figure 3.47. To set the axis of the flip, you first need to position the X-point. You can click on the Scale, Rotate, Skew, or Perspective tool to do this.

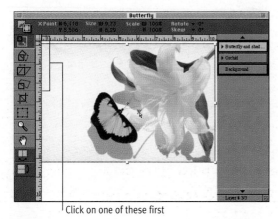

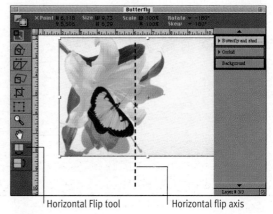

Click on one of these first

Horizontal Flip tool — Horizontal flip axis

Figure 3.47 Positioning the X-point before flipping an image

Figure 3.48 Horizontal flip

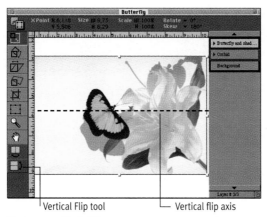

Vertical Flip tool   Vertical flip axis

Figure 3.49   Vertical flip

34. In the toolbar, click on the Horizontal Flip tool. The orchid image flips along the horizontal axis defined by the X-point.

35. Click on the Horizontal Flip tool to flip back to the original position.

36. In the toolbar, click on the Vertical Flip tool. The orchid flips along the vertical axis defined by the X-point.

By completing this exercise, you have used all the positioning tools. You are now able to reposition an image, several images, or any type of layer, such as a shadow contained in a layer of paint.

OPACITY CONTROL

Use the Opacity control to change the opacity of an image globally when you insert it. It's great for positioning an image over other images. By setting the opacity at 50%, you can see both the image and the layers beneath it. When you finish positioning the image, slide the opacity back to 100%.

The Opacity tool is only available in Insertion mode (for more information, see Chapter 7, "Inserting Images"). If you toggle to the positioning tools later on, the tool is not available.

Click here and drag

Figure 3.50   Opacity control with Opacity slider extended

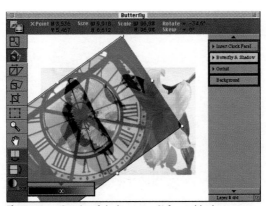

Figure 3.51 Opacity of clock set at 50% for positioning

> **TIP**
>
> To change the global opacity of an image after insertion, use the Marquee with the Fill option and the Opacity slider.

To modify the opacity of part of an image, you can use the Brush (see "Brush" earlier in this chapter).

In Image Insertion and Image Distortion layers, if you want to leave image opacity at 50% or any other percentage, set the opacity at the desired setting and toggle to creative mode. The image remains at the opacity selected.

In an Image Silhouette layer, the opacity is used only for positioning. When you toggle to creative mode, image opacity is reset at 100% to allow you to silhouette the image.

Figure 3.52
The view toolbar

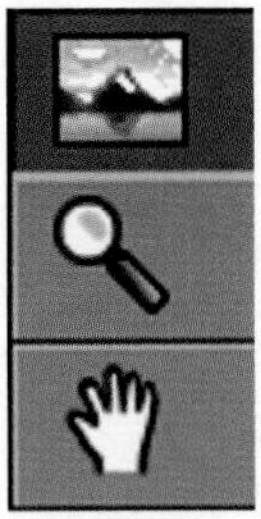

THE VIEW TOOLS

The view tools allow you to create and edit views. Views are described fully in Chapter 6, "Using Views."

To enter view mode, choose Add/Edit in the View menu. The view toolbar appears.

To leave view mode, click on the mode toggle.

THE COLOR TOOLS

Live Picture offers a full range of tools for selecting colors: color bar, Live Picture color picker, Apple color picker with Pantone colors. You can also take colors directly from your composite, or from anywhere on your screen.

In addition, Live Picture supports Apple ColorSync 2.0. ColorSync is designed to maintain color accuracy from scanning to output. For more information, see Chapters 28 and 29, "Building Outputs and Printing" and "Quality Color Separations in Less than One Minute."

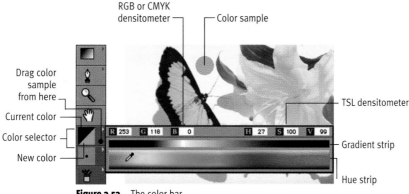

Figure 3.53   The color bar

The color bar

The color bar is the tool to use for quickly selecting colors. It contains a hue strip and a gradient strip.

Special features include the following:

- Alternate color bars: Each time you click on the spacebar, the palette of colors changes: RGB, CMYK, electric, pastel, dark colors, light colors, and more.

- Color sample: Click and drag out the color sample. Place it against an object you want to match. As you drag the eyedropper along the color bar, the color sample changes to reflect the current color. To remove the color sample, click on the small circle on the Color Selector.

The Live Picture color picker

This is the most complete color tool. Use this color picker to enter specific color values in RGB, HSV, or CMYK. You can also save and reload colors in the color palette.

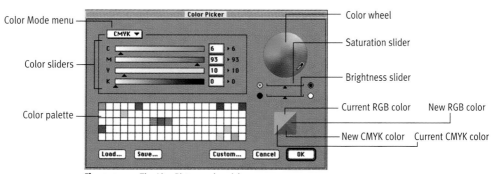

Figure 3.54   The Live Picture color picker

Click here
for Pantone
color pickers

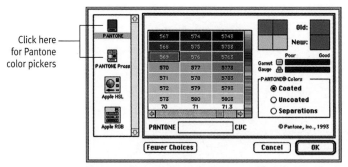

Figure 3.55 The Apple color picker

The Apple color picker

Use the Apple color picker to enter specific colors values in HSV or RGB, or to select Pantone colors.

Picking colors directly from the composite

Use the eyedropper to pick colors directly from the composite or anywhere on the screen.

TIP

You can place a color sample from any software, color swatch, or palette anywhere on your screen, and pick it up in Live Picture using the eyedropper.

ACCESSING THE COLOR TOOLS

The basic way to access the color tools is through the color selector:

- Press and drag to access the color bar.

- Click once to display the Live Picture color picker.

- Click twice to show the Apple color picker (or click Custom in the Live Picture color picker).

You can also access the color bar and color pickers via the color controls in Multicolor and Colorize gradient boxes. For more information, see Chapter 17, "Creating Gradients."

To take a color directly from the composite or anywhere else on your screen, pull out the color bar and drag the eyedropper anywhere on your screen.

In a Multicolor or Colorize layer, you can also press the Option key to activate the eyedropper.

TIP

To keep a color picker on your screen at all times, create a Multi-color gradient outside your main view (see figure 3.56). Then pick colors directly from the gradient in a Multicolor or Colorize layer using the Option key (see Chapter 17, "Creating Gradients").

Create a Multicolor layer

Figure 3.56 Using a Multicolor gradient as a custom color picker

CHAPTER 4

THE LAYERS REVEALED

This chapter describes the basic uses for each type of layer. The figures show examples of how each layer is used. At the end of each layer section, you'll find a reference to other chapters for a full description, or more specific or advanced applications.

If you are already familiar with each layer type, check this chapter for interesting additional information in the notes and tips.

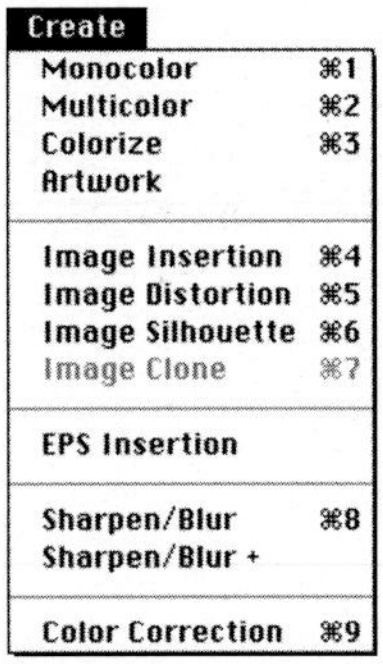

Create	
Monocolor	⌘1
Multicolor	⌘2
Colorize	⌘3
Artwork	
Image Insertion	⌘4
Image Distortion	⌘5
Image Silhouette	⌘6
Image Clone	⌘7
EPS Insertion	
Sharpen/Blur	⌘8
Sharpen/Blur +	
Color Correction	⌘9

Figure 4.1 The Create menu is used to create the layers

ABOUT THE LAYERS

The breakdown of layers in this chapter is slightly different from that found in the Create menu (see figure 4.1). It begins with the three layer types used to insert IVUE images, and then covers the Image Clone layer used to copy image matter. The next section describes the EPS Insertion layer, which allows you to import PostScript text and graphic files created in illustration and page layout programs. Then come the layers used to apply color, followed by the layers used to modify color. The former are used to paint, while the latter are used to change the color of images without modifying their texture. The last section deals with Sharpen/Blur layers.

LAYERS FOR INSERTING IMAGES

Three types of layers are available for inserting IVUE images: Image Silhouette, Image Distortion, and Image Insertion.

Once an image is inserted in a given layer type, you cannot change the layer type. Therefore, before creating a layer, take a moment to think about what you want to do with your image.

To combine the tools of different image layers, such as silhouetting and distortion, use the methods and tricks described in this chapter, and in Chapters 9 and 11, "The Great Silhouetting Lab" and "Distorting Images."

Image Silhouette

Use Image Silhouette layers to isolate images from their background using color-sensitive tools. For silhouetting to be effective, you need some color contrast between the object you want to keep and the background you want to discard.

British designer Helen Hann silhouetted the orchid and the clock face (see figures 4.2 to 4.4). The completed image, "The Wedding of Brother Wolf" (see figure 4.5), was created using these silhouettes, along with other images inserted in Image Insertion layers.

When you silhouette an image, the part of the image silhouetted is generally opaque. In this composite, Helen ghosted the orchid and clock face afterward; she created transparency in some areas (see figure 4.4).

For a full description of the silhouetting tools, see Chapter 8, "Isolating Images from their Background," and especially Chapter 9, "The Great Silhouetting Lab."

Figure 4.2   Clock Face

Figure 4.3   Clock silhouetted and ghosted into sky background image

Figure 4.4   Orchid

Figure 4.5   "The Wedding of Brother Wolf" with orchid silhouetted

Figure 4.6   Pipe bent using distortion tools

Image Distortion

Use Image Distortion layers if you want to distort parts of your image using a brush. Create this type of layer if it's possible you'll want to use distortion at some point. Otherwise, create an Image Insertion layer. "Raychem Cable," by American photographer John Lund, illustrates one kind of distortion you can create in an Image Distortion layer (see figure 4.6).

To learn how to use the distortion tools, see Chapter 11, "Distorting Images."

Image Insertion

Create Image Insertion layers when you don't need to create Image Silhouette or Image Distortion layers. Such cases include inserting a full image to use as the backdrop for a composite, using the Path tools to cut out part of an image, and inserting and ghosting images with the Brush, Palette Knife, and Marquee.

The images in figures 4.7 to 4.9 were inserted in Image Insertion layers. Figure 4.7 was inserted with an opacity gradient. It was used as the backdrop for "The Wedding of Brother Wolf" (see figures 4.3 and 4.5 earlier in this chapter). Figure 4.8 was also inserted using an opacity gradient, and parts of it were then brushed in manually. Figure 4.9 was ghosted entirely with the Brush.

Image Insertion layers also have a nice little option called Outline, which has some degree of color sensitivity. You could call it the poor man's silhouetting tool, but it can work quite well for small areas if you zoom in. The tool is described in full in Chapter 9, "The Great Silhouetting Lab," because it's often used as a tool for retouching silhouetted images. However, it can be used even if the image has not been silhouetted.

Figure 4.7   Sky used as backdrop and inserted with opacity gradient

Figure 4.8   Wolf

Figure 4.9   Roman Floor inserted entirely with the Brush

NOTE: At first glance, Image Insertion layers seem to be Image Distortion layers without the distortion tools. However, Image Insertion layers offer several advantages over Image Distortion layers: 1) The Outline options; 2) The ability to convert paths to masks (you can only convert paths to stencils in Image Distortion layers); and 3) Image Distortion masks are not compatible with the masks in frequently used layers, such as Monocolor and Color Correction layers. (For more on masks and stencils, see Chapter 10, "Sources, Masks, and Stencils Revealed.") So don't create Image Distortion layers unless you plan to use the distortion tools.

For more information on Image Insertion layers, see Chapter 8, "Isolating Images from Their Background."

Figure 4.10 Original image of apple

Figure 4.11 Apple after cloning

LAYER FOR ADDING OR REMOVING MATTER (CLONING)

Image Clone layers are used to remove unwanted objects, dust, spots, and scratches from scanned images. They can also be used for creative effects.

In figures 4.10 and 4.11, cloning was used to remove imperfections on the apple.

To perform cloning, first select the image layer you want to clone. If you do not, the image clone option is grayed out. See Chapter 12, "Cloning," for a step-by-step exercise, along with a wealth of information and tips on how to maximize cloning efficiency.

LAYER FOR IMPORTING EPS FILES

Create an EPS Insertion layer to import text or graphics saved as Encapsulated Post-Script (EPS) files. Page layout programs such as QuarkXPress, and graphics applications such as Freehand and Illustrator allow you to save text and graphics as EPS files.

EPS Insertion layers allow you to insert PostScript files in the same composite with IVUE files. The EPS files and the IVUE files can then be output at different resolutions. This allows you to retain the highest quality for your images, text, and graphics. It also turns Live Picture into a powerful page-layout program and design tool, where you can mix high-resolution images with PostScript graphics.

TIP

The definition of the EPS preview displayed in Live Picture depends on the size of the EPS file when saved. Scale up the EPS before saving it in your graphics program to improve display definition.

When Live Picture opens an EPS file, it uses the 72-dpi preview to create a temporary IVUE file for viewing and positioning. When you build your output file and send it to a PostScript output device, the EPS file is substituted for the temporary IVUE and output at the resolution of the PostScript device. For more information, see Chapter 28, "Building Outputs and Printing."

EPS Insertion layers are somewhat different from all other layers (called "FITS" layers). The text and graphics remain in Postscript form. You cannot edit an EPS Insertion layer

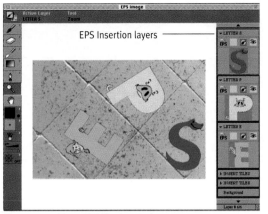

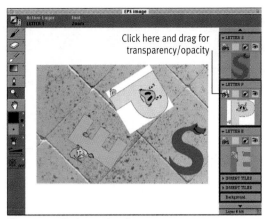

Figure 4.12 Three EPS files inserted

Figure 4.13 Background made opaque

using the creative tools, because the mask is not accessible. For example, you cannot modify the opacity of an EPS file. However, you can reposition an EPS Insertion layer by using the positioning tools (except the Perspective tool).

Figure 4.12 shows three EPS files composited above two image layers. Each letter is a separate EPS file inserted in a separate EPS Insertion layer. The letters are scaled and rotated.

You can make the white areas in an EPS layer transparent or opaque. In Figure 4.13, the Transparent Background icon is dragged to create an opaque background. The background of the EPS thumbnail in the layer bar also becomes opaque. The Transparent Background option only affects the screen display. It does not affect how the file will output on a PostScript output device.

EPS layers always appear on the top of the layer stack, and remain there. You can group EPS layers, but you cannot group EPS layers with FITS layers. For more information on the layer stack and grouping, see Chapter 5, "Handling Layers."

Important: The EPS file is not actually contained in the FITS file. To reopen the FITS file or build an output, keep the original EPS files.

. . . .

NOTE: To open a Photoshop-compatible EPS file (pixel-based as opposed to PostScript), use the Acquire command in the Converter menu and save it as an IVUE file. You can then insert it in a FITS image layer and use the creative tools.

. . . .

LAYERS FOR APPLYING COLOR

The three layers for applying color are Monocolor, Multicolor, and Artwork. These layers can be used to paint, fill text and other shapes, or create gradients.

Also, see Chapters 16 and 17, "Creating Type" and "Creating Gradients."

Figure 4.14   Composite before drop shadow was created

Figure 4.15   Drop shadow added

Figure 4.16   Final image, with Monocolor gradients of light

Monocolor

Use Monocolor layers to paint with a single color. The limitation is that you are restricted to using one color. The advantage is that you can change the color anytime you want, and everything you've done in that layer will automatically change to the new color. You don't have to brush again or redraw fills or gradients.

If you need to use more than one color, each color will be in a separate layer. This means that each color can be changed independently, as well as modified, erased, repositioned, and so on.

To change a color, activate the Monocolor layer and choose a new color. (To activate a layer, double-click the layer bar. See Chapter 5, "Handling Layers.")

TIP

Use Monocolor layers if you're creating drop shadows or text in one color.

Figures 4.14 to 4.16 show how French Photographer Thierry Petillot used two Monocolor layers in "Information Superhighway No. 3." In figure 4.15, the Monocolor layer was used to create a drop shadow for the boy and woman. In figure 4.16, the Monocolor layer was used to create a lighting effect.

Another advantage of Monocolor layers over Multicolor layers is that its masks are compatible with those of the most frequently used layers. For more information, see Chapter 10, "Sources, Masks, and Stencils Revealed."

Multicolor

In a Multicolor layer, there is no limit to the number of colors you can use. The flip side is that, unlike a Monocolor layer, you can't automatically change the color of what's already been done. Each time you change colors, whatever has been painted remains as is, and any new painting is in the new color.

Use Multicolor layers for skies, colorful backdrops, gradients or text in more than one color, or any time you just feel like painting without any hindrance to your artistic expression.

Figure 4.17 Green gradient for ocean, plus image of sky inserted with opacity gradient

Figure 4.18 Blue gradient behind sky image extends and darkens sky

Figure 4.19 Final composite: the green gradient is mixed with a gray textured image

In figures 4.17 to 4.19, American photographer David Bishop used two Multicolor gradients to serve as the backdrop for the water and sky in "Electronic Musician."

For more information, see Chapter 17, "Creating Gradients."

Artwork

Artwork is much like a Monocolor layer. You can use one color per layer, and one pattern per layer. Choose the patterns by dragging out the Patterns palette in the control bar (see figure 4.20). Everything done in the layer changes if you change the color or pattern.

The interesting parts of an Artwork layer are the areas that contain transparency. In Artwork, transparency can be obtained only along the edges of the brush stroke, or using gradients. If you create a 100%-opacity fill with Artwork, it will look just like a Monocolor fill. To play with the opacity and push the patterns around, try using the Palette Knife, or the Eraser at low pressure.

Click here and drag to select pattern

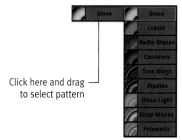

Figure 4.20 The Patterns palette

Figure 4.21 Bubble created with Artwork and Multicolor

Figure 4.22 Images of Lolita and computer inserted behind bubble

Figure 4.23 Final composite

In this ad for IBM (see figure 4.23), David Bishop used Artwork and Multicolor layers to create the bubbles.

LAYERS FOR MODIFYING COLOR

Colorize and Color Correction layers are designed mainly for changing the colors in images. Their effects are either subtle or invisible on paint.

Colorize

Colorizing is similar to using a photographic filter. It colors images while increasing their contrast. Use Colorize layers to add color and contrast to color images, to colorize black and white images, or to lighten or darken images. It's a beautiful creative tool, whether you use the Brush or create fills and gradients.

For more information on colorizing, see Chapters 14, 15, and 17, "Making Selective Color Corrections," "Playing with Color and Light," and "Creating Gradients."

TIP

Colorize layers can be used to brush in contrast. To do this, choose gray (in HSV mode, S=0 and V=50) and select the Paint option.

TIP

Colorization is generally too strong at 100% opacity. Opacities in the 15-40% range are usually more appropriate.

Figure 4.24 Original image

Figure 4.25   Green colorize fill applied to water

Figure 4.26   Blue-to-green colorize gradient applied to sky and trees

Color Correction

Use Color Correction layers to selectively modify image colors. The Selective Color Correction dialog box contains a wide range of options. You can shift reds to magenta, saturate light blues, lighten or darken areas, and so on. Selectively modifying colors with the Brush offers unprecedented creative freedom.

You can also use Color Correction layers non-selectively to modify all the colors in your composite.

In "Old and Young" (see figure 4.27), Thierry Petillot used three Color Correction layers to change Gérard's eye color, whiten his teeth, and change his shirt color.

For a full description of Color Correction layers, see Chapters 14 and 15, "Making Selective Color Corrections" and "Playing with Color and Light."

Figure 4.27   Original face

Figure 4.28   Retouched eyes and teeth

Figure 4.29 After creating "old" mask

Figure 4.30 In the final image, shirt changed from gray to green

LAYERS FOR SHARPENING, BLURRING, BLENDING, AND SMUDGING

Use Sharpen/Blur layers to sharpen and blur images using the Brush, a fill, or a gradient. The Palette Knife also offers two important options: Blend and Smudge. Blending can be used to soften sharp lines and attenuate relief; for instance, to retouch a face. Smudging can be used to simulate motion.

In the "Watch" image, French photographer Jean-Luc Michon used the Marquee/Fill option at 15% opacity to slightly sharpen the image (see figures 4.31 and 4.32). After some color-correcting, he used the Brush to blur the edges of the image and parts of the watchband (see figure 4.33). In the completed image, a white Monocolor layer was brushed in to create a soft, cottony effect (see figure 4.34).

Figure 4.31 Watch

Figure 4.32 Entire image slightly sharpened

Figure 4.33 After color correction, blur applied with brush

Figure 4.34 Final image, surrounded by cloud of white paint

Another French photographer, François Marquet, used the Blend option to create a simple, yet touching, image. First, he inserted the eye in an Image Silhouette layer and created a luminance mask. Luminance masks are partially transparent (see figure 4.35). In a Sharpen/Blur layer, he then used the Palette Knife with the Blend option to create the soft, gentle effect on the eyelid (see figure 4.36).

A peculiar characteristic of a Sharpen/Blur layer is that it actually contains an imprint of the sharpened or blurred images. This imprint is determined by what layers are displayed in your composite at the time you create the Sharpen/Blur layer. This can lead to some surprises, particularly if you decide to change images beneath a Sharpen/Blur layer. This is the one exception to the rule that you can reorder any layers at any time.

Figure 4.35 Eye silhouetted with luminance mask

Figure 4.36 Eyelid blended using Blend option

Figure 4.37   Original parrot

Figure 4.38   Sharpened parrot

Figure 4.39   Virtual parrot on blue background

You can use this "imprint" phenomenon to create interesting creative effects. In figure 4.38, the image was purposely over-sharpened (Sharpen fill using Marquee at 100%). In figure 4.39, the image of the parrot was deleted. A dark blue Monocolor layer was inserted in its place. You see the sharpened imprint of the parrot against a blue background. The actual image is no longer in the composite.

NOTE: Sharpness without an image is only visible against a dark background, which is why dark blue was used. On the other hand, blur without an image can only be seen on a light background.

The Sharpen/Blur+ layer is the same as the Sharpen/Blur layer, except the effect is stronger.

CHAPTER 5

HANDLING LAYERS

This chapter explains all the basics for handling layers. The first part will answer any questions you may have about activating and selecting layers. The second part tells you how to change layer names, substitute images, duplicate and group layers, and more.

ACTIVE VS. SELECTED

A layer can be active, selected, or both. What's the difference? Table 5.1 summarizes the key points concerning active and selected layers.

Figures 5.1 and 5.2 illustrate two common reasons for activating or selecting a layer.

For more information, read the rest of this section.

Figure 5.1 Activate a layer to use the creative tools, such as the Brush

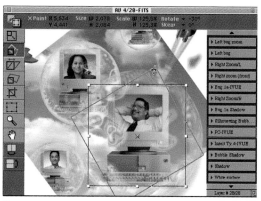

Figure 5.2 Select a layer to reposition it

TABLE 5.1 ACTIVE VS. SELECTED QUICK REFERENCE

	Active Layer	Selected Layer
Activate/Select to	Use the creative tools (Brush, and so on)	Reposition layers
	Change the color of a Monocolor or Artwork layer	Convert path to mask/stencil
		Retrieve path
	See layers above currently active layer	Get Info
		Delete
	Visualize stencil	Show/Hide
	Insert new layer directly above	Group/Ungroup
		Make IVUE Corrections
		Apply filter plug-ins
Activate/Select by	Double-clicking	Clicking
	Selecting and choosing Activate (Layer menu)	Command-click or Shift-Click for more than one layer
Visualized by	Uppermost layer with dark gray border	Blue border
Maximum no.	1	Unlimited

Using active layers

There are five reasons to activate a layer:

- To use the creative tools in that layer

- To change the color of a Monocolor or Artwork layer

- To see a layer that is not hidden, but is nevertheless not displayed on the screen

- To visualize a stencil

- To insert a new layer directly above it

USING THE CREATIVE TOOLS

To use the Brush, Eraser, Palette Knife, or Marquee to modify a layer, you must *activate* that layer first. These tools only affect the *active* layer. When you create a new layer, it is automatically active, so it seems like you don't have to do anything. But when you create a new layer, to rework a previous layer you need to activate that previous layer.

CHANGING COLORS OF MONOCOLOR OR ARTWORK LAYERS

To change the color of a Monocolor or Artwork layer, activate the layer. Then select a new color using the color selector. All paint in that layer changes automatically to the new color.

DISPLAYING A LAYER

When a layer is active, you see that layer and all underlying layers. Any layers above the active layer are not displayed on the screen. Therefore, sometimes you'll need to activate a layer just to see what the complete composite looks like. (Sometimes layers are not displayed because they are hidden; this is another matter. For more information, see "Hiding/Showing" later in this chapter.)

VISUALIZING A STENCIL

Sometimes it's helpful to actually see a stencil on the screen. By default, stencils are transparent, but you can use the Stencil Color command in the Mask menu to give it a color. The layer containing the stencil must be active, *and you must also click on one of the top four creative tools.*

INSERTING A NEW LAYER

When you create a new layer, it is automatically inserted above the active layer. In most cases, it is not very important where the layer is created, because you can easily reorder layers. However, Sharpen/Blur layers will be different depending on where they are created in the layer stack. Such layers must be inserted in the right order in the layer stack.

Using selected layers

To do any operations with a layer other than those listed in "Using active layers" earlier, it must first be *selected.*

Select a layer to:

- Reposition a layer using the positioning toolbar. Select the layer to be repositioned before or after you toggle to the positioning tools.

- Convert a path to a mask or stencil. Select the layer you want the mask or stencil to be created in before choosing Mask->Path or Stencil->Path (Mask menu).

- Retrieve a path already converted to a mask or stencil. Select the layer containing the path before choosing Path->Mask or Path->Stencil (Mask menu).

- Use the commands in the Layer menu. These commands include Activate, Get Info, Delete, Show, Hide, Group, Ungroup, IVUE Correction, and Filter Plug-ins. They are described in "Operations On Layers" later in this chapter.

Activating/deactivating layers

To activate a layer, do one of the following:

- Double-click on the layer bar
- Select the layer and choose Activate in the Layer menu

When you activate a layer, the previously active layer is deactivated. If you don't want to see a layer, hide it by clicking on the Eye icon in the layer panel.

Selecting/deselecting layers

To select a layer, click on it. The layer is framed in blue.

To deselect a layer, do one of the following:

- Press and hold Command and click on the selected layer
- Click on the bottom default layer (called "Background") or anywhere beneath the bottom default layer in the layer stack; this deselects all layers
- Select another layer

Finding the active layer

When a layer is bordered in dark gray, it is displayed in your composite. The active layer is the top layer bordered in dark gray. Layers bordered in light gray are not currently visible (see figure 5.3).

The active layer is also indicated in the control bar when you're in creative mode (see figure 5.4).

NOTE: The Live Picture interface was designed to avoid colors from the screen affecting our perception of colors in the image. That explains all the gray.

Figure 5.3 The active layer is the uppermost layer bordered in dark gray

Finding the selected layer(s)

Selected layers are bordered in blue (see figure 5.5).

Name of active layer

Figure 5.4   Active layer indicated in control bar

Figure 5.5   A selected layer

Figure 5.6 Several selected layers, one active layer

Number of active or selected layers

Only one layer can be active at a time. Any number of layers can be selected at a time.

To select more than one layer, do one of the following:

- Press the Command key and click on the layers you want to select
- Press the Shift key and click on the first and last layer of a series; all layers in between are selected.

Figure 5.6 shows several selected layers and one layer that is active and selected.

The active layer is selected also, which makes it a little hard to see that it's active. If ever in doubt, check the control bar in Creative mode.

OPERATIONS ON LAYERS

Live Picture allows you to easily perform a series of operations on the layers in your composite. Table 5.2 contains the basic information you need to perform these operations.

The following sections provide additional information and tips on these operations.

Getting information

The Get Info dialog box (see figure 5.7) allows you to give any layer a name. For image layers, it also shows the current position of the image and the size of the IVUE file on disk. The Substitute button allows you to switch IVUE images.

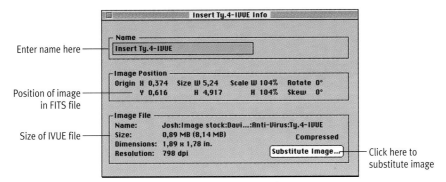

Enter name here

Position of image in FITS file

Size of IVUE file

Click here to substitute image

Figure 5.7 Get Info dialog box in an image layer

Changing name

Use names that will quickly remind you what was done in the layer. The name field readily visible in the layer panel is limited, so don't bother to include information that is already provided in the layer panel. For example, in a Monocolor layer, it's more important to write "stencil on pear" than to indicate "white coloring." Monocolor is by definition color, and the Source icon shows both the layer type and the color used.

TABLE 5.2 LAYER OPERATIONS QUICK REFERENCE

To	Do This
Get information on a layer	Choose Get Info in the Layer menu (Command-I)
Change the name of a layer	Choose Get Info in the Layer menu (Command-I) and enter a new name in the name field
Substitute an image	Choose Get Info in the Layer menu (Command-I), click on the Substitute button, and open a different IVUE image
Change the order of the layers	Drag the layer to a new position
Hide/Show a layer	Click on the Eye icon in layer panel
	Or, select the layer(s) and choose Hide/Show in the Layer menu
Duplicate a layer	Option-drag the layer to a new position
Group/Ungroup layers	Select the layers (or layer group) and choose Group (or Ungroup) in the Layer menu (Command-G/U)
Delete a layer	Select the layer and choose Delete in the Layer menu (Command-D)
Insert a layer	Activate a layer; the new layer created is inserted above the active layer
Select all layers	Choose Select All Layers in the Layer menu (Command-Y)
Make an IVUE Correction	Select a layer and choose IVUE Correction in the Layer menu; then choose a sub-option from the submenu
Apply a filter plug-in	Select a layer and choose Filter Plug-ins in the Layer menu; then choose a filter plug-in from the submenu

Substituting images

When you substitute an image, the IVUE file is replaced by the new IVUE selected. Substituting can be used to

- Replace low-resolution images with high-resolution images

TIP

If you substitute an image that was sharpened or blurred, delete the Sharpen/ Blur layer and re-create it. See Chapter 4, "The Layers Revealed."

- Replace JPEG-compressed IVUEs with non-compressed IVUEs (see Chapter 30, "Compression, CD-ROMs, and Networking")

- Replace one IVUE image with any other IVUE image

Figure 5.8 shows David Bishop's "IBM Anti-Virus Package." The sky in figure 5.9 was used as the backdrop for the bubbles. By using the Substitute button, you can very quickly obtain a variation such as that shown in figure 5.11, using the image in figure 5.10.

When you substitute one IVUE for another, the mask, stencil, position, and any IVUE corrections are reapplied to the new image. In this example, the sky was rotated 90° and skewed 180° when it was composited and the sky was colorized to increase saturation. When the galaxy image was substituted for the sky, it was also rotated and skewed by 90° and 180° respectively, and colorized.

Figure 5.8 "IBM Anti-Virus Package"

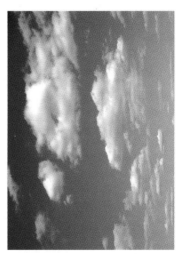

Figure 5.9 Original sky

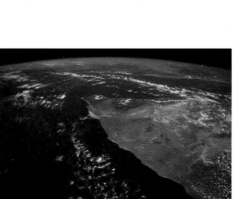

Figure 5.10 New background substituted for original sky

Figure 5.11 New composite

Click here to hide layer

Figure 5.12   Layer shown

Click here to show layer

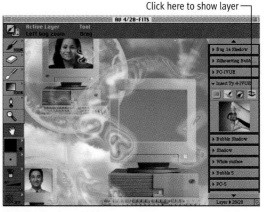

Figure 5.13   Layer hidden

If the new image is not the same size as the image it is replacing, it is scaled to the size of the original image. In other words, the proportions of the new image will change to fit the proportions of the original image.

Changing layer order

Drag the layer to its new position in the layer stack. When a light gray line appears between two layers, release the stylus. The layer moves to its new position.

Hiding/Showing

When you build an output, hidden layers do not appear in the output. This is useful for creating multiple versions of an image. Hiding layers also allows you to speed up the screen rendering (see figures 5.12 and 5.13).

Duplicating

When you duplicate a layer, you won't notice any difference initially on your screen because it is positioned directly above the original. Use the positioning tools to reposition the duplicate.

Grouping/Ungrouping

Grouping is used only to make layer handling easier. It does not actually merge layers. If you want to move two layers simultaneously, you can either group them or select them both. It's exactly the same thing. Grouping ensures that when you reposition a layer, you don't leave any associated layers behind.

In figure 5.14, each image associated with a bubble was grouped together. Each group contains the layer with the computer, the layer with the person, the layer with the bubble, and any other related layers, such as lightening or shadow.

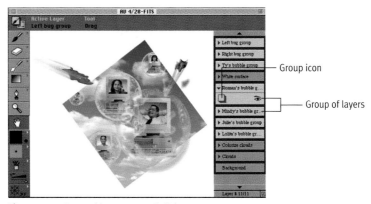

Figure 5.14   Grouped layers appear in light gray

You cannot activate a group because you can't activate more than one layer. To activate a layer in a group, ungroup the layers first. When you ungroup, you recover each layer with its name.

Deleting

If you delete a layer, it's gone—so be careful. You can recover it by pressing Command-Z if it's the last action you've done. An alternative to deleting layers is to hide them temporarily using the Eye icon.

Inserting

When you create a new layer, it is automatically inserted above the active layer. If you want to insert it elsewhere, first activate the appropriate layer. This is particularly important when you create Sharpen/Blur layers.

Making IVUE Corrections

IVUE Corrections are used to correct the colors in an image layer globally. You can only use IVUE Correction on image layers. For more information, see Chapter 13, "Making Global Color Corrections."

Applying filter plug-ins

Third-party filter plug-ins can be applied to image layers. For more information, see Chapter 18, "Using Filter Plug-ins."

PART ii

WORKING WITH IMAGES

USING VIEWS

This chapter describes the different uses of views, as well as how to create and modify them. To build an output file, you need to define a view. Views can also be used for quick zooming, creating grids, and applying Photoshop-compatible filter plug-ins.

BUILDING OUTPUTS

The main purpose of a view is to determine what part of your document you build into an output. Unlike pixel-based programs, a document in Live Picture has no size and no resolution. It is an infinite, resolution-independent space. Views allow you to define a two-dimensional portion of that space, such as an 8 1/2" × 11" page or an 8" × 10" transparency.

A document can contain several views. When you build the output, you select the view you want to build.

In figure 6.1, French photographer Jean-Luc Michon used the view "Complete image" as his final output for "Ilse on Motorcycle." However, he also could build the view "3 bikes," in which case his final output would look like figure 6.2.

By creating several views, you can use the FITS file to output as many different "crops" as you like.

Figure 6.1 "Ilse on Motorcycle"

Figure 6.2 Output of "3 bikes" view

PRECISION ZOOMING

The second use of views is to create pre-established zooms. The Go To command in the View menu (see figure 6.3) allows you to fill the document window with a view.

Each motorcycle in this composite is a separate image (the same model, Ilse, appears in every image). Jean-Luc used the view "Front bike" (see figure 6.4) to immediately zoom to the foreground and blend the front motorcycle into the background with the Brush. He could have done the same thing with the Zoom tool. However, by creating views beforehand of the areas that he knew he had to work on, he didn't have to worry about framing zooms precisely. This allowed him to concentrate on the creative aspect of his work.

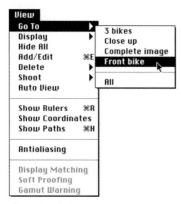

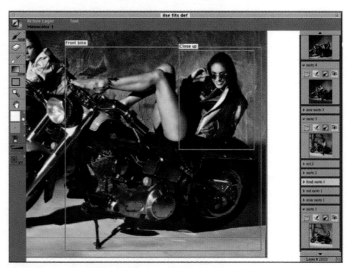

Figure 6.3   Using the Go To command to jump to a view

Figure 6.4   View used for precise zooming

CREATING AND MODIFYING VIEWS

Figure 6.5   View menu

The View menu contains the commands for working with views.

Table 6.1 shows what each command in the View menu is used for.

You can also create a default view with the Document Setup command in the File menu. For example, if you usually output a 4" × 5" transparency, you can create a view that size in the Document Setup dialog box. Each time you create a new document, the 4" × 5" view will appear. For more information, see Chapter 7, "Inserting Images."

USING THE ADD/EDIT COMMAND

Use the Add/Edit command in the View menu to create and modify views. When you choose this command, you enter View mode, and your screen looks like figure 6.6.

In View mode, you can drag open a view manually, or you can enter the view dimensions and X-Y coordinates in the control bar. The X-point works just like the X-point in the positioning toolbar. Use this to position views with precision.

Use the Line Color control (see figure 6.7) and Line Width control (see figure 6.8) to control the color and width of the view lines. This can be helpful for differentiating views, or to make some views stand out more than others.

TABLE 6.1 THE VIEW MENU COMMANDS

Use	To
Go to	Fill the document window with a view
Display	Hide or show individual views
Hide All/Show All	Hide or show all views
Add/Edit	Create or modify views
Delete	Delete views
Shoot	Build a 72-dpi output of a view without using the Build dialog box
Auto View	Automatically create a view for each image inserted; the view is the exact size of the image

Figure 6.6 View mode

Figure 6.7 Line Color control

Figure 6.8 Line Width control

Table 6.2 summarizes the procedures for creating and editing views in View mode.

TABLE 6.2 CREATING AND EDITING VIEWS IN VIEW MODE

To	Do This
Create a view	Drag open the view or enter view dimensions in the control bar
Select a view	Click on the view lines
Deselect a view	Click outside the view lines
Scale a view and change the proportions	Drag a handle
Scale a view and keep the proportions	Press Shift and drag a handle
Name a view	Click on the view name and enter a new name
Delete a view	Select the view and click on the Backspace key
Quit View mode	Click on the mode toggle in the control bar

USING VIEWS AS GRIDS

One special use of views is to create grids for precise positioning of objects such as images and gradients. The following procedure shows how to use views for positioning. It will also get you familiar with the tools for creating and modifying views.

Suppose you are creating an 8 1/2" × 11" page. Your client has asked for a 2" × 8" blue fill. She wants the top right corner of the fill positioned 1 1/2" down from the top of the page and 7" to the right.

To position an object with precision, follow these steps:

1. In the File menu, choose Document Setup. The Document Setup dialog box appears (see figure 6.9).

2. In the Document Setup dialog box, enter 8 in the Width field (W) and 11 in the Height field (H). Click on Define Initial View if it is not checked. The view should appear in the small document window in the dialog box.

3. Click on New. A new document opens with your initial view (see figure 6.10).

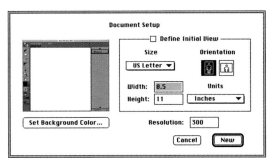

Figure 6.9 Document Setup dialog box

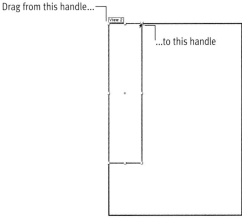

Figure 6.10   Initial view

4. In the View menu, choose Add/Edit. The screen switches to View mode.

5. In the control bar, enter 2 in the Width field and 8 in the Height field (see figure 6.11).

6. Press Return. The view appears. You have defined the size of the view. Now you will position it.

7. Drag the X-point from the upper left corner to the upper right corner of the view (see figure 6.12). The X-point snaps onto the handle.

8. In the control bar, enter 7 for the X-coordinate and 1.5 for the Y-coordinate.

Drag from this handle...

...to this handle

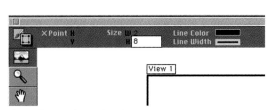

Figure 6.11   Defining view size

Figure 6.12   Moving the X-point

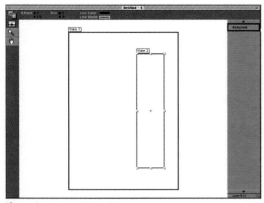

Figure 6.13 Repositioned view

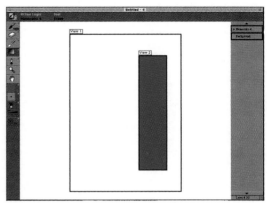

Figure 6.14 View used to position blue fill

9. Press Return. The view is positioned (see figure 6.13).

10. In the Create menu, choose Monocolor.

11. In the creative toolbar, click on the Marquee and choose the Fill option.

12. In the creative toolbar, click the color selector and drag to choose a blue from the color bar.

13. Drag open the Marquee along the lines of the view. When you release the stylus, the view is filled with blue (see figure 6.14).

To erase any unwanted blue near the view lines, click on the Marquee and choose the Erase option. Then drag the Marquee over the areas you want to erase.

You created the view to position the gradient. You don't need the view anymore.

14. In the View menu, choose Display/View 2 to temporarily hide the view, or choose Delete/View 2 to delete it.

USING VIEWS TO APPLY FILTER PLUG-INS

When you apply a Photoshop-compatible filter plug-in to a FITS file, Live Picture builds a new IVUE. As for any build, a view is required. For more information, see Chapter 18, "Using Filter Plug-ins."

CHAPTER 7

INSERTING IMAGES

In this chapter, you'll learn how to obtain IVUE files, the image format used in Live Picture. Then we'll go through the procedure for creating documents and opening images. It is helpful to have at least a basic understanding of views and their purpose.

Following that, we'll pick apart the much-discussed concept of resolution independence, and find out what implications it will have for your work. The chapter also includes a number of tips for working with images.

USING THE PROPER FORMAT

To use images in Live Picture, they must be in the IVUE format. You can either scan directly to the IVUE format, or convert images from other formats.

NOTE: You can also insert EPS (Encapsulated PostScript) files directly in a composite. Because these files are not pixel images and therefore not fully editable, they are not covered in this chapter. For more information, see Chapter 4, "The Layers Revealed."

Scanning directly to IVUE

If you have a scanner that can be driven by a Photoshop-compatible plug-in, you can scan directly to the IVUE format.

To scan directly to IVUE:

1. Place the scanner plug-in in the Live Picture Plug-ins folder. If you currently scan your images using a pixel-based software such as Adobe Photoshop, copy the plug-in from the Photoshop plug-ins folder to the Live Picture plug-ins folder.

2. In the Edit menu, choose Preferences/Files & Folders. You are going to tell Live Picture where to look for the plug-ins.

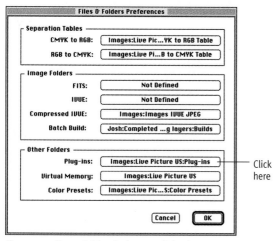

Figure 7.1   Files & Folders Preferences dialog box

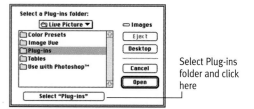

Figure 7.2   Plug-Ins Folder dialog box

3. In the Files & Folders dialog box, click on the Plug-ins field.

   If the Plug-ins folder is already located, as is the case in figure 7.1, skip steps 4 to 7.

4. In the Plug-ins Folder dialog box, locate the folder called Plug-ins and select it. It is located in the Live Picture folder (see figure 7.2).

5. Click on the Select "Plug-ins" field (see figure 7.2). The dialog box closes.

6. In the Files & Folders Preferences dialog box, click on OK.

7. Quit Live Picture and launch the program again.

8. In the Convert menu, choose Acquire, and select the scanner plug-in from the Acquire submenu (see figure 7.3).

....

NOTE: You can also use the separate application Image Vue supplied with Live Picture. You can install it on another Macintosh or give it to your scanner operator if you outsource scanning.

....

9. The scanner plug-in dialog box appears. Select an image, enter your scanning parameters and click on OK or Scan. The Save As dialog box appears (see figure 7.4).

   For more information on scanning, consult your scanner or plug-in documentation.

Figure 7.3   Selecting a scanner plug-in

10. Select a destination folder, and enter a name for the IVUE file. Then click on Save.

    The image will be scanned and saved directly as an IVUE file in the destination folder. Unlike pixel-based software, no new document is created when you scan an image.

Important: In Live Picture, compositing, retouching, and building output files are not affected by the size of the images used. Furthermore, image size has no effect on the amount of RAM required. Therefore, scan as large as you need to work comfortably and create high-definition images. For more information on scan size, see "Doing input, thinking output" later in this chapter.

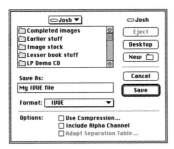

Figure 7.4 Save As Dialog box

Converting files from other formats to IVUE

To use a file that is not in the IVUE format, you must first convert it to IVUE. For example, your images may come from a scanner that does not support the plug-in architecture, or you may have obtained them from a CD.

TIP

If you have a choice, use TIFF files. They are faster to convert than other formats.

Once a file has been converted to IVUE, you don't need to keep the original (for example the TIFF, Photoshop 3.0, or other format). No data loss occurs during the conversion, and you won't need the original once you begin working with Live Picture. While IVUE files are in RGB, they are 1/3 larger than their RGB TIFF counterparts, and the same size as a CMYK TIFF.

There are two slightly different procedures, depending on the file type you are converting. TIFF and Photo CD use one procedure, while EPS (Photoshop-compatible), DCS, Photoshop 3.0, and Scitex CT formats require another.

You can also use the separate application Image Vue, which can be installed on another Macintosh.

To convert TIFF and Photo CD (Kodak) files:

1. In the Convert menu, choose Open. The Open Image dialog box appears (see figure 7.5).

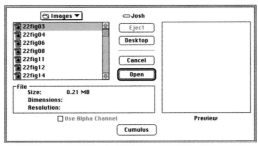

Figure 7.5 Open Image dialog box

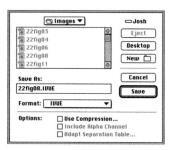

Figure 7.6 Save As dialog box

2. Select an image and click on Open. (There is no image preview for TIFF files.) The image opens on your screen.

   If you acquire images from a Photo CD, open the folder on the CD called "PHOTO_CD." Then open the folder called "IMAGES," select an image, and click on Open. When acquiring from a Photo CD, the largest version of the image is automatically used.

   If you use Pro Photo CD, the largest image may not be available using the Open command. In that case, try the Open As command.

3. In the Convert menu, choose Save As. The Save As dialog box appears (see figure 7.6).

4. Select a destination folder and image name. Then click on Save. The image is converted to IVUE.

To convert EPS, DCS, Photoshop 3.0, and Scitex CT files:

1. In the Convert menu, choose Acquire and select the appropriate plug-in (see figure 7.7).

   The Acquire dialog box appears.

2. Select an image and click on Open. The Save As dialog box appears. The image does not appear on your screen.

....

NOTE: If you get an error message when opening an EPS file, it is probably a PostScript file. Use the EPS Insertion command in the Create menu.

....

3. Select a destination folder and image name.

4. Click on Save. The image is converted to IVUE.

Figure 7.7 Selecting the EPS/DCS plug-in

Performing batch conversions

Image Vue has a limited batch conversion capability. Batch conversion allows you to convert several images simultaneously. The Image Vue application allows you to batch-convert TIFF files. Therefore, if you have your images scanned on a drum scanner that doesn't support Photoshop-compatible plug-ins, have them scanned in TIFF when possible. (Even if you don't use the batch conversion feature, TIFF files are faster to convert than other file formats.)

Figure 7.8 Dialog box for batch
conversion

Figure 7.9 Batch Save dialog box

Batch conversion with Image Vue cannot be performed when you are using your Macintosh. However, unless you have a large number of large images, converting to IVUE is relatively fast (from TIFF RGB, very roughly 20-40 MB per minute on a Power Mac, depending on the model. CMYK files take slightly longer).

To use batch conversion:

1. Select and drag all TIFF files onto the icon of the application called "Image Vue." This launches the application. A dialog box appears (see figure 7.8).

2. In the dialog box, click on Save All. The Batch Save dialog box appears (see figure 7.9).

   This dialog box allows you to automatically delete the original TIFFs after they are converted to IVUE.

3. Click on Save. All TIFFs are converted to the IVUE format.

CREATING A NEW DOCUMENT

In Live Picture, you insert IVUE images in a document, much as you would import images in a page layout program. So before you open an image, you need to create a document. In this exercise, we're going to use the Document Setup command to create a new document. We'll assume that we need a full-page output at 300 dpi.

To create a new document:

1. In the File menu, choose Document Setup. The Document Setup dialog box appears (see figure 7.10).

2. In the View pull-down menu, choose US Letter (see figure 7.10). The initial view should always be the size of your final output.

   Check that Define Initial View is selected. If it is not, click to select it.

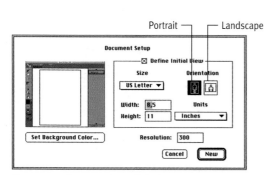

Figure 7.10   Document Setup dialog box

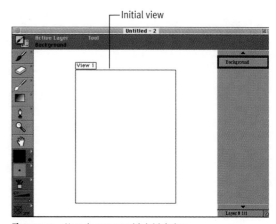

Figure 7.11   New document with initial view

3. Under Orientation, select the Portrait icon (see figure 7.10).

4. In the Units pull-down menu, choose inches.

5. In the Resolution field, enter 300. Always enter the resolution of your final output.

6. Click on New. A new document opens. The view you defined fills the document window (see figure 7.11).

   To reuse the same settings for your next document, choose New in the File menu. The new document uses the settings entered in the Document Setup dialog box.

   To change the document settings, open the Document Setup dialog box, change the settings, and click on New (all documents must be closed to use the Document Setup command). All new documents will have the new settings.

   You can also change document settings after opening a document.

   ■ Use the Add/Edit command in the View menu to delete, modify, or create a new view.

   ■ Use the Preferences/General command in the Edit menu to change units.

   ■ Use the Set Resolution command in the Edit menu to change document resolution.

OPENING AN IMAGE

Once you have images in the IVUE format, you are ready to insert them in a document. When working with images in Live Picture, there are two basic cases:

1. You know the size needed for your final output. In this case, use the Document Setup command to create an initial view the size of your output. See "Creating A New Document" earlier in this chapter.

2. You are retouching a single image. The size of the final output will be the size of the image. In this case, use the Auto View command to create a view the size of the image.

The next section, "Using an initial view" describes the procedure for Case 1. It is followed by "Using Auto View," which describes the procedure for Case 2.

....

NOTE: In this section, we will deal with two terms: document resolution and output resolution. Document resolution refers to the resolution of the FITS file. In reality, a FITS file has no resolution, but setting a document resolution provides a yardstick that is needed to work with pixel images (IVUE files). Output resolution is the resolution used to build the output file.

   In general, document resolution and output resolution are the same. However, if you change the output resolution, the document resolution is not updated automatically. For example, you may want to output your image at several different resolutions. In this case, update the document resolution to check the degree of interpolation that will occur before actually building the output. This is discussed in the next section, "Using an initial view." For more information on building outputs, see Chapter 28, "Building Outputs and Printing."

....

Using an initial view

Follow this procedure to composite several images. The initial view and document resolution are used to determine the size and resolution of your output file.

To insert images using the initial view:

1. After your launch Live Picture, choose Document Setup, from the File menu. You want to create an 8.5" × 11" output image at 300 dpi.

2. Repeat steps 2 to 6 in "Creating A New Document" earlier in this chapter. The settings in the Document Setup dialog box should be identical to figure 7.10 earlier.

   The initial view appears in the new document window. This view will be your output page. Everything inside the view will be included in the output file. Anything falling outside the view will not be included.

3. In the View menu, check that Auto View is deselected. We are using the initial view defined in the Document Setup dialog box as the area for the final output. Creating an additional view would clutter up the screen unnecessarily.

4. In the Create menu, choose Image Insertion. The Insert Image dialog box appears (see figure 7.12).

   Image Insertion is the standard layer for inserting images. The basic procedure for opening an image is the same in all image layers.

5. In the Insert Image dialog box, locate the image "Parrot" in the IVUE folder on the CD.

6. Auto Insert should not be selected. If it is, click on the Auto Insert box to deselect it.

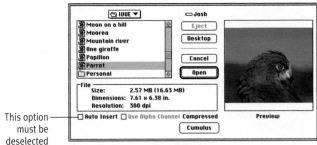

This option must be deselected

Figure 7.12   Insert Image dialog box

7. Click on Open.

The image fills the document window. The positioning tools appear to the left. You are in Insertion mode.

Notice the scale percentage in the control bar. It is 179.1% in figure 7.13. The scale percentage may be slightly different in your control bar. That's because, when Live Picture opens an image, the image is not opened at 100% of its initial size. Rather, the image fills the document window. So the initial scale percentage will depend in part on the size of your document window.

The scale percentage also depends on the document resolution. In the Document Setup dialog box, we set document resolution at 300 dpi, because we want a 300 dpi output file. If you change the document resolution, the image is not affected. This is due to the fact that a FITS file is resolution-independent. However, the scale percentage changes.

8. Tab to the Scale field and enter 100% in both fields. Then press Return (see figure 7.14). You have just scaled the image to 100% of its size for a 300 dpi output.

Enter 100% here...   ... and here

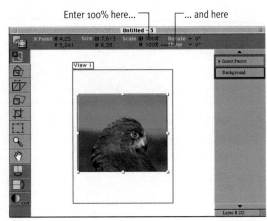

Figure 7.13   Image in Insertion mode

Figure 7.14   Image inserted at 100%

The image is now smaller than the view. If you enlarge the image to fill the view, the scaling percentage will rise above 100%. If you then output the view at 300 dpi, interpolation will occur because the image is scaled larger than its initial size (more than 100%).

9. Click on the mode toggle to use the creative tools.

   After you've inserted all your images and completed the composite, build the initial view to create your output. For more information on building, see Chapter 28, "Building Outputs and Printing."

TIP

If you decide to increase output resolution after inserting your images, change the document resolution to the new output resolution. Then check the scale percentages of the images to avoid excessive interpolation.

You are not obliged to insert an image at 100%. You can insert it at less than 100%. In this case, the image contains more information than needed for the output, so this is not a problem.

Furthermore, in most cases, you can scale images up to 200%. In other words, generally, you can safely interpolate up to twice the size of the original image. The main point is to be aware of the insertion percentage so that you know whether interpolation will occur, and how much.

In practice, it is more intuitive to just insert an image, position it as you wish, and check the percentage afterward. This puts less of a damper on your creativity. You can scale down the image at any time if needed.

To check the scale percentage of an image, select the image layer and toggle to the positioning tools. The percentage is always indicated in the control bar.

You can also change the document resolution at any time using the Set Resolution command in the Edit menu. If you do, the scale percentage of the images inserted will change to reflect the new resolution.

Using Auto View

TIP

If you don't know the resolution of the image, create an Image Insertion layer and check the resolution in the Insert Image dialog box. Then click on Cancel and enter the resolution in the Document Setup dialog box.

Follow this procedure to open a single image, retouch it, and output it at the same size and resolution as the original. Auto View and document resolution are used to determine the size and resolution of your output file.

To insert an image using Auto View:

1. In the File menu, choose Document Setup. The Document Setup dialog box appears.

2. Enter the resolution of the image. In this case, it will be 300 dpi.

3. Check that Define Initial View is not selected. We will use the Auto View to define the final output. An initial view would therefore serve no purpose.

4. Click on New. A new document appears. It does not contain a view (see figure 7.15).

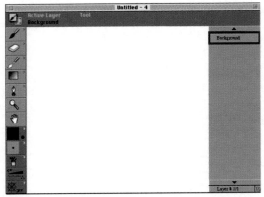

Figure 7.15 New document without initial view   **Figure 7.16** Selecting Auto View

TIP

You zoomed out in step 8 because otherwise the image would have become larger than the document window. You can zoom out after scaling to 100% but it takes longer.

5. In the View menu, check that Auto View is selected. If it isn't, select it (see figure 7.16). Auto View creates a view exactly the size of the image being inserted.

Important: You can create a view at any time. However, using Auto View is the only way to create a view exactly the size of the image. Auto View must be selected before you insert the image.

6. In the Create menu, choose Image Insertion. When the Insert Image dialog box opens, make sure that Auto Insert is not checked. If it is, click to deselect it.

7. In the Insert Image dialog box, select the image "Parrot" in the IVUE folder on the CD. Then click on Open. The image opens in the center of the document window (see figure 7.17).

   In figure 7.17, the scale percentage is approximately 50%. However, this percentage will vary depending on the size of your screen and your level of zoom.

8. If the scale percentage in the control bar is less than 100%, click on the Zoom tool, press and hold the Option key, and click once in the center of the image to zoom out.

9. In the control bar, click on the Scale W (width) field and enter 100%. Tab to the Scale H (height) field and enter 100% (see figure 7.19). Then press Return. The image is scaled to 100%.

Scale percentage ⎯

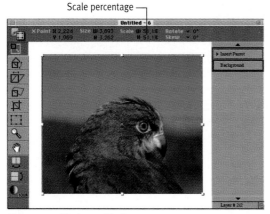

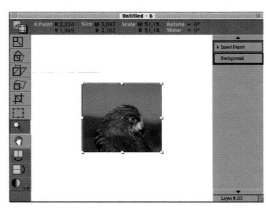

Figure 7.17   The image fills the screen

Figure 7.18   Screen after zooming out

Enter 100% here... ⎤   ⎡ ... and here

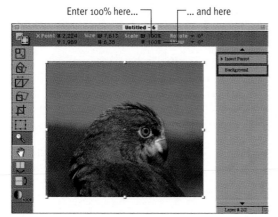

⎯ Automatic view named "Parrot"

Figure 7.19   Scaling image to 100%

Figure 7.20   Automatic view fitting image

10. Click on the mode toggle to switch to Creative mode. The Auto View appears around the Parrot image. By default, the view is given the name of the image.

After you retouch the image, build the view called "Parrot" to create your output. For more information on building, see Chapter 28, "Building Outputs and Printing."

TIPS ON INSERTING IMAGES

This section contains more information on image insertion.

Auto Insert

When you open an image, an option called Auto Insert is available in the Insert Image dialog box (refer to figure 7.12). If you select Auto Insert, the image opens in Creative mode and fills the document window. If you don't use Auto Insert, the image opens in Insertion mode, and also fills the document window (see figures 7.21 and 7.22).

The difference is that Auto Insert bypasses Insertion mode and goes directly to the creative tools. If you toggle back to the positioning tools, you will be in Positioning mode, not Insertion mode. See the next section.

Auto Insert is a quick way to insert images. It can be useful, for example, for silhouetting images, because in that case you want the image to fill the document window.

Insertion mode vs. Positioning mode

When you open an image without using Auto Insert, you are in Insertion mode (see figure 7.22). Once you toggle to the creative tools and toggle back to the positioning tools, you are in Positioning mode. Insertion mode is only available when you first insert the image.

There are several advantages to opening an image in Insertion mode (without Auto Insert):

- The Opacity tool is available only in Insertion mode (see figure 7.22).

— Creative mode

— Insertion mode

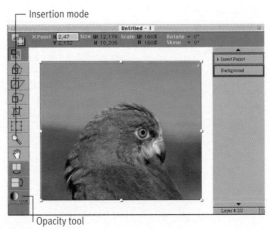

Opacity tool

Figure 7.21 Image inserted with Auto Insert

Figure 7.22 Image inserted without Auto Insert

TIP

In Insertion mode, zoom out so the whole image being inserted is visible, before you toggle to the creative tools. If you do lose part of an image, use the Marquee/Fill option to recover it.

- Repositioning an image is faster in Insertion mode because the image is not yet "pasted" into the composite.

- If you use the Auto View option, in Insertion mode, the automatically created view follows the image as you reposition it. In Positioning mode, the view does not follow the image. If you want to output an image at its original size using Auto View, do not use Auto Insert (see "Using Auto View" earlier in this chapter).

The disappearing image

When you toggle from Insertion mode to Creative mode, only the areas of the image in the document window remain visible. If you zoom out, the rest of the image is gone. This "disappearing act" does not occur when you toggle from Positioning mode to Creative mode.

THE WHOLE IMAGE, ALL THE TIME

In Live Picture the entire image is always there. You can crop out part of an image, use an Image Silhouette layer to remove a background, or simply remove parts using the Eraser. In every case, all you're doing is modifying the mask or stencil that allows you to see the image. You're not actually erasing the image.

Keeping the entire image in a file is all to your advantage. It won't slow down processing, because only a screenful of data is loaded in RAM, no matter what the size of the image. On the other hand, it allows you to recover the parts of an image that you or your client finally decide you'd like to include in the composite.

Figure 7.23 shows "The Wedding of Brother Wolf," created by British designer Helen Hann. In this image, the clock face was silhouetted to remove the background, and only part of the image was used in the composite. Figure 7.24 shows the original clock face.

Figure 7.23   "The Wedding of Brother Wolf"

Figure 7.24   Original clock face

Figure 7.25 Alternate version, with parts of clock reinserted

However, Helen could easily reinsert the background and use more of the image if necessary (see figure 7.25).

RESOLUTION INDEPENDENCE?
THERE'S NO SUCH THING!

Many of you may have heard that Live Picture works with resolution independence. To understand what this means, let's first see what it does not mean.

Resolution independence does *not* mean that the digital images you've been working with will suddenly be resolution-free. Each image has a given amount of data. If you retouch an image in Live Picture and output it at four times its original size, interpolation will occur; in other words data will have to be created that was not contained in the original image file.

What resolution independence *does* mean is that the resolution of anything you create inside Live Picture is not calculated until you build your output. So all the masks and stencils—meaning all image masks, paint, color corrections, and effects created in Live Picture—are resolution-independent.

In figure 7.26, a stroke of red paint was added to the composite. Figure 7.27 shows a zoom far into the edge of the paint. No pixels appear, because the paint has no resolution.

You can create several outputs at different resolutions. Each time, the masks, paint, and effects created in Live Picture are recalculated at the resolution you choose. There is never any quality loss.

The tools also are resolution-independent. A brush in Live Picture is not measured in pixels. It has no minimum or maximum size. If you zoom in or out, the displayed size of your composite changes, but the brush size remains the same.

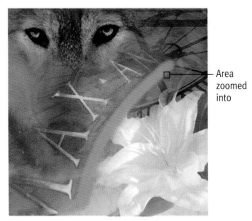

Area
zoomed
into

Figure 7.26   Red paint

Figure 7.27   No pixels appear in effects
generated in Live Picture

In figure 7.28, the circle shows the size of the largest brush. Figure 7.29 shows the same brush just after zooming out. The composite has gotten smaller, but the size of the brush is the same. This composite contains 5 images totaling 135 MB. By zooming, you can cover the entire image in a single brush stroke, in real time. This would still be the case if the image files totalled 500 MB or more.

Resolution independence also means that each image opened in Live Picture retains its original resolution, until you build the output. So you can open several images with different resolutions in a single document, without having to make them all conform to the resolution of the main image. The document, or FITS file, has no resolution. It is resolution-independent.

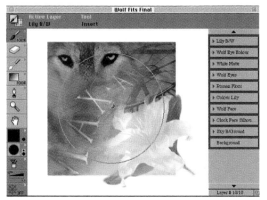

Figure 7.28   Circle shows largest brush size

Brush size remains constant

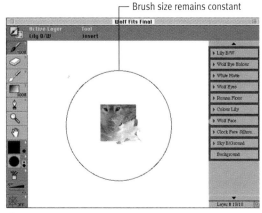

Figure 7.29   Same brush after zooming out

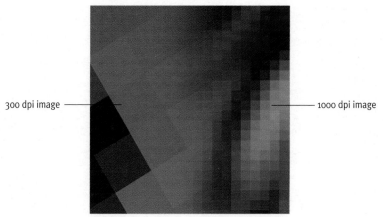

300 dpi image ————————   ———— 1000 dpi image

Figure 7.30   Each image retains its resolution

Figure 7.30 shows a zoomed-in view of two images with different resolutions. The image to the left is a 1 MB file scanned at 300 dpi. It was inserted in a new document (document resolution 300 dpi) and scaled to 100%. The image to the right is a 53 MB file, scanned at 1000 dpi. It was inserted in the same document, and scaled to 100%. The size of the pixels is different, because the resolution of each image is different. In addition, the 300 dpi file was rotated, so the orientation of the pixels is different.

In pixel-based software, the 1000 dpi image would be downsized to match the size of the first image. The extra data contained in the file would be lost. If you then decided to scale the image up, new data would be created, which means quality loss. With the FITS resolution-independent approach, the image retains its original resolution. The extra data is preserved and used, for example, if you increase the size of the image. No information is ever lost.

There are many other advantages to this resolution-independent approach. They are discussed in the rest of this chapter, and in Chapter 27, "The Most Flexible Software You've Ever Seen." It's important to understand these advantages to grasp what this software is really all about.

Doing input, thinking output

Since the IVUE images you insert are not resolution-independent, you still need to think about final output size when you scan. However, Live Picture introduces a new approach to scanning images.

PIXEL-BASED APPROACH

Your client wants a 300 dpi output. Scan all your images at 300 dpi and build a 300 dpi output. The idea is to keep scan size to the absolute minimum needed, because larger images take more time to open and edit.

LIVE PICTURE APPROACH

Scenario: On a recent job, you did a full-page ad for a client. The client called back a month later and asked for the same image for a two-page spread. You had to rescan the images at a larger size and redo the composite. Time spent: two long days. Money spent: cost of scans.

With Live Picture, scan your images at twice the size needed or more. Create the ad and build a full-page output. The IVUE files used retain their original resolution and dimensions. If the client asks for a two-page spread, double the size of the view, and output the new view—a very short and easy process!

Tips for viewing images at a 1:1 ratio

Viewing at a 1:1 ratio means that your screen displays one image pixel for each screen pixel. It allows you to know exactly what your final output will look like.

Viewing at 1:1 is important if your composite contains relatively sharp edges, such as silhouetted images or text. These edges don't look exactly the same at every level of zoom. Furthermore, if you are removing scratches on an image, it helps to know "how deep" you should go into the image before you stop cleaning up the image. Some scratches may not be visible in the output because they will be too small, so you could be wasting your time.

You can have several image resolutions in a Live Picture document, so there is no ready-made system for viewing images at a 1:1 ratio. Live Picture does offer an Antialiasing command in the View menu. Antialiasing smoothes the screen display and brings you closer to what your final output will look like. Still, this is not 1:1.

There are two work-arounds to view your image at exactly 1:1. For both procedures, it is helpful to know how to build output files.

....

NOTE: Unlike pixel-based software, Live Picture's screen display offers excellent quality at low viewing ratios, such as 1:8. This makes it possible to view the entirety of a large file on your screen with minimum quality loss. See "The three types of files" in Chapter 2, "An Overview."

....

The following procedure allows you to quickly view a small section of your composite.

To view a section of your composite at 1:1:

1. In the View menu, choose Add/Edit. The screen switches to View mode (see figure 7.31).

2. Drag open a view around a critical area, such as a hard edge or a silhouetted image. In figure 7.32, a view is created to check the silhouetted edge of the orchid.

3. Click on the mode toggle to switch back to Creative mode.

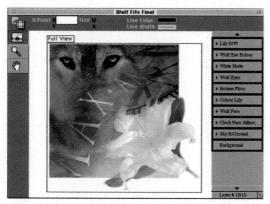

Figure 7.31   View mode

Figure 7.32   View for checking silhouetted edge ⌐ View

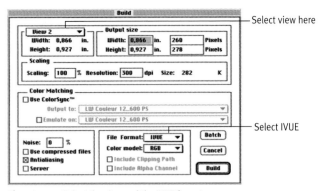

Select view here

Select IVUE

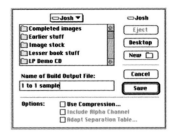

Figure 7.33   Select the view and the IVUE format

Figure 7.34   The Build Output dialog box

4. In the File menu, choose Build. The Build dialog box opens (see figure 7.33).

5. In the view pull-down menu, select the name of the view you created to check the edge. In this case, the name of the view is View 2. In the Export To menu, choose IVUE (see figure 7.33).

The size of the view selected is shown in inches and kilobytes.

6. Make sure the resolution indicated in the dialog box is the resolution of your final output. Then click on Build. The Build Output dialog box appears (see figure 7.34).

7. Enter a name for the output file, choose a destination folder, and click on Save. The Build progress bar appears.

8. When the build is completed, choose Open in the Converter menu. Choose the image you just built and click on Open. The image is opened on your screen.

IVUE 100% indicates that the image is displayed at a 1:1 ratio. If the percentage is less than 100%, the view is too large. In that case, create a smaller view and repeat steps 3 to 8.

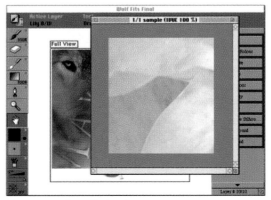

Figure 7.35   View 2 displayed at 1:1

Figure 7.36 Viewing an image at 1:1 with Image Vue

The next procedure allows you to view the entire composite at 1:1. You can only do this after you've completed your composite and built the entire image.

To check your final composite at 1:1:

1. Build the final output view at the final resolution. Build to IVUE.

2. Launch the application Image Vue. It is located in the Live Picture folder.

3. Choose Open in the File menu and open the IVUE.

4. In the View menu, choose Zoom Factor 1:1. The file is displayed at a 1:1 ratio (see figure 7.36).

5. Use the Pan tool to check the image.

Pixel measurements in a pixel-free world

In some dialog boxes, you have the option of entering a number of pixels. In pixel-based software, pixels refer to image pixels. In Live Picture, this is never the case, because you can have several images with different resolutions in one document. Depending on the dialog box, the term *pixel* may refer to document pixels, screen pixels, or output pixels.

Knowing what the term *pixel* refers to is not always essential. For instance, when you convert a path to a stencil, you enter a pixel value for the feather, but it's the visual result that counts. However, this section will help you better understand the use of the term *pixel* in Live Picture.

DOCUMENT RESOLUTION PIXELS

When you convert a path to a mask or stencil, and when you convert a mask or stencil to a path, the term *pixel* refers to document resolution pixels (see figures 7.37 and 7.38).

For example, if the document resolution is 300 dpi (dots- or pixels-per-inch) and you enter a feather value of 3 pixels in the Convert Path dialog box, then the feather will be 1/100th of an inch (300 divided by 3 = 100).

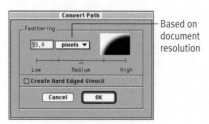

Figure 7.37 Convert Path dialog box

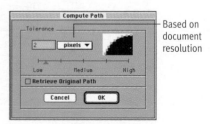

Figure 7.38 Compute Path dialog box

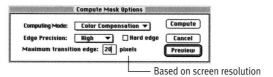

Based on screen resolution

Figure 7.39   Maximum Transition Edge option

. . . .

NOTE: Feathers and tolerances are calculated based on document resolution. They are not updated if you change the document resolution in the course of your work.

. . . .

SCREEN PIXELS

In an Image Silhouette layer, Maximum Transition Edge is calculated in screen pixels (see figure 7.39). The default value is 20. If you want some idea of what 20 screen pixels represents, it's about 1/4″ on your screen (20 pixels divided by 72, because most computer monitors are roughly 72 dpi). For more information, see Chapter 9, "The Great Silhouetting Lab."

OUTPUT PIXELS

The pixels in the Build dialog box refer to the number of pixels in the output file.

CHAPTER 8

ISOLATING IMAGES FROM THEIR BACKGROUND

This chapter provides an overview of the various ways to isolate part of an image from its background. It begins by exploring the intuitiveness and sensitivity of the Brush and Eraser. Then it shows images isolated using the powerful automatic Silhouetting tools and the Path tools. The chapter ends by demonstrating how several tool sets can be combined.

USING THE BRUSH AND ERASER

Inserting an image with a brush or eraser is a unique feature of Live Picture. The resolution-independent tools guarantee smooth edges at any size output. And because the size of the tools is unlimited, you can brush a smooth stroke over an entire image, no matter what its size.

To insert an image with a brush, follow these steps:

1. In the Create menu, choose Image Insertion. The Insert Image dialog box appears.

2. If the Auto Insert option is checked, click to deselect.

3. Open the image on the CD called "Watch," located in the IVUE folder. The image fills your document window (see figure 8.1).

4. In the positioning toolbar, click on the Opacity control and drag the Opacity cursor to 0% (see figure 8.2).

When you release the cursor the image becomes transparent, because overall image opacity is equal to 0%. You see the background beneath the image.

5. Click on the mode toggle to switch to Creative mode.

6. In the creative toolbar, click on the Size control and select the largest brush (see figure 8.3).

....

NOTE: Brush size is based on screen pixels. Therefore, depending on the size of your screen, the brush may be larger or smaller than in figure 8.3.

....

Figure 8.1 "Watch" in insertion mode

Figure 8.2 Dragging Opacity cursor to 0%

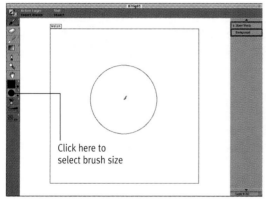

Figure 8.3 Selecting brush size

Figure 8.4 Ghosting in an image

7. Gently brush in parts of the image (see figure 8.4).

- Vary the amount of pressure you apply to the stylus.

- To brush in the image more gradually, decrease the pressure setting on the Pressure control.

- If you brush in too much of the image, click on the Eraser (or press and hold the Command key) and erase parts gradually.

- Slide the Brush Opacity cursor to 50%. Now try brushing in areas already visible as well as parts of the image not currently visible.

To create "Balloon" (see figure 8.11 and the cover of this book), German photographer Uve Ommer began by sketching his acrobatic vision on paper. He then took the shots shown in figures 8.5 to 8.10.

Under Uve's direction, I created Balloon (see figure 8.12) by assembling these images. Each image was inserted in an Image Insertion layer. I erased the parts not needed manually with the Eraser, and blended the parts used with the Brush. Precise erasing around the edges of the woman's body was not necessary, because all the shots had roughly the same background. The trick here was to find the points enabling each image to be brought together seamlessly, to reconstruct an apparently unified body. There was a constant play between brush, eraser, and pressure on the stylus.

....

NOTE: The last composited image (see figure 8.11) was hand-painted by Uve and scanned. To make the background more uniform, I placed figure 8.11 at the top of the composite and inserted it at an opacity of 20%. I then erased the painting manually wherever it covered the woman's body and the balloon.

....

Figure 8.5

Figure 8.6

Figure 8.7

Figure 8.8

Figure 8.9

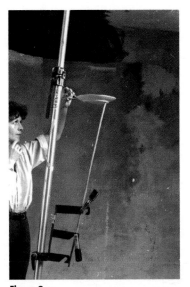

Figure 8.10

Figure 8.11 Hand-painted texture

Figure 8.12 "Balloon"

USING THE SILHOUETTING TOOLS

The Silhouetting tools allow you to automatically isolate an object from its background. Silhouetting works by recognizing differences in color. Therefore, the greater the color contrast between an object and its background, the more effective these tools are.

American photographer David Bishop used an Image Silhouette layer to isolate the computer monitor from its background and screen content (figures 8.13 and 8.14).

Figure 8.13   Original image

Figure 8.14   Silhouetted image

Figure 8.15   Monitor composited with transparency

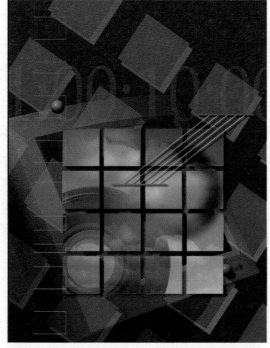

Figure 8.16   "Sybex Multi-Media Textbook" completed

The Image Silhouette layer was inserted on top of several layers of computer-generated images created using Live Picture and other software. The opacity of the monitor frame was then decreased (see figure 8.15).

The resulting transparency makes the monitor look like it's floating somewhere between the various objects, whereas it's actually located on top. This interplay of layers and transparency serves as the backdrop for "Sybex Multi-Media Textbook," the final image (see figure 8.16).

For a full description of the Silhouetting tools and exercises using images contained on the CD, see Chapter 9, "The Great Silhouetting Lab."

USING THE PATH TOOLS

Use the Path tools (see figure 8.17) to isolate an object by drawing a path around it. The part of the image inside the path is retained, and the part outside is discarded.

The Path tools are especially useful when there is not enough color contrast to use the Silhouetting tools. They are also well adapted to cutting out fairly regular geometric shapes such as boxes and containers, bottles, cars, and other smooth objects. To isolate the gargoyle from its background (see figure 8.18), French photographer Thierry Petillot used the Path tools due to the poor color contrast between the gargoyle and its background (see figure 8.19).

Figure 8.17   Path tools palette

Figure 8.18   Original image with path   **Figure 8.19**   Path alone

Figure 8.20   Convert Path dialog box

Figure 8.21   Gargoyle isolated on black background

Figure 8.22   Gargoyle on new background in "Paris"

The Convert Path dialog box appears before you transform the path into a mask or stencil (see figure 8.20).

You can select a hard edge for the mask or stencil, or you can enter a feather value. Feathering creates a gradual transition between the image and its new background. One advantage of the Path tools over Silhouetting is that you can experiment with a wide range of feathered edges until you obtain the precise edge you want.

Figure 8.21 shows the gargoyle after its original background was removed. For the sake of clarity, the image is placed on a black background. However, when Thierry was actually working on the image, the feathering was chosen with the gargoyle inserted in the composite to ensure a photorealistic blend between the image and its apocalyptic Parisian setting (see figure 8.22).

A full description of the Path tools is provided in the Live Picture User Guide.

USING THE OUTLINE TOOLS

Use the Outline tools, like the Silhouetting tools, to differentiate between object and background based on differences in color. The Outline tools are not as powerful as the Silhouetting tools, but they can be used at any time and are very flexible.

TIP

Try the Outline tools if silhouetting is difficult without zooming, and if the Path tools are too time-consuming (hair, and so on).

The Outline tools are generally used to retouch a silhouetted image, so they are described more fully in Chapter 9, "The Great Silhouetting Lab." That chapter provides information on these tools and two silhouetting exercises.

COMBINING TOOLS

Each set of tools described in this chapter can be combined in a variety of ways:

- Use the Silhouetting tools and finish up using the Outline tools.

- Use the Silhouetting tools for part of an image and the Path tools for the rest (see the following section, "Combining the Silhouetting and Path tools").

- Use the Path tools and then use the Brush, Eraser, or Marquee to modify image opacity.

- Use the Silhouetting tools and the Brush or Eraser (see "Combining silhouetting and the Brush/Eraser" later in this chapter).

Combining the Silhouetting and Path tools

In some cases, part of an object is easily isolated using the Silhouetting tools, while another part is more easily isolated using the Path tools.

To combine the Silhouetting tools and the Path tools:

1. Silhouette the part of the object that has strong color contrast.

2. Compute the mask.

3. Use the Mask –>Path command in the Mask menu to convert the mask to a path (use a low tolerance).

4. Continue the path using the Path tools.

5. Convert the path to a mask or stencil.

Combining silhouetting and the Brush/Eraser

This section illustrates the use of the Silhouetting tools combined with the Brush and Eraser.

To create "Blue Book," Thierry Petillot first used traditional photographic techniques to obtain an image of a book with blurred pages (see figure 8.23).

He then inserted the image in an Image Silhouette layer and removed the background using the automatic Silhouetting tools. After the image was silhouetted and positioned in its new background (images of microphone and compact disc), he used the Brush and Eraser to modify the transparency of the book in areas (see figure 8.24).

Figure 8.23 Image of blurred book

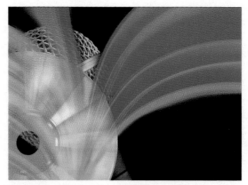

Figure 8.24 Book with variable transparency

Figure 8.25 "Blue Book" containing 225 MB of image files

By brushing and erasing manually, he made the book more or less transparent just where he wanted. The visibility of the microphone and CD are completely controlled, and the result is instantaneous, despite the fact that the two background images total 110 MB and the book is a 20 MB file.

Thierry then added a 95 MB file of a sharper book to create the illusion that some of the pages are turning (see figure 8.25).

CHAPTER 9

THE GREAT SILHOUETTING LAB

Silhouetting is one of Live Picture's most stunning and powerful features. It allows you to isolate an object by automatically detecting color differences between the object and its background. This chapter is divided into two parts:

- "A jump-start course on silhouetting" demonstrates the use of the Silhouetting tools. It contains a step-by-step procedure for silhouetting two images contained on the CD.

- "Silhouetting dissected" provides full details on the tools and technology used to silhouette. It contains many tips to help you get the most out of the Silhouetting tools to be more productive. Look for the answers in this section if you have any questions after completing "A Jump-Start Course on Silhouetting," or if you already know how to silhouette but want more information on specific areas.

A JUMP-START COURSE ON SILHOUETTING

To silhouette an image means to select an object in the image and separate it from its background. The object can then be placed on a new background, such as a gradient or another image. It can also be exported into a page layout program.

Some of you may have seen spectacular demos with Live Picture silhouetting 150 MB images in the space of a few seconds. The Silhouetting tools are indeed extremely powerful. However, the speed and ease at which you silhouette an image depends on the colors in the image. That's because, to isolate an object from its background, the Silhouetting tools analyze the differences in color between the two.

Two exercises are provided on the following page. The first one uses the image "Earth," which has strong color contrast between background and object. This exercise provides a simple framework for learning the basic silhouetting skills.

The second exercise makes use of the image "Woman in White Bathrobe." In this image, the white background and the bathrobe are almost the same color. Silhouetting this image brings into play most of the options you'll use to silhouette a wide variety of images. It also contains a number of useful tips.

To silhouette the image "Earth," follow these steps:

1. In the Create menu, choose Image Silhouette.

   The Insert Image dialog box opens.

2. Select the image Earth, located on the CD, in the IVUE folder. If the Auto Insert option is not selected, click on the box to select it (see figure 9.1).

3. Click on Open. The image opens and fills the document window (see figure 9.2).

4. In the control bar, click on the Outside control. It should now be framed in red, as shown in figure 9.3.

   By clicking on Outside, you are telling Live Picture that you want to select the part of the image you want to discard. In this case, it's the background.

5. In the creative toolbar, click on the Brush and choose the Auto option. Then draw a line as shown in figure 9.4.

When you release the stylus, all the colors drawn over are selected throughout the image, as shown in figure 9.5.

6. In the control bar, click on the Inside control.

7. In the creative toolbar, click on the Marquee and choose the Fill option. Then draw a rectangle over the entire image so that the whole earth is selected in red, as shown in figure 9.6.

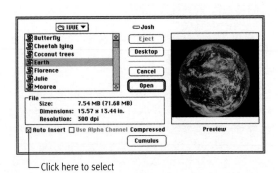

Click here to select

Figure 9.1 Insert Image dialog box with Auto Insert selected

Figure 9.2 "Earth" in Image Silhouette layer

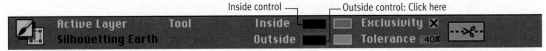

Inside control —— ┌— Outside control: Click here

Active Layer	**Tool**	**Inside**
Silhouetting Earth		**Outside**

Exclusivity ✕
Tolerance 40%

Figure 9.3 Control bar in Image Silhouette layer

Figure 9.4   Selecting colors with Auto option

Outside selection in green

Figure 9.5   Creating Inside selection

Marquee — Inside selection in red

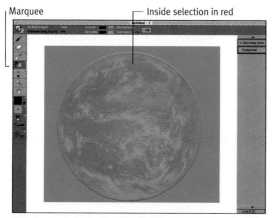

Figure 9.6   Creating Outside selection

Click here

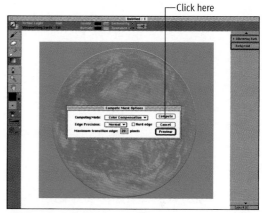

Figure 9.7   Compute Mask Options dialog box

Figure 9.8   Silhouette completed

8. In the control bar, click on the Compute Mask icon. The Compute Mask Options dialog box appears.

9. In the Compute Mask Options dialog box, click on Compute (see figure 9.7).

The cursor computes the mask. When it stops, the black background is removed and the earth is ready to be inserted on a new background (figure 9.8).

Congratulations! You've just silhouetted "Earth," a 71 MB file!

To silhouette the image "Woman in White Bathrobe," follow these steps:

1. In the Create menu, choose Image Silhouette.

2. In the dialog box, check that Auto Insert is not selected. Open the image called "Woman in White Bathrobe," located on the CD in the IVUE folder. You are in Insertion mode.

3. Using the positioning tools, position the image so that it fills your document window. Then toggle to the creative toolbar. Your screen should be similar to figure 9.9.

Important: At this stage of silhouetting you cannot zoom, so make sure to position the image properly before you toggle to the creative toolbar, using the Pan and Zoom tools. If you toggle before you are satisfied with your positioning, press the Escape key. Then delete the layer (Command-D) and start again.

4. In the control bar, click on the Outside control (see figure 9.10).

5. Press the Outside color sample and choose dark blue from the pop-down menu. In this image with its light colors, dark blue stands out more than the default green (see figure 9.11).

6. Click on the Brush and choose the Auto option. Then select a range of whites by dragging the Brush, as shown in figure 9.12.

When you release the Brush, all of the values dragged over are selected throughout the image, the including part of the bathrobe sleeve, which we don't want to select.

Outside selection in blue

Figure 9.9 Image ready to be silhouetted

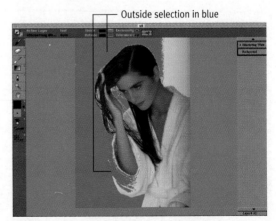

Figure 9.11 Selection created by brush stroke

Click here — — Press here and select dark blue

	Active Layer	Tool	Inside	⬛	⬜ Exclusivity ✕	
	Silhouetting Wh...	Auto	Outside	⬛	⬜ Tolerance 40%	--->ε---

Figure 9.10 Changing the color of the selection

Click here and drag cursor to 20%

Figure 9.12   Brushing with the Auto option

Figure 9.13   Selection with a lower tolerance

7. Press Command-Z to undo the brush stroke. Click and drag the Tolerance slider in the control bar from 40 to 20 (40 is the default setting). Then repeat the brush stroke. Your screen should look something like figure 9.13.

   Part of the sleeve is still selected, but most of the selection is not too close to the edge of the bathrobe.

   Each time the Auto option eats too far into the subject, press Command-Z, lower the tolerance and brush again. When the tolerance gets so low that this option becomes ineffective, use another option (for example, the Fill option described in Step 8).

8. Click on the Marquee and choose the Fill option. Drag open the Marquee as shown in figure 9.14.

   When you release the Marquee, your screen should look like figure 9.15.

Figure 9.14   Dragging open the Marquee

Figure 9.15   Selection created with Marquee

TIP

The Marquee can be used to fill in large areas which are not too close to the edge. It is much faster than using the brush.

TIP

The Fill option is quicker to use than the Selective option, used in step 10. On images with many colors, selecting each color is time consuming. Use the Fill option (Brush or Marquee) to create most of the selection, and the Selective option along the edge of the object.

9. Click on the Brush and choose the Fill option. Now fill in the background areas not selected by the Marquee. Brush near the woman, but don't attempt to brush up to the edge. The Fill option is not color-selective. Wherever you brush, you extend the selection. When you're finished brushing, your screen should be similar to figure 9.16.

10. Click on the Brush and choose the Selective option. Then set the tolerance to 25%.

11. Click near the edge of the bathrobe, *and without releasing the pressure on the stylus,* brush. (see figure 9.17). The color clicked is the color selected. The color appears in the Outside color box in the control bar.

    Brush right up to the bathrobe and all around the woman's head. Your Outside selection should be similar to figure 9.18.

    A 25% tolerance allows you to remove most of the white background, but some white remains along the edges of the woman's hair.

12. To remove the remaining white, increase the tolerance to 65%. Then click on the white background and brush over the hair, face, and hand.

    Remember, the first click defines the color selected. So always click in the white background. If you click on the hair or skin, the hair or skin color is selected (which isn't what you want). Figure 9.19 shows the brush being dragged over the hand, but the initial click was in the white background.

    Do not brush over the bathrobe. At a tolerance of 65%, the white of the background and the white in the bathrobe are too similar, so the bathrobe would be selected too.

13. Click on the Palette Knife to use the Clean Up option. Then brush the Palette Knife over the entire image. Isolated unselected spots in the background are selected, and isolated selected spots on the bathrobe are erased (see figure 9.20).

Figure 9.16 Filling with the Brush

Click here and drag cursor to 25%

Figure 9.17 Brushing with the Selective option

— Always click first on white background

Figure 9.18   Brushing near the edge

—Click-drag to 65%

Figure 9.19   Removing white background around the hair

NOTE: For your technical information, the Clean Up option only selects or erases isolated spots of 4 screen pixels or less. Any spot larger than 4 screen pixels is not affected.

---

14. Click on the Eraser and choose the Remove option. Erase the blue selection on the bathrobe sleeve, but don't go too close to the edge, or you'll also erase the blue selection on the background. Your image should look like figure 9.21.

    The Remove option using the Eraser is the opposite of the Fill option using the Brush. It erases. The option does not recognize differences in color. The only safe-guard against erasing the wrong parts is your own dexterity.

15. Click on the Eraser and choose the Selective option. In the control bar, click and drag the Tolerance slider to 20%.

— Brush over entire image

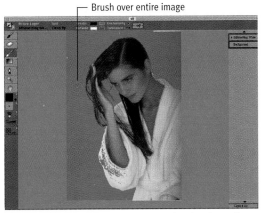

Figure 9.20   Selecting small spots using the Clean Up option

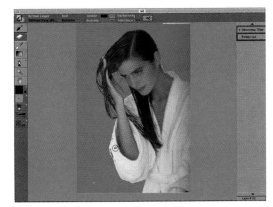

Figure 9.21   Erasing unwanted selection

TIP

You can use the Brush/Auto option instead of the Marquee. Drag the Brush over the inside until the whole object is selected in red. This may result in a smoother silhouetted edge.

16. Click on the bathrobe and remove any remaining blue selection along the edge of the sleeve (see figure 9.22).

Because the bathrobe and the background are very similar in color, some of the blue selection on the background may also be erased. To avoid this, run the edge of the Eraser along the edge of the bathrobe (check the Size Circle before you apply pressure). Erase slowly and carefully: in this case, the selectivity helps you, but dexterity is also necessary to avoid removing the existing selection.

You have now finished creating your Outside selection. Creating the Inside selection will be very quick.

17. In the control bar, click on the Inside control.

18. Click on the Marquee and choose the Fill option. Then drag a rectangle over the entire image. When you release the stylus, any part of the image not painted in blue becomes the Inside selection, displayed in red (see figure 9.23).

NOTE: The Exclusivity option in the control bar must be selected.

19. In the control bar, click on the Compute Mask button. The Compute Mask Options dialog box appears.

20. Click on Preview. A preview of the mask is displayed (see figure 9.24).

When you click on Preview, the Preview button changes to Retouch (see figure 9.25).

21. In the Compute Mask Options dialog box, click on Retouch.

22. Click on the Brush. The Retouch option is the default option. Then click on the white in the bathrobe. Without removing the pressure on the stylus, run the Brush

❷ Click-drag to 20%

❶ Click bathrobe first

Figure 9.22   Erasing using the Selective option

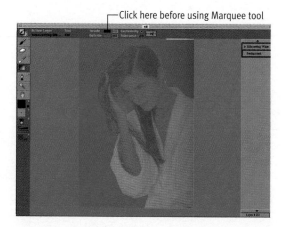

Click here before using Marquee tool

Figure 9.23   Creating the remaining selection

carefully along the edge of the sleeve (see figure 9.26). This will fully reveal the bathrobe in areas where it's somewhat transparent. In other words, brush in the bathrobe in areas where the new blue background is showing through.

Compute Mask button

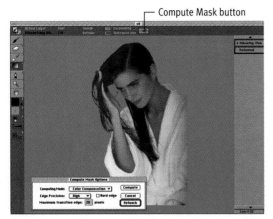

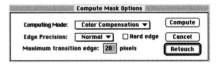

Figure 9.24   Subject with background removed

Figure 9.25   Compute Mask Options dialog box with Retouch option

If the original white background is reappearing, press Command-Z and move the Pressure control cursor all the way to the left. Also, apply less pressure with your stylus. The less you press, the more selective the Retouch option is.

Make sure you're not releasing pressure on the stylus after you click on the bathrobe. If you reclick on the background, you're telling Live Picture that you want to reinsert the background.

If you accidentally reinsert parts of the original background (white), click on the Eraser and use the Retouch option. It works just like the Brush/Retouch option, except it erases instead of revealing.

Figure 9.26   Retouching the preview

23. Click on Compute in the Compute Mask Options dialog box. The cursor moves across the screen to indicate that Live Picture is calculating the resolution-independent mask.

You have silhouetted the woman in the white bathrobe. The rest of this exercise shows you how to zoom and rework the finer details of the mask. For high-quality silhouetting, this will often be necessary.

24. Zoom into the hand and hair, as shown in figure 9.27.

25. Click on the Eraser and choose the Outline option.

26. Press and hold the Option key. The eyedropper appears. Still pressing the Option key, click on a strand of hair (see figure 9.27).

This defines what you don't want to erase. The color clicked appears in the control bar, across from the Brush icon.

27. Release the Option key. Then click in between the strands of hair where white remains from the original background, and drag to erase the white (see figure 9.28).

Like the Retouch option, the Outline option is affected by the last color clicked, the Pressure control in the creative toolbar, and the pressure applied by your hand.

TIP

If the white areas are too small to allow you to click with precision, you can also zoom in, then click.

If the white area is too small to click precisely on a white, click in a different, larger background area, and drag lightly across the hair to the area you want to erase. Though you can't see it, the original background is still there, and the color clicked is the color of the original image before it was silhouetted. You can verify this in the control bar by looking at the color across from the Eraser. The color box always shows the last color clicked (see figure 9.29).

Color appears here

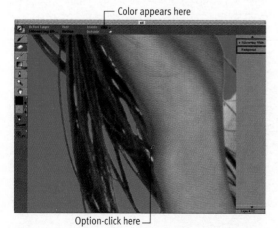

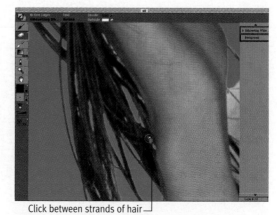

Option-click here ⌐

Click between strands of hair ⌐

Figure 9.27 Indicating color to not erase

Figure 9.28 Erasing using the Outline option

Color being erased appears here

Color appears here   Option-click here

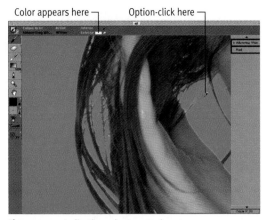

Figure 9.29   Clicking-dragging to define color to erase

Figure 9.30   Indicating color to not reinsert

TIP

Since the Outline options are color-sensitive, you have to click and drag for each color. For images with many colors, it can be faster to zoom in and use the Insert and Erase options (Brush and Eraser respectively).

28. Click on the Brush and choose the Outline option. Outline with the Brush is the exact opposite of Outline with the Eraser.

29. Press and hold the Option key. When the eyedropper appears, click right next to a strand of hair that you want to make reappear (see figure 9.30). When you Option-click, you define what you don't want to make reappear (in this case, the original white background).

30. Find a strand of hair that was partly erased when the mask was computed. Click on the strand of hair and drag to reinsert it (see figure 9.31).

31. When you have cleaned up the hair sufficiently, zoom out (see figure 9.32). You have successfully silhouetted the image "Woman in White Bathrobe."

Color being brushed in appears here

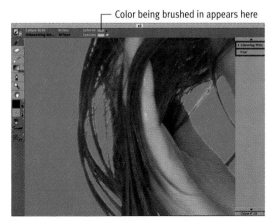

Figure 9.31   Brushing using the Outline option

Figure 9.32   Completed silhouette

SILHOUETTING DISSECTED

The "jump-start course on silhouetting" in this chapter is designed to get you up and running with the Silhouetting tools. However, not all the intricacies and tips for efficient, quality silhouetting could be demonstrated. This section provides an overall view and fuller understanding of the Silhouetting tools.

One of the things that surprises users when they silhouette an image for the first time is that they cannot zoom—at least at the beginning. This would be a major handicap in a pixel-based application, but the Live Picture technology is quite different. Understanding and getting familiar with the advantages and limitations of each stage of this technology will increase your efficiency. This will help you be timely at each stage and get the most out of each set of tools. Then you can view this "zoom disability" in its proper perspective.

There are three basic stages to silhouetting. They are summarized in table 9.1 and then described in further detail.

Helpful preliminaries

Silhouetting is a beautiful piece of technology, but once it takes off it's difficult to stop it. However, you can prepare yourself properly. Table 9.2 provides a list of things you cannot do once you begin silhouetting, why they are important, and how to prepare yourself beforehand.

Once you have completed the first two stages of the silhouetting process (see table 9.1), you will again be able to perform the operations listed in the first column of table 9.2.

TABLE 9.1 THE THREE SILHOUETTING STAGES SUMMARIZED

Stage	Tools selective based on color differences?	Zooming?	Use
Creating two selections	Yes	No	Basic silhouetting
Retouching the mask	To a certain degree	No	Removing transparency in mask
Detailed retouching: • Outlining	To a certain degree	Yes	Zooming in to work on detail too small to silhouette in the two previous stages.
• Inserting	No	Yes	

TABLE 9.2 SILHOUETTING PRELIMINARIES

Things you can't do	Why they are important	How to prepare beforehand
Change background color	If the Image Silhouette layer is the first layer in your composite, the subject, once isolated, is set against the background color. Selecting a strongly contrasting color makes it easier to visualize the silhouetted edges and use the Retouch option.	Set the background color before you create the Image Silhouette layer. To check image colors: • Open the image in an Image Insertion layer, check image colors and delete the layer; or • Use the preview in the open image dialog box of any layer and then click on Cancel; or • Use the Open command in the Converter menu. Then select a strongly contrasting color and choose Set Background in the Edit menu.
Change the Cursor icons	It's easier to select precise colors if the Cursor Icon option is deselected.	Choose the Preferences/General command in the Edit menu and deselect the Cursor Icon before you create the Image Silhouette layer.
Zoom	To display the object to be silhouetted as large as possible	Silhouette first, position after **Basic method** 1) If the document window isn't opened to maximum screen size, drag it to cover your entire monitor. 2) In the Open Image dialog box, select Auto Insert. When opened, the image will fill the document window. 3) After you compute the mask, position the image. **Special methods** Do not use Auto Insert. For portrait formats on a horizontal screen, you can rotate the image 90° and scale to get the most out of your screen area. If you want to silhouette only a small object in an image, zoom or scale so that the object fills the document window. Areas you want to discard can be off-screen. NOTE: Always leave at least a 1/2" of empty space along each edge. The tools cannot brush right up to the edge of the document.

TIP

Do not try to create two perfect selections if the details are too small to work on without zooming. You'll only waste time. Instead, do what you can at this level of zoom, and perfect the details later using the Zoom tool and the Insert and Outline options (see "Zooming and Reworking the Mask" later in this chapter).

Creating the Inside and Outside selections

This is the basic and most powerful stage of the silhouetting process. However, this is only the first stage. You create two selections, an Inside selection and an Outside selection. Live Picture then calculates the mask.

The rest of this section is organized in the form of questions and answers.

What's the difference between Auto, Fill, and Selective?

These are the three Brush options, though they are also available when using the Eraser and Marquee (figures 9.33, 9.34, and 9.35).

■ Fill does not recognize differences in color. Wherever you brush, the area is selected. Use it for filling in areas that aren't too close to the edge of the object.

■ Auto covers the entire image. You select a range of color values by dragging the Brush over those colors. When you release pressure, the colors are selected throughout the image.

■ Selective is the same as Auto, but areas are only selected if you actually brush them. You click and drag without releasing the pressure on the stylus. As you drag, the colors the same as the color originally clicked are selected.

How do you use the Selective option with the Marquee?

1. Click the Marquee and choose the Selective option.

2. Press and hold the Option key. With the eyedropper, click on the color you want to select.

3. Drag open the Marquee. The color will be selected within the Marquee.

4. To add to the selection, choose another color with the eyedropper. Then press and hold the Shift key, and drag open the Marquee. If you don't press the Shift key, the new selection will replace the former selection.

How can I control the range of colors selected?

Several ways, depending on the option used.

■ Tolerance control: The Tolerance control in the control bar affects the Auto and Selective options. A tolerance set at 40% will select a wider range of colors than a tolerance set at 10%. Values between 20 and 40% are the most frequently used (see figure 9.36). Values below 10% are too selective to pick up anything. At 100%, you lose all selectivity—all areas are selected. Tolerance has no effect on the fill option.

Figure 9.33   Brush silhouetting options

Figure 9.34   Eraser silhouetting options

Figure 9.35   Marquee silhouetting options

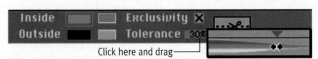

Figure 9.36   The Tolerance control

The tolerance values (0-100%) do not correspond to any absolute values, such as luminance. They are relative figures. Finding the right tolerance mostly comes with experience.

....

NOTE: The tolerance setting is less selective in Auto than in Selective. Ten percent is usable in Auto, but it's too sensitive if you're using the Selective option.

....

- Brush stroke: With the Auto option, select a wide range of colors by dragging over many colors, or a small range by dragging over just a few colors. For the smallest range, you can click on just one color.

- Pressure: With the Selective and Fill options, applying more pressure or increasing the Pressure control setting in the toolbar "fattens" the Brush stroke, much like painting with a real brush. However, it does not affect the range of colors selected. Pressure has no effect on the Auto option.

Why does the edge of my mask look rough and jagged?

This is not the mask you're looking at. It's still just a selection. Live Picture is going to use the selections to calculate the mask. Once the mask is computed, zoom in and check the edge of the silhouetted object. It should be smooth.

Why must I create two selections?

Live Picture analyzes the colors selected as the Inside and the colors selected as the Outside. Based on these two selections it finds its own edge! So, it doesn't simply transform the Inside selection into a mask. It uses both the selections to create the mask.

For some images, it is difficult if not impossible to create precise selections. One example is hair blending into the background colors. You can create approximate selections and let Live Picture find the edge for you.

The image in figure 9.37 is not very sharp, and the colors of the giraffe are similar to the background colors. Rather than spending lots of time perfecting the selections, the Marquee/Fill option was used to fill in the large areas, and the Brush/Fill option was used near the edge of the giraffe. Both the Inside and Outside selection were created in this manner. A space or "no man's land" was left near the edge (see figure 9.38).

Figure 9.39 shows the preview before any retouching was done. Figure 9.40 shows what the image looked like after brief retouching.

After the mask was computed, the giraffe was cleaned up using the Insert option and zooming. Notice the giraffe's mane against a white background (see figure 9.41). Aside from some final retouching, the edge of the mane was computed by the software based solely on the two selections. Figure 9.42 shows the giraffe inserted on a new background.

Figure 9.37   Original image

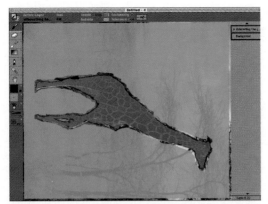

Figure 9.38 Image with Inside and Outside selections

Figure 9.39 Preview before retouching

Figure 9.40 Preview after using Retouch option

Figure 9.41 Silhouetted giraffe after using the Insert option

Figure 9.42 Giraffe on new background

Check here before silhouetting ⎯⎤

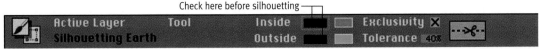

Active Layer **Tool** **Inside** **Exclusivity** ☒
Silhouetting Earth **Outside** **Tolerance** 40%

Figure 9.43   Checking the Selection control

How do I know whether I'm working on the Inside or Outside selection?

Remember, "outside" refers to the Outside selection, not any particular part of the image. Live Picture doesn't know what part of the image you consider the Outside selection until you compute the mask.

Here are a few tips to avoid confusion:

- You can begin with the Inside selection or Outside selection. Before you create a selection, check the control bar and make sure the appropriate color box is selected (see figure 9.43). If the wrong color box is mistakenly selected, there is no way to switch after the selection has been created.

- If you have created both selections and want to rework one of the selections, it can get a bit confusing. So, check the colors instead of trying to figure out which selection you want to work on. Example: You want to erase a bit of the green selection. Look in the control bar, check which selection is green, and make sure the color box across from green is selected. Then erase.

- To replace a red selection with a green selection, for instance, first select the red selection and erase the red, then select the green selection and add green.

What if I don't want to silhouette an image anymore?

Press the Escape key, then delete the layer.

The Compute Mask options

The Compute Mask options allow you to define the type of mask you want to create, control edge hardness, and preview the silhouette.

When you have created the Inside and Outside selections, click on the Compute Mask button in the control bar. The Compute Mask Options dialog box appears (see figure 9.44).

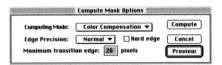

Figure 9.44   Compute Mask Options dialog box

Computing mode

- Standard calculates a mask based on the Inside and Outside selections.

- Color Compensation does the same, but creates some transparency on the edge of the silhouetted object. In photographs, objects reflect the colors of their original backgrounds, especially along their edges. By creating a minute degree of transparency along the edge of the silhouetted object, the colors of the new background are reflected along its edges. The result is a more photorealistic composite. Images don't look cut out.

- Luminance takes the brightness values of the Inside selection into account when calculating the mask. The opacity of each point in the mask is based on the brightness values of the image. The result is a mask of variable opacities. For more information, see Chapter 23, "Luminance Masks and Texture Revealed."

- Alpha Channel allows you to import an alpha channel created in pixel-based software and transform it into a FITS resolution-independent mask.

Table 9.3 tells you when to use each computing mode.

Edge precision

Edge precision refers to the width of the mask edge. Technically speaking, it's the distance over which mask opacity drops from 100% to 0% along the edge of the object. In visual terms, a more precise edge is a sharper edge. Moreover, the higher the edge precision, the longer it takes Live Picture to compute the mask.

TABLE 9.3 Computing Mode Summary

Choose	For
Color Compensation	All cases *except* those listed below.
Standard	Silhouetting objects with many edges, such as a straw hat with tiny holes, or an image containing many small objects. Color Compensation might create too much transparency for small objects.
Luminance	Creating relief, creating textures, special effects. See chapter 23, "Luminance Masks and Texture Revealed."
Alpha Channel	Images imported with alpha channels.

Figure 9.45   Original image

Figure 9.46   Mask computed using low edge precision

Figure 9.47   Mask computed using high edge precision

Edge precision depends on the image being silhouetted, and the new background you plan to use. For instance, if the new background image is not as sharp as the silhouetted image, then Medium or Low precision probably would provide the best photorealistic blend. However, if both images are sharp, high-res images, then High precision will create the best result.

A mask computed for the same image (see figure 9.45) using low and high edge precision is shown in figures 9.46 and 9.47. A Multicolor gradient was inserted behind the image. Because clouds are by nature soft, low edge precision creates a more natural blend in this case.

HARD EDGE

Hard Edge creates a hard, cut-out look and often results in jaggies. It can be used to silhouette geometric objects or very small objects. Hard Edge overrides the computing mode and edge precision options.

MAXIMUM TRANSITION EDGE

I like to call this "Distance analyzed." This option does not affect the width of the edge. Rather, it refers to the number of pixels Live Picture analyzes between the Inside and Outside selections to calculate the edge of the mask.

The default value is 20. This means that, by default, Live Picture analyzes 10 pixels into the Inside selection and 10 pixels into the Outside selection to calculate the edge. The only reason you should change this default value is if you leave a space between the two selections (see figure 9.38). In this case, increase the "Maximum Transition Edge" to 40 or 60 pixels. The pixels here are screen pixels, so 72 pixels equals about 1" on your screen. Try previewing different values.

The preview

When you have finished selecting the Mask Compute Options, you can ask Live Picture to calculate the mask, or you can first see a preview to check the silhouette. *Always ask for the preview.* Remember, the mask is not an exact replica of the Inside selection. Some retouching, however minor, is usually required.

You can also use the preview to see what the silhouette looks like using different Mask Compute options. Each time you change an option, the Preview button can be clicked again.

....

NOTE: For some options, the difference you'll notice on the screen is very slight, and sometimes not apparent at all. However, the difference will be more marked on the final output, or if you zoom into the image—which you cannot do at this stage. Read "The Mask Compute options" earlier in this section to understand what to expect in the final image.

....

After you check the preview, you have two options:

- Click on Silhouette. This brings back the Inside and Outside selections. You can continue to create and modify the selections. This is generally not the most efficient approach. As mentioned earlier in this chapter, it is better to not spend too much time perfecting the selections.

- Click on Retouch.

Retouching

The importance of the Retouch option is often overlooked. When Live Picture calculates a mask based on the Inside and Outside selections, there are almost always areas within the mask that are somewhat transparent. It is this transparency that allows the photorealistic compositing of different images. However, sometimes underlying layers or the background color show through the image in unwanted areas. Conversely, parts of the background you want to discard may appear in the preview. The Retouch option allows you to clean up these areas.

The Retouch option can save you a great amount of time. If you don't use the Retouch option, you can retouch later using the Insert and Outline options. However, these tools are most effective when you zoom. The Retouch option, on the other hand, allows you to quickly retouch most of the image without zooming. Only small areas of detail will need to be reworked with the Insert and Outline options.

The Retouch option works somewhat like the Selective option when you are creating your Inside and Outside selections. However, you directly modify the opacity of the mask, rather than working on a selection. So, you reveal the image fully where it is semitransparent, and you erase any remaining background.

There is no tolerance bar for the Retouch option. However, there are two ways to control tolerance:

TIP

Only use Retouch *if no further changes will be made* to the Inside and Outside selections. If you click on Silhouette in the dialog box, you can modify the selections, but all retouching is lost.

- To make retouching more selective, press lightly on the stylus. *This is the real key to selectivity.*

- To make the Retouch option yet more selective, move the pressure setting in the toolbar to the left. To make the Retouch option less selective, move the pressure setting to the right. I suggest starting with the setting all the way to the left.

Computing the mask

Let's summarize.

1. Create the Inside and Outside selections.

2. Check the preview.

3. To rework the selections, click on Silhouette, modify the selections and click on Preview again.

4. Use the Retouch option.

5. Click on Compute.

The cursor moves across the screen.

Important: Once you click on Compute, you can no longer access the Retouch option or return to the Inside/Outside selections. Other tools, described below, allow you to continue reworking your mask. But when you click on Compute, you permanently exit Silhouetting mode.

The rest of this section is organized in the form of questions and answers.

What's happening when the cursor moves across the screen?

Live Picture is calculating the mask at another mathematical level, taking the full resolution of the image into account, and creating an antialiased (smooth) edge.

Why does my mask still look a little rough?

To see the smoothed edge, you first need to regenerate the screen, by zooming, for example. The more you zoom in, the smoother the edge becomes and the more it resembles your output.

You can also use screen antialiasing. This option offers the highest display quality. Turn it on temporarily to view the mask edge. Since it slows down Live Picture, turn it off when you are finished checking the edge. The Antialiasing command is located in the View menu.

To view the mask edge at a 1:1 ratio, see Chapter 7, "Inserting Images."

Why have the tool options in the creative toolbar changed?

Once the image is silhouetted, the Image Silhouette layer becomes an Image Insertion layer. The tool options are the same as those found in any Image Insertion layer. (The only difference is that no Crop tool is available in Positioning mode.)

What if I want to silhouette the image again or silhouette another image already inserted in the composite?

The Silhouetting tools are only available when you first insert an image. However, there are ways to get around this constraint. See "More silhouetting tips" at the end of this chapter.

Can I zoom now?

Yes, you can. Two options are now available to rework the silhouetted mask: Insert and Outline.

Zooming and reworking the mask

Live Picture offers two options for reworking a silhouetted mask: Insert and Outline. Use both of these options for work on detail while zoomed in.

Important: The clean edges created using the Silhouetting tools become fuzzy if you work at a low magnification level with these options, for example with the full image visible on the screen. For this type of work, use the Retouch tool, which is available before you click on Compute (see "Retouching" earlier in this chapter).

Table 9.4 indicates when each option is appropriate. You can combine Outline and Insert.

USING THE OUTLINE OPTIONS

With the Outline options, differentiating between inside and outside allows you to erase unwanted background without erasing the silhouetted object. Conversely, you can use Outline to reinsert parts of an object without reinserting the background. In the first

TABLE 9.4	**USING OUTLINE AND INSERT**	
Use	**To**
Outline (color sensitive)	Work along edges, especially to remove colors remaining from the original background.
Insert and erase (not color sensitive)	• Fill in transparent or semitransparent areas missed with the Retouch option, and which are not too close to the edge of the mask (Insert option). Use erase to remove bits of background not too close to the edge.
	• Work on edges containing many colors. The Outline options would take too long, since you have to select each color.

case, use the Eraser/Outline option. In the second, use the Brush/Outline option. These options are very helpful for work on detail.

To erase colors remaining from the original background:

1. Click on the Eraser/Outline option.

2. Option-click on a color *you do not want to erase.*

   The idea here is to first tell Live Picture what colors *should not be erased.* By clicking, you are "protecting" that color. The colors that most need that protection are the colors close to the area you will be erasing. So click close to that area. When you Option-click, the color clicked appears in the control bar, across from the tiny Brush icon.

3. Click on a color you want to remove and drag to erase.

   This option functions much like the Selective option during silhouetting. If you remove the pressure from the stylus and press down again, the new color clicked is the color erased. You can see the most recent color clicked in the control bar, across from the tiny Eraser icon.

To make parts of the image reappear:

1. Click on the Brush/Outline option.

2. Option-click a point you do *not* want to reappear.

   The idea here is to tell Live Picture what colors *should not reappear.* By clicking, you are "locking out" that color, in other words preventing it from reappearing. The colors that most need to be "locked out" are the colors close to the part of the edge you are working on. So click close to that area. Remember that, even though only part of the original image is now visible, the entire image is still there. If you do not "lock out" areas currently invisible, they will reappear.

   When you Option-click, the color appears in the control bar, across from the tiny Eraser icon. The color you see is the color of the original background, as if the image had never been silhouetted. Even though this color may not be visible in your image, it's there. The whole image is and always will be there (see Chapter 7, "Inserting Images").

3. Click on a color you want to make reappear and brush to insert.

   Each time you remove the pressure from the stylus and press down again, the new color clicked will be the color brushed back in. You can see the most recent color clicked in the control bar, across from the tiny Brush icon.

Tolerance: To increase color-sensitivity, that is, to affect fewer colors, move the Pressure cursor to the left. To decrease color-sensitivity, that is, affect more colors, move it to the right. Stylus pressure has no effect on Outline tolerance.

This option takes a bit of practice. Since the colors change as you move through the image, you have to keep updating the colors. You may find it helpful to talk yourself through this process. Click on the Brush/Outline and ask yourself:

1. "What area do I not want to reappear?" (Option-click it).

2. "What area do I want to reappear?" (Brush the area back in).

   Move up or down along the edge of the mask and repeat.

3. "What area do I not want to reappear?" (Option-click it).

4. "What area do I want to reappear?" (Brush the area back in).

   And so on as you move along the edge of the mask.

TIP

When zoomed in, this option can be very effective and quick to use because you don't need to select colors.

USING THE INSERT/ERASE OPTIONS

The Insert/Erase options are purely manual. They do not recognize differences in color. Any area brushed using the Insert option reappears (including the background you just got rid of). Any area erased using the Erase option disappears.

And now, some answers to the questions most frequently asked.

Why is almost nothing happening when I use Outline?

It's probably because the colors keep changing. When you click and brush, you brush in only the color clicked. If there are several colors or shades, they will not all reappear. You have to click and insert each color separately. You can insert a wider color range by moving the Pressure cursor to the right. If it still takes too long, zoom and brush carefully using the Insert option.

Why have the edges of my mask suddenly gotten fuzzy?

There are two possibilities:

■ You did an Undo (Command-Z or Edit menu). The edges look ragged. This is just a display effect that disappears as soon as the screen is regenerated.

■ You are not zoomed in enough. The Insert and Outline options are most effective when zoomed in. Otherwise, you'll lose the photorealistic edge you obtained using the Silhouetting tools.

When should I stop retouching the mask?

If you zoom in and use the Insert option to correct the edge of the mask, you'll notice when you zoom out that the part you reworked may be "cleaner" or sharper than the original silhouetted edge. Usually, automatically calculated edges are more photorealistic than the sharper edge obtained by zooming and brushing manually. So don't make the edge any sharper than the automatically computed edge.

Why do I notice transparent areas when I zoom?

Masks created using the Silhouetting tools are sometimes not fully opaque in all areas, especially near the edge. Often, you don't notice this until after you zoom. That's why I recommend briefly brushing the entire image with the Retouch option before computing the mask. Otherwise, you can fill in these areas with the Brush (Insert or Outline options). Remember, though, that slight transparency near the edges often results in a more photorealistic composite than a fully opaque edge.

More silhouetting tips

This section contains tips on handling images after they are silhouetted. Most of the tips require skills described elsewhere in this book. While references are made to the appropriate chapters, these tips will be easier to understand after you have acquired these skills.

"Saving" a mask by copying to the stencil

When you silhouette an image, Live Picture creates a mask. Chapter 10, "Sources, Masks, and Stencils Revealed," shows that a mask can be easily modified, either purposely or accidentally.

To avoid this, whenever you finish retouching and reworking a silhouetted mask, copy it to the stencil in the same layer (see figure 9.48).

This ensures that you keep a copy of the original mask. You can retrieve the original mask by copying the stencil back to the mask. See Chapter 10 for more information on copying masks to stencils and vice-versa.

Viewing a mask

In Live Picture, you cannot view a mask without the image. A trick to get around this is to create a Monocolor layer and copy the mask from the Silhouette layer to the mask of the Monocolor layer. This creates a colored fill that is a replica of the mask. Then hide the Image Silhouette layer.

Option-drag from here... ⎯⎯ ⎯⎯ ...to here

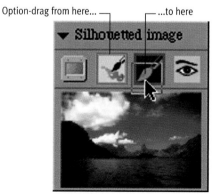

Figure 9.48 Copying a silhouetted mask to a stencil

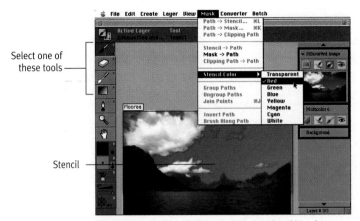

Select one of
these tools

Stencil

Figure 9.49   Stencil of silhouetted image colored in red

By changing the color of the Monocolor layer, you can change the color of the fill. This method allows you to see if areas of transparency remain.

Another way to view a mask in Live Picture is to display the stencil. First, copy the mask to the stencil (in the Image Silhouette layer). Then display the stencil using the Stencil Color command in the Mask menu. To use the Stencil Color command, activate the layer and select one of the four top tools in the creative toolbar.

In figure 9.49, the sky was removed by silhouetting. After copying the mask to the stencil, the stencil was colored red. When you activate another layer, the stencil becomes transparent again.

REMOVING UNWANTED EDGE COLORS USING COLOR CORRECTION LAYERS
In some cases, to remove unwanted colors along the edge of a mask, it's easier to use a Color Correction layer than to use the Outline option. For an illustration of this procedure, see "More color correction tips" in Chapter 14, "Making Selective Color Corrections."

TRANSFORMING FUZZY SILHOUETTES INTO SHARP OUTLINES
To obtain a uniform edge on images that are difficult to silhouette, use the commands in the Mask menu: convert the mask to a path and then convert the path back to a mask, using a small feather. The edge will probably still need reworking, but this is a quick way to remove fuzziness.

TO SILHOUETTE AN IMAGE ALREADY INSERTED IN A COMPOSITE
This is one of the more constraining areas of Live Picture, but there are ways to get around the problem.

Case 1: You've silhouetted an object, and you later decide to keep only part of the object. You'd like to remove the unwanted parts using silhouetting.

1. Hide all existing layers and choose a background color in sharp contrast with the colors of the silhouetted object (this will facilitate step 4).

2. Build the silhouetted image in IVUE format.

3. Reinsert the IVUE in an Image Silhouette layer in the composite. To reposition the newly built image in its original position, use the Get Info dialog box (see Chapter 20, "One Image, Two Layers").

4. Silhouette the image again, selecting the parts you want. Since you selected a background color in sharp contrast with the object, removing the background is easy. You only have to concentrate on silhouetting the unwanted parts of the object.

5. When you are finished silhouetting the image, delete the original Image Silhouette layer.

Case 2: You've distorted an image and you want to silhouette it.

This is basically the same as Case 1. You build out the distorted image to IVUE format, reinsert the image and silhouette it. However, you cannot apply any more distortion. For more flexibility, silhouette the image first and then distort it. This requires using an alpha channel. See "Using brush distortion and a mask" in Chapter 11, "Distorting Images."

Case 3: You've inserted an image in an Image Insertion layer, and you want to do some silhouetting.

Again, this is the same as Case 1. However, it may be easier to simply delete the image and start silhouetting from scratch.

TIP

At any point, you can use the Path tools or combine the Outline and Insert options without having to build out an image and redo the silhouette. See "Combining tools" in chapter 8, "Isolating Images from Their Background."

CHAPTER 10

SOURCES, MASKS, AND STENCILS REVEALED

The source, the mask, and the stencil are three elements that define what you see in a layer in Live Picture. This chapter describes each of these elements and explains how they interact. In particular, a step-by-step exercise demonstrates the fundamental difference between a mask and a stencil.

SOURCE: THE SUBSTANCE OF A LAYER

Each layer has a source. The source is the "substance" of a layer, what it consists of. In a Monocolor layer, the source is one color of paint. In a Sharpen/Blur layer, the source is sharpening and/or blurring. In an image layer, the source is the image.

While the source is always there, by itself it is not visible. We could say that the source is latent. To become visible, to be revealed, it needs a mask.

MASK: THE "REVEALER"

The mask "reveals" the source. It may seem strange that the term mask is equivalent to visibility. Mask generally expresses the idea of hiding or invisibility. In reality, the word mask conveys two indissociable ideas:

- The mask makes the source visible
- The mask hides or "masks" the layers beneath it

Mask and source in a Monocolor layer

Figures 10.1 and 10.2 illustrate the source and mask interaction in a Monocolor layer. In figure 10.1, a Monocolor layer has been created on a black background. The layer panel shows that the color of this layer is red. So, the source of this layer is red paint.

Source of a Monocolor layer ⌐

Mask ⌐

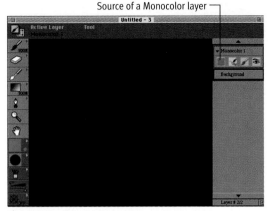

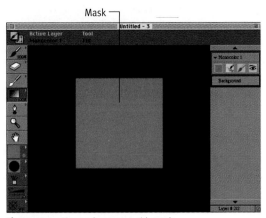

Figure 10.1   Monocolor source

Figure 10.2   Monocolor source with mask

The document window is entirely black. Having a source (red paint) is not enough to see it. You need a mask to reveal the source. In figure 10.2, the Marquee was used to create a rectangular fill. This fill is nothing other than a mask. It reveals the source of the layer it was created in—in this case, red paint. And it hides or "masks" anything underneath that layer: the black background is no longer visible beneath the mask.

Mask and source in an Image Insertion layer

When you create an image layer, the image is generally inserted by default with a mask. Let's examine the case of an image with a mask, and then see what happens when there is no mask.

Figure 10.3   Image Insertion source with mask

When you open an image in an Image Insertion layer without using Auto Insert, the Opacity control appears at the bottom of the positioning toolbar (see figure 10.3). If you leave the opacity at 100%, it is not readily apparent that a mask has been created, but in fact it has.

In image layers, the image is the source. One hundred percent opacity means there is a 100%-opacity mask covering the source, or image. You see the image at full opacity, but you don't see what's behind it.

Setting the opacity at 0% is like removing the mask. The layer exists, the image is still there, but it is invisible. Anything beneath the image is visible, in this case the black background (see figure 10.4).

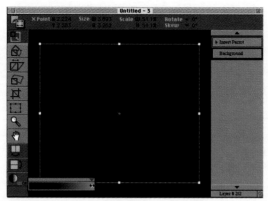

Figure 10.4 Image Insertion source without mask

STENCIL: A HOLE TO BE FILLED

A stencil is a hole defining a shape. It functions much as a stencil does in the traditional graphic arts. The shape of the hole defines what you see. But if you create a stencil by itself, you won't see anything. You still need a mask to reveal the source. The stencil constrains the visibility of the source and mask.

Understanding the difference between a mask and a stencil is not always easy. The following two exercises are designed to help you understand masks, stencils, and how they interact.

To create a stencil in a Monocolor layer, follow these steps:

1. In the File menu, choose New. A new document is created.

2. In the Create menu, choose Monocolor. A Monocolor layer is created.

3. In the creative toolbar, click on the Color Selector and drag to select a blue from the color bar. The color of the Monocolor layer is now blue.

4. In the creative toolbar, click on the Path tool and select the Oval tool (see figure 10.5).

5. Drag open an oval. In the Mask menu, choose Path −>Stencil (see figure 10.6).

   The Convert Path dialog box appears. Drag the Feathering cursor to Low and click on OK. The path disappears but nothing happens. This creates a stencil, but not a mask yet.

6. Now, click on the Marquee and choose the Fill option. Drag a rectangle over the entire document window. A circle the shape of your stencil appears. So, the mask fills the stencil (see figure 10.7).

Oval tool

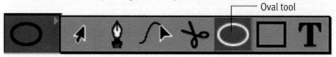

Figure 10.5 Selecting the Oval tool

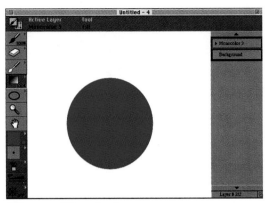

Figure 10.6   The Path —>Stencil command

Figure 10.7   Filling a stencil

Remember, though, that with just the stencil you don't see anything. You always need a mask to see the source (in this case blue paint). The stencil is used to constrain the visible area of the source.

To create a stencil in an Image Insertion layer, follow these steps:

1. In the File menu, choose New. A new document is created.

2. In the Create menu, choose Image Insertion. If Auto Insert is not already checked, click on it to select it. On the CD, select any image from the IVUE folder and click on Open.

3. In the creative toolbar, click on the Path tool and select the Oval tool.

4. Drag open an oval. In the Mask menu, choose Path —>Stencil (see figure 10.8).

   The Convert Path dialog box appears.

5. Drag the Feathering cursor to Low and click on OK. The image is now visible only through the oval stencil (see figure 10.9).

Oval path

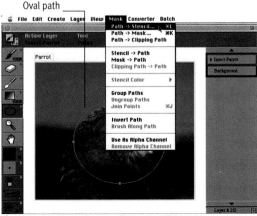

Figure 10.8   Converting a path to a stencil

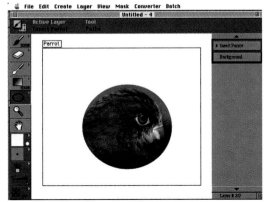

Figure 10.9   Stencil in an image layer

The image is visible through the stencil because there is a mask. The mask comes as a default when you open an image using Auto Insert.

6. Now, click on the Marquee and choose the Erase option. Drag a rectangle over the entire document. The image is no longer visible because you have just erased the mask, but the stencil remains.

So, if anything is visible in any type of layer, then that layer has a mask. Conversely, if you create a stencil and you don't see anything, you need to create a mask.

COMBINING A MASK AND A STENCIL

To summarize: The mask reveals the source of a layer, and hides what is underneath that layer. The stencil constrains the visibility of the source and mask.

In each layer panel, the source, mask, and stencil are represented by an icon. To open the layer panel, click on the layer toggle (see figure 10.10).

In image layers, the layer panel also contains a thumbnail of the source image (see figure 10.11).

The following exercise further explores masks, stencils, and how they can be combined.

To combine a mask and a stencil:

1. In the File menu, choose Open FITS.

2. In the Copy me to Hard Drive folder, choose "Earth Silhouetted" and click on Open. This FITS file contains a single Image Silhouette layer. The source image "Earth" has been silhouetted and is ready for use in a composite (see figure 10.12).

   To demonstrate the use of masks and stencils, we're going to blend the earth into the white background using an opacity gradient.

3. In the creative toolbar, click on the Marquee and choose the Horizontal Gradient option (see figure 10.13).

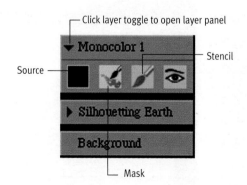

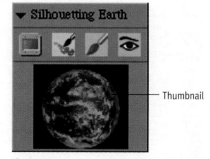

Figure 10.10 Layer panel of a Monocolor layer   **Figure 10.11** Layer panel of an image layer

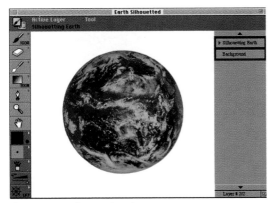

Figure 10.12 Silhouetted earth

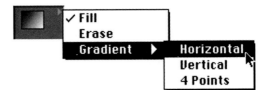

Figure 10.13 Selecting Horizontal Gradient

4. Drag open the gradient box so that it covers the earth.

5. Leave 100% in the left opacity control, tab to the right opacity control, and enter 0%, as shown in figure 10.14.

6. Click inside the gradient box. Your screen should look like figure 10.15.

   Notice that the black from the original background (before silhouetting) has reappeared. That's because when you silhouette an image, you create a mask. And when you use any of the top four tools in the creative toolbar, you also create or modify a mask. So you replaced the first mask (obtained by silhouetting) with another mask (the rectangular gradient).

7. Press Command-Z to undo the gradient.

8. Click on the layer toggle to open the layer panel. Then press and hold the Option key and drag the Mask icon to the Stencil icon (see figure 10.16).

Click and enter 0% here ⌐

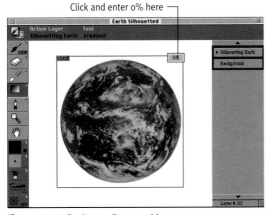

Figure 10.14 Setting gradient opacities

Click here ⌐

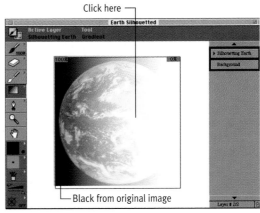

Black from original image

Figure 10.15 Previewing the opacity gradient

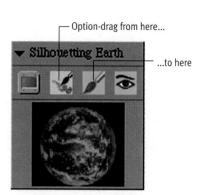

Option-drag from here...

...to here

Figure 10.16 Copying the mask to the stencil

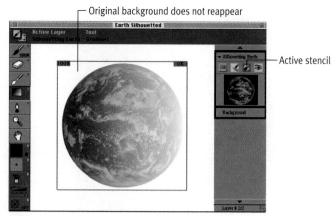

Original background does not reappear

Active stencil

Figure 10.17 Redoing the opacity gradient

You have just copied the mask to the stencil: the mask remains unchanged, and the stencil becomes the same shape as the mask. So, for the time being, the mask and the stencil are the same.

9. Now repeat steps 3-5. Then click inside the gradient box. Your screen should look like figure 10.17.

This time, the black background does not reappear. The opacity gradient affects only the earth. The stencil used was copied from the mask of the earth, so it protects the areas outside the earth.

By using a stencil, you have complete freedom to modify the opacity of your mask quickly an unlimited number of times. The stencil hides any mask created outside the stencil.

10. Now turn the stencil off by dragging the Stencil icon to the Deactivated Stencil icon, as shown in figure 10.18.

The black background reappears (see figure 10.19). When you created a rectangular gradient, you modified the mask, but the mask outside the earth wasn't visible because you created a stencil first. If you deactivate the stencil, you see the full mask.

The key point here is that stencils are fixed, whereas masks are modified each time you use the Brush, Eraser, Palette Knife, or Marquee. Being fixed, a stencil allows you to experiment freely with the mask and its opacity.

CREATING MASKS AND STENCILS

There are several ways to create masks and stencils.

To create a mask, you can:

- Use one of the top four tools in the creative toolbar: Brush, Eraser, Palette Knife, and Marquee.

Figure 10.18   Deactivating the stencil

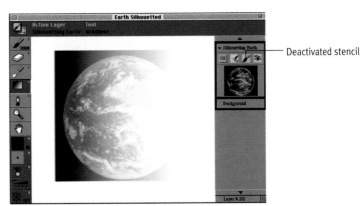

Deactivated stencil

Figure 10.19   Deactivated stencil

- Convert a path to a mask (certain layers only*).
- Copy a mask to a mask (certain layers only**).
- Copy a stencil to a mask (certain layers only**).
- Compute a mask in an Image Silhouette layer.
- Insert an image in an Image Insertion or Image Distortion layer (in this case, a default mask is created which covers the image).

To create a stencil, you can:

- Convert a path to a stencil.
- Copy a mask to a stencil (certain layers only***).
- Copy a stencil to a stencil.
- Insert an image in an Image Insertion or Image Distortion layer (in this case, a default stencil is created that frames the image).
- Crop an image in an Image Insertion or Image Distortion layer (by cropping, you are in fact modifying the default stencil).

COPYING MASKS AND STENCILS

Masks and stencils can be copied from one layer to another (see "Creating masks and stencils" for the exceptions).

---

* If you cannot convert a path to a mask, the Path –>Mask command in the Mask menu will be grayed out.

** If you cannot copy a mask or stencil to a mask, the Mask icon you are copying to in the layer panel will not turn dark gray.

*** If you cannot copy a mask to a stencil, the Stencil icon you are copying to in the layer panel will not turn dark gray.

You can copy a mask to the following:

- a mask in another layer

- a stencil in another layer

- the stencil in the same layer

You can copy a stencil to the following:

- a stencil in another layer

- a mask in another layer

- the mask in the same layer

When you copy to a mask, the new mask takes on the opacity of the mask or stencil being copied.

When you copy to a stencil, the new stencil takes on the opacity of the mask or stencil being copied. However, stencils are not visible by themselves. When we speak of the opacity of a stencil, we are referring to the maximum opacity at which it can be filled with a mask.

To copy to a mask or a stencil, follow these steps:

1. In the File menu, choose Open FITS.

2. In the Copy me to Hard Disk folder, choose the file named "Earth Silhouetted" and open it.

3. In the Create menu, choose Image Insertion.

4. On the CD, in the IVUE folder, choose the image named "Florence." Check that Auto Insert is not selected, and click on Open.

5. In the positioning toolbar, click on the Opacity control and drag the Opacity slider to about 70%. This will allow you to position Florence in relation to the earth beneath her (see figure 10.20).

6. In the control bar, click on the "Rotate" arrow and select 90° in the pop-down menu. The image rotates to a vertical position.

7. Drag the image down so that Florence's face more or less fills the earth. If Florence is too large or too small in relation to the earth, drag one of the corner handles to scale Florence. Your screen should approximate figure 10.21.

8. Once Florence is positioned, click on the Opacity control and drag the Opacity slider to 0%. Then click on the mode toggle to switch to the creative toolbar.

   The image "Florence" is now completely invisible. The image (source) is still there, and positioned as you left it, but by setting the opacity at 0%, you removed the mask. We're now going create a new mask.

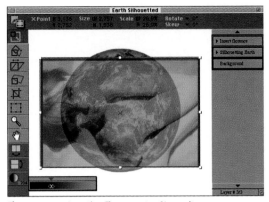

Figure 10.20   Inserting Florence at 70% opacity

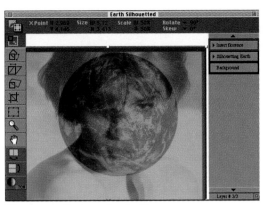

Figure 10.21   Moving and scaling Florence

9. In the layer stack, click on the layer toggles of both layers to open the respective layer panels.

10. Press and hold the Option key. Then drag the Mask icon from the "Silhouetting Earth" layer to the Mask icon in the "Insert Florence" layer (see figure 10.22).

   A new mask is created in the "Insert Florence" layer. It has the same shape and opacity (100%) as the mask in the "Silhouetting Earth" layer (see figure 10.23).

11. Click on the Brush and drag the Opacity slider to 50% to ghost the image. Notice what happens when you brush near the edge of the earth. You reveal parts of the image outside the mask. That's because you are modifying the initial mask with the Brush.

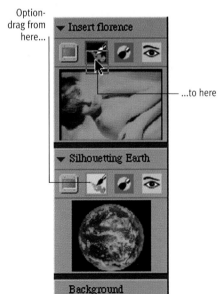

Figure 10.22   Copying a mask to a mask in another layer

Figure 10.23   Two identical masks

12. In the "Insert Florence" layer, click on the Mask icon to select it. It is framed in red. If anything else is selected, deselect first by clicking on "Background" in the layer stack.

13. In the Layer menu, choose Delete (Command-D). The mask is deleted. The image "Florence" becomes invisible. You have removed the mask, not the image.

14. Press and hold the Option key. Then drag the Mask icon from the "Silhouetting Earth" layer to the Stencil icon in the "Insert Florence" layer (see figure 10.24).

    A new stencil is created in the "Insert Florence" layer. It has the same shape as the mask in the "Silhouetting Earth" layer. However, the image "Florence" is not visible because there is no mask to reveal it. A stencil alone does not reveal an image.

15. Click on the Brush and drag the Opacity slider to 70%. Brush in the image gradually. Even if you brush near the edge of the earth, the image appears within the stencil only (see figure 10.25).

    Adjust opacity, pressure, and brush size. Make some areas more transparent than others. Try using the Eraser, Palette Knife, and Marquee. Experiment with these until you obtain an image you like.

    The stencil was created from the mask of the earth. Since this mask had an opacity of 100%, you can fill the stencil up to 100%. If the mask of the earth had an opacity of 50%, you could fill the stencil up to an opacity of 50% only.

To sum up this exercise, a mask is immediately modified with the creative tools. A stencil provides a fixed shape. Inside that shape, you can experiment and modify the mask indefinitely. For this reason, you gain more flexibility by copying masks and stencils to stencils, rather than to masks.

Option-drag from here...

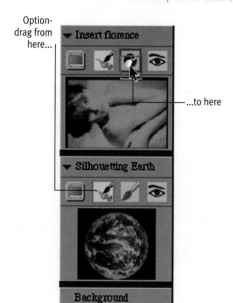

...to here

Figure 10.24 Copying a mask to a stencil in another layer

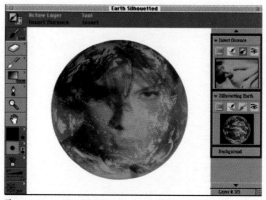

Figure 10.25 Brushing in an image inside a stencil

CONVERTING PATHS TO MASKS AND STENCILS

Paths can be converted to masks or stencils. When you convert a path to a mask, the path is filled 100% with the source (see figure 10.26). When you convert a path to a stencil, you create or modify the stencil.

Convert to a mask if you want to fill a path 100%. Convert to a stencil if you want to create the mask by using the Brush, Marquee, or other creative tools. A stencil also gives you the freedom to modify your mask at a later time.

The process for converting paths to masks and stencils is dealt with in detail in the Live Picture User Guide.

INVERTING STENCILS

Another advantage of a stencil is that it can be inverted (see figure 10.27).

Masks cannot be inverted.

One practical use of an inverted stencil is to create a frame, or matte, for your on-screen image. When you output a view, the output file or printed image is cropped along the lines of the view. However, the screen image is not cropped. For viewing purposes, it sometimes helps to create a matte, so the screen image is framed just like the output image.

To create a matte:

1. Create a Monocolor layer at the top of the layer stack.

2. Click the color selector and drag to select the background color using the eyedropper.

3. Using the rectangular Path tool, drag a rectangular path along the lines of the view. Be as precise as possible.

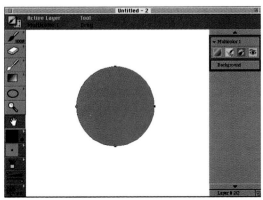

Figure 10.26   Stencil created from a circular path

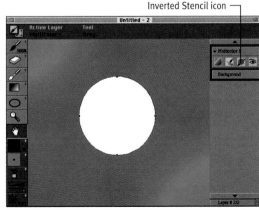

Figure 10.27   Inverted stencil

4. Select the Monocolor layer.

5. Convert the path to a stencil using the Path –>Stencil command (Mask menu). Select Create Hard Edge.

6. Invert the stencil.

7. Using the Marquee/Fill option, drag a rectangle over the view and surrounding area. Areas outside the view are painted the same color as the background.

8. Before you build your output, hide the Monocolor layer. It may slightly overlap the view. When you build the output, let the view do the cropping. For more information, see Chapter 28, "Building Outputs and Printing."

CHAPTER 11

DISTORTING IMAGES

Several types of distortion are possible in Live Picture. Certainly, the most stunning is distortion created using the Brush. However, you can create powerful distortion effects using the Perspective tool. And the Scale tool allows you to distort images in more "conventional" ways. This chapter covers all the types of distortion available.

DISTORTING WITH THE BRUSH

Figure 11.1 Brush tool options

The Brush offers unprecedented freedom to change the shape of objects intuitively. To distort with the Brush, first create an Image Distortion layer. Once the image is inserted, four options are available in the Brush tool menu (see figure 11.1).

Freehand, Radial, and Shimmer are all distortion options, which are described and illustrated in the following information. The first option, Insert, is not a distortion option. It is used to insert an image or modify its opacity with the Brush.

The Freehand option

The Freehand option is the most frequently used distortion option. Use it to distort an image by pushing it.

The image used to illustrate the Freehand option was created by American photographer John Lund for Raychem™. John created an alpha channel for the image of the cable shown in figures 11.2 and 11.3. (For more information on alpha channels, see "Using brush distortion and a mask" later in this chapter.) He then inserted the image with the alpha channel into a FITS file already containing six layers. With the Freehand option, John gently brushed the cable, "bending" it into the shape he wanted.

Figure 11.2 Original image

Figure 11.3 Image with alpha channel

Figure 11.4 Cable before distortion

Figure 11.5 Cable after Freehand distortion

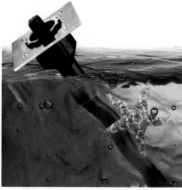

Figure 11.6 "Raychem Cable" completed

TIP

When you use the distortion tools, select a low pressure setting on the Pressure control. Otherwise, you might "rip" a hole in the image.

At first glance, you might think that John used distortion to magnify the length of cable beneath the water. In fact, he used a technique described in Chapter 20, "One Image, Two Layers."

The three image files used in this composite total 148 MB. In addition, two of the images were inserted more than once.

The Radial option

Use the Radial option to enlarge or shrink objects. It's best suited for round or roundish objects, but with practice you can use it for other shapes as well.

To use the Radial option, follow these steps:

1. Create an Image Distortion layer. The Insert Image dialog box appears.

2. Check that Auto Insert is selected and open the image on the CD called "Julie" located in the IVUE folder (see figure 11.7).

Figure 11.7   "Julie" before distortion

Figure 11.8   Brush size for radial
distortion

Figure 11.9   Radial option used
counterclockwise

3. In the creative toolbar, click on the Brush and choose the Radial option.

4. Choose a brush that is slightly larger than the area you want to distort. In this case, the brush should be a bit larger than the eye (see figure 11.8).

5. In the control bar, set the pressure on the lowest or second lowest setting, depending upon how sensitive your digitizing tablet is. (To change the sensitivity of your digitizing tablet, read the documentation that comes with it.)

6. Drag the brush counterclockwise around Julie's eyes. Follow a path just beyond the edge of the eye (see figure 11.8 for a good starting point). Do this slowly and gently, and as evenly as possible. As you drag, the eyes get larger (see figure 11.9).

Several factors affect the Radial option: pressure setting, brush size, where you draw the circular path made with the Brush, and the amount of pressure applied to the stylus. By learning to balance these parameters, you'll gain increased control over radial distortion.

7. In the creative toolbar, click on the Marquee and choose the Undistort option. Then drag a rectangle over the image to remove all distortion.

8. Now, repeat step 5, but this time drag the brush clockwise. The eye gets smaller (see figure 11.10).

Figure 11.10   Radial option used
clockwise

The Shimmer option

Create ripple effects with the Shimmer option. David Bishop used Shimmer to create a water-like effect for the cover of the September 1995 issue of the magazine *Electronic Musician* (shown in figure 11.11).

First, David created an Image Distortion layer and inserted the image of the staff (see figure 11.12). He then brushed over the staff using the Shimmer option, gradually reducing the ripple as he moved toward the end (see figure 11.13). This allowed him to mimic the ripple pattern in the composite, where the ripples fade into the distance.

The rest of the process used by David is a bit more complex. It isn't necessary to create distortion, but it demonstrates more possibilities available.

After applying the shimmer effect, David built out the image by itself as an IVUE file. He opened a new FITS file and created a green gradient. He then inserted the shimmered image into the new composite, in an Image Silhouette layer. After silhouetting the staff, he created a Multicolor layer. At this point, he copied the mask from the silhouetted image onto the stencil of the Multicolor layer, and filled it with light blue at a low opacity.

Why all this? By silhouetting the distorted image and using the silhouetted mask in a Multicolor layer, David was able to experiment with any color he wished. Had he just used the image, he would have been stuck with black. (He could have done a color correction, but that's never easy with black.) This way, the multicolor stencil was the shape of the staff, and all he had to do was fill it with the color of his choice. Though David settled for a transparent light blue, he can still change his mind.

Figure 11.11   Cover of September 1995 issue of *Electronic Musician*

Figure 11.12   Image Distortion Layer

Figure 11.13   Using the Shimmer Option

Undoing and softening distortion

One of the great things about brush distortion is that it can be undone gradually. Almost everything in Live Picture can be undone gradually, but undoing and softening distortion deserves a special mention because of its uniqueness.

You have unprecedented control over where and how much distortion you apply, with the capability to undo distortion progressively on the parts of the image you want. Blend and Undistort are the two basic options for undoing distortion.

To undo distortion in an image, follow these steps:

1. Create an Image Distortion layer. Check that Auto Insert is selected and open the image on the CD called "Julie" located in the IVUE folder.

2. In the creative toolbar, click on the Brush and choose the Freehand option.

3. Set a medium or low pressure setting. Then choose a brush that basically covers the distance from the top to the bottom of Julie's mouth.

4. Position the brush on the right part of Julie's lips and gently brush outward, so that her lips move outward and form a soft smile (see figure 11.14). Don't worry if you push the lips a bit too far. We'll work on that in the next step.

5. In the creative toolbar, click on the Palette Knife and choose the Blend option. Brush over the distorted part of the mouth. Blending allows you to subtly soften the distortion created using the Brush. By blending the distorted part of the lips, you move back closer to the initial proportions of the lips. At the same time, not all the distortion is removed (see figure 11.15).

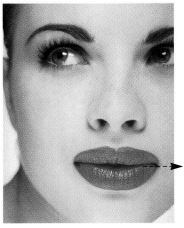

Figure 11.14 Lips slightly "pushed" to the right

Figure 11.15 The distortion on the lips is "blended"

Figure 11.16   Distortion partially removed using the Undistort option

6. In the creative toolbar, click on the Eraser and choose the Undistort option. Gently brush the distorted part of the mouth. Undistort gradually removes the distortion and you eventually retrieve the original undistorted image (see figure 11.16).

NOTE: When you use Undistort, you are not reversing each brush stroke of distortion applied, one at a time. The undo is not linear. When you undistort, you are just as free as when you applied the distortion because FITS recalculates the image each time you stroke your with the stylus.

7. To quickly remove all distortion, click on the Marquee and choose the Undistort option in the creative toolbar. Drag open a rectangle that covers the entire mouth. When you release the stylus, all distortion is removed, and you're back to your original image.

NOTE: The Erase option (using the Eraser or Marquee) erases the image, not the distortion. These options are the opposite of the Insert and Fill options available with the Brush and Marquee.

Using paths to distort images

Distortion can be constrained to a path. This is true of any brush stroke, but constraining to a path can be particularly interesting for distortion.

To apply distortion along a path, follow these steps:

1. Create an Image Distortion layer. Check that Auto Insert is selected and open the image on the CD called "Julie," located in the IVUE folder.

2. In the creative toolbar, click on the Path tool and select the Pen tool.

3. Create four paths as shown in figure 11.17. Create the first point next to the mouth, and the second point farther away from the mouth. When you have created the first two points, press and hold the Command key and click outside the path to deselect the path. Then release the Command key and create two new points, and so on until you have four distinct paths with two anchor points each.

4. In the creative toolbar, click on the Brush and choose the Freehand option.

5. Click on the Pressure control to select the second-highest pressure setting.

6. Choose a brush size that roughly spans the mouth from top to bottom.

7. On your digital keypad, press 6. Brush strokes along paths are generated automatically, not applied with the stylus. The digital keypad enables you to set the pressure you would like to apply. It works in conjunction with the Pressure control in the creative toolbar.

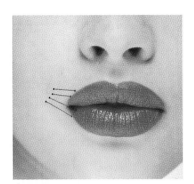

Figure 11.17   **Figure 11.18**

8. Press Command-A to select all the paths.

9. In the Mask menu, choose Brush Along Path. The distortion is automatically applied along the four paths (see figure 11.18). If the distortion is not strong enough, choose Brush Along Path again. If it is too strong, press Command-Z to undo the stroke, choose a lower pressure setting or a lower number on the digital keypad, and choose Brush Along Path again. You can also erase along a path. Click on the Eraser and choose the Undistort option before you choose Brush Along Path. You can also try changing tool size.

DISTORTING BY CHANGING IMAGE PROPORTIONS

While less spectacular than using the Brush, changing the proportions of an image is also a form of distortion.

To change the proportions of an image, follow these steps:

1. In the File menu, choose Open FITS. All other documents must be closed for this command to be active. The Open dialog box appears.

2. Select "Silhouetted Veggies" in the Copy me to Hard Drive folder.

3. Click on Open. The FITS file opens on your screen (see figure 11.19).

    This FITS file contains two layers: a green Monocolor opacity gradient and an image layer where the pressure cooker was silhouetted.

4. In the layer stack, select the layer "Silhouetted Veggies."

5. Click on the mode toggle to switch to the creative toolbar. The Scale tool is selected by default.

Drag upward

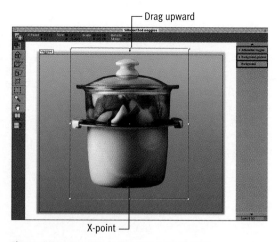

X-point

Figure 11.19 "Silhouetted Veggies"

Figure 11.20 Pressure cooker stretched heightwise

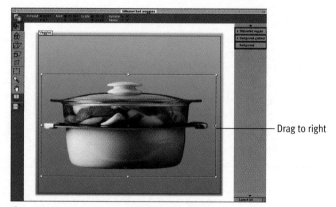

Drag to right

Figure 11.21 Pressure cooker stretched lengthwise

6. Drag the X-point from the center of the image to the bottom of the pressure cooker (see figure 11.20).

7. Then drag the top middle handle of the Positioning Box upwards to stretch the image heightwise, as shown in figure 11.20.

8. Press Command-Z to undo the scale. Then drag the right middle handle of the Positioning Box to the right to stretch the image lengthwise, as shown in figure 11.21.

DISTORTING WITH THE PERSPECTIVE TOOL

Powerful distortion can be applied quickly and easily using the Perspective tool. This type of distortion is particularly effective on silhouetted images (see the following exercise).

Drag upward

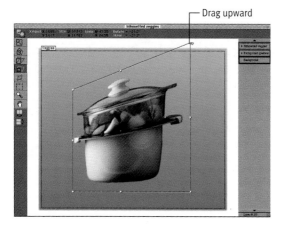

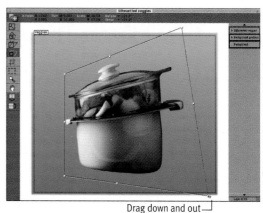

Drag down and out

Figure 11.22   Dragging upward

Figure 11.23   Dragging down and to the right

Figure 11.24   Pressure cooker distorted using the Perspective tool

To distort an image using the Perspective tool, follow these steps:

1. In the File menu, choose Open FITS. All other documents must be closed for this command to be active.

2. In the Open dialog box, choose "Silhouetted Veggies" from the Copy me to Hard Disk folder.

3. Click Open. The FITS file opens on your screen.

4. In the layer stack, select the layer "Silhouetted Veggies."

5. Click on the mode toggle to switch to the creative toolbar.

6. In the creative toolbar, click on the Perspective tool.

7. Drag the top right handle upwards, as shown in figure 11.22.

8. Then drag the bottom right handle downward and a bit to the right, as illustrated in figure 11.23.

9. Repeat steps 7 and 8 for the within a mask means that you will not be distorting the edge of a mask. For instance, if we had silhouetted the face of "Julie" used earlier in this chapter, the edge of the silhouetted mask would not be affected by distorting her eyes or mouth.

TIP

To distort an object further than the Perspective tool will allow, create the maximum perspective possible, hide all other layers, and build out the image in IVUE format. Then reinsert the image and use the Perspective tool again.

....

NOTE: If you drag the handles of the Positioning Box to extreme positions, parts of the object being distorted may disappear. In that case, press Command-Z and don't drag the handles so far.

....

USING BRUSH DISTORTION AND A MASK

Each image layer has distinct funtions in Live Picture. An image Distortion layer all ows you to distort images with the Brush, but not silhouette them. An Image Silhouette layer allows you to silhouette images, but not distort them with the Brush.

The purpose of this section is to help you work around these constraints. The procedure will be different,depending on whether you want to distort the image within a mask (as we did for the eyes of "Julie," figures 11.7 to 11.10) or outside the mask (as for the cable in John Lund's image, figures 11.2 to 11.6).

The solutions offered here also apply to images cut out using path tools.

Distorting within a mask

Distorting within a mask means that you will not be distorting the edge of a mask. For instance, if we had silhouetted the face of "Julie" used earlier in this chapter, the edge of the silhouetted mask would not be affected by distorting her eyes or mouth.

To distort within a mask, follow these steps:

1. In the File menu, choose Open FITS. All other documents must be closed for this command to be active.

2. In the Open dialog box, choose "Silhouetted Veggies" from the Copy me to Hard Disk folder. Click on Open.

3. Create an Image Distortion layer.

4. Deselect the Auto Insert option. Then open the image "Veggies" contained on the CD in the IVUE folder.

5. Position "Veggies" at the exact same position as the silhouetted image, using the Get Info command. For more information, see "Breaking down an image into background and foreground," (steps 6 to 10) in Chapter 20, "One Image, Two Layers."

6. Check that the Opacity tool is set at 100%. Then click on the mode toggle to switch to Creative mode.

7. Copy the mask from the "Silhouetted Veggies" layer to the stencil of the "Distort Veggies" layer.

8. Hide or delete the "Silhouetted Veggies" layer. You don't need it anymore. The silhouetted mask is now contained in the "Distort Veggies" layer.

9. Click on the Brush and choose the Freehand option. Then distort the pressure cooker as shown in figure 11.25. Do not distort the edges of the pressure cooker.

Distorted image — Mask

Figure 11.25 Silhouetted image distorted inside mask

Figure 11.26 Silhouetted image distorted outside mask

Distorting the edge of a mask

To understand what happens when you distort the edge of a masked image, repeat the exercise above, but this time distort the edge of the pressure cooker. The result is illustrated in figure 11.26. Remember, in Live Picture, the whole image is always there, all the time. So the original background reappears (in this case, black), and the image disappears because there is no mask where it has been pushed (cover handle is no longer in view).

The solution to this problem is to create an alpha channel. This was the solution adopted by John Lund in "Raychem Cable" (refer to figures 11.2 and 11.3). When you import an alpha channel in an Image Distortion layer, the alpha channel is not resolution-independent; rather, it is linked to specific pixels in the image. When you distort the image, the alpha channel moves with it, so the problem encountered in figure 11.26 doesn't occur.

To distort using an alpha channel, follow these steps:

1. Create an Image Silhouette layer and silhouette your image.

2. In the Mask menu, choose Use As Alpha Channel. This transforms the mask into an alpha channel when you build the output.

3. Build the image to IVUE format. Remember to select Include Alpha Channel in the Build dialog box.

4. Reinsert the image in an Image Distortion layer.

5. Delete the original image layer.

6. Distort the image with the alpha channel.

NOTE: You can use any mask or stencil to create an alpha channel. This includes masks and stencils made using the Path tools.

CHAPTER 12

CLONING

This chapter explains how to use the Image Clone layer. A simple exercise is included to familiarize you with the cloning tools. The chapter also discusses the pros and cons of cloning with Live Picture and contains helpful tips for more efficient cloning.

THE PURPOSE OF CLONING

In image editing software, to *clone* means to copy part of an image to another area in that same image. In a sense, you are copying image matter.

The most basic use of cloning is to remove scratches, spots, and dust marks found on scanned images. You choose a clean area next to an unwanted mark and copy the clean area onto the mark.

Another common use of cloning is to remove unwanted objects from an image. In figure 12.1, I cloned the background shrubs to the left of the cheetah onto the truck to the right of the cheetah to remove it from the scene of this Kenyan wildlife reserve (see figure 12.2). (I also lightened and sharpened the cheetah's fur.)

Figure 12.1   Original image

Figure 12.2   Truck removed using cloning

Figure 12.4   Close-up of skirt

Figure 12.3   Original image

Figure 12.5   Close-up of cloned skirt

Sometimes you need more matter in an image. For instance, the image in figure 12.3 was given to French photographer François Marquet to be used on a box for Nur Die, the leading German stocking company. He was asked to "extend" the image by adding "ground" to the bottom and "skirt" to the top.

By copying bits of existing skirt, François was able to re-create the material and extend the skirt (figure 12.5). By using the same method for the background and pavement, he "grew" the entire image (see figure 12.6).

Cloning can also be used to adjust colors, as shown in the following exercise.

USING AN IMAGE CLONE LAYER

Cloning uses layers. To clone an image, first select the image you want to clone and then create an Image Clone layer.

An Image Clone layer contains three basic brush options: Clone, Restore, and Rework (see figure 12.7).

The following exercise demonstrates what each option is for and how to use it. The image used, "Choice Fruit 1," was created by British designer Helen Hann for the University of Salford's 1996 undergraduate course catalog.

Figure 12.6   "Nur Die" after cloning

Figure 12.7 Clone brush options

A slightly modified version, called "Opple," was created for this exercise.

To use an Image Clone layer, follow these steps:

1. In the File menu, choose Open FITS. All FITS files must be closed, or this command is grayed out.

2. Open the FITS file called "Opple" from the Copy me to Hard Drive folder. This composite contains four layers: a monocolor layer for the shadow and three image layers.

3. Press and hold the Option key, and click on any layer toggle. All the layer panels open, showing you the source image used in each layer. Notice that the top part of the orange pulp is lighter than the rest (see figure 12.8). We are going to use cloning to adjust the pulp's color.

   Zoom in so that the "Opple" fills your document window.

   In this image, Helen silhouetted the apple and created a drop shadow. She then inserted the image of an orange in two different layers. In each layer, she brushed in the parts of the orange she wanted. In addition, the mask of the apple was copied to the "Left Quarter" and "Right Quarter" layers to ensure that none of the orange would appear outside the apple.

4. In the layer stack, select the layer "Right Quarter." This selects the layer to be cloned.

5. In the Create menu, choose Image Clone. An Image Clone layer is created and appears at the top of the layer stack. This layer contains a clone of the image "Right Quarter."

6. In the toolbar, click on the Brush. The Clone option is selected by default.

7. Press and hold the Option key. Then drag the stylus from the darker area of the right quarter to the lighter area, as shown in Figure 12.9.

   You are cloning matter from one point to another. The Size Circle shows where you are cloning from. The end of the vector shows where you are cloning to.

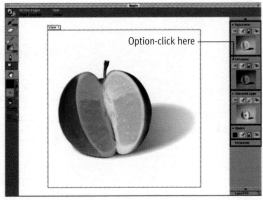

Figure 12.8 "Opple"

Image Clone layer

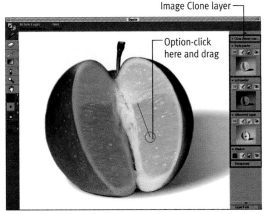

Option-click
here and drag

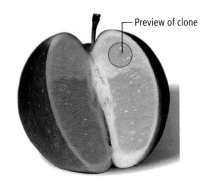

Preview of clone

Figure 12.9   Defining a cloning vector

Figure 12.10   Do not press to preview the clone

8. Without applying pressure to the stylus, position it above the light area (see figure 12.10). Within the Size Circle, you see what will appear if you actually brush.

9. Brush in the darker pulp of the orange over the lighter pulp (see figure 12.11).

....

NOTE: If you brush outside the pulp, the rest of the orange appears. When you define a cloning vector, you are creating a complete copy of the image at another position. By drawing the cloning vector shown in Figure 12.9, you are copying the entire image of the orange at a higher position. It's then up to you to insert the parts of the clone you want. If you brush in too much of the clone, use the Eraser to remove those parts.

....

10. Now select the layer "Left Quarter."

11. In the Create menu, choose Image Clone to create a new cloning layer. This time, the layer cloned will be "Left Quarter."

12. Press and hold the Option key. Then drag the stylus as shown in figure 12.12.

Second Image Clone layer

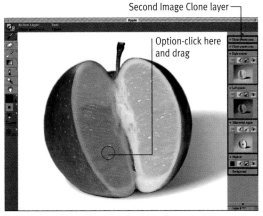

Option-click here
and drag

Figure 12.11 Darker pulp cloned onto lighter pulp

Figure 12.12 A second Image Clone layer is created

13. Brush in the darker pulp in the left quarter.

    This completes the basic exercise on cloning. For a full description of how an Image Clone layer works, continue with step 14. Otherwise, skip to step 19.

14. For the sake of illustrating the Prohibit cursor, the following exercise is included. Suppose that you want to whiten the edge of the Opple. Press and hold the Option key and drag a cloning vector as shown in figure 12.13.

15. Attempt to brush in the white matter over the yellow matter. The Prohibit cursor appears (see figure 12.14). That's because you can't clone to an area you've already cloned to. Because we already brushed in the darker pulp in essentially the same area, we can't clone there again. The solution would be to create a new Image Clone layer. But let's continue with this layer.

16. Using the Option key, create another cloning vector, as shown in figure 12.15. Then brush to remove the small, dull white area. This time, the Prohibit cursor does not appear because you cloned to another area. The fact that you cloned *from* the same area does not cause the Prohibit cursor to appear. Therefore, you can clone more than once in an Image Clone layer, unless you are cloning *to* the same area.

17. To further illustrate the Prohibit cursor, the following steps are included. Go back to the area you already cloned and brush in the orange pulp along the edge of the apple, as shown in figure 12.16. The Prohibit cursor appears again. That's because you're going back to an area to perform additional cloning after creating another cloning vector in step 16.

18. Click on the Brush and choose the Rework option. Then brush in the area you attempted to brush in step 17. This time, the Prohibit cursor doesn't appear.

    Use the Rework option to go back to an existing clone and brush in more of it. With Rework selected, you can brush in more of any clone in a layer. To create a new cloning vector, reselect the Clone option.

Option-click
here and drag

Figure 12.13 Drag a cloning vector

Prohibit cursor

Figure 12.14 Prohibit cursor

Figure 12.15 Two clones in one Image Clone layer

Preview of
Restore option

Figure 12.16

Figure 12.17 Preview before restoring an
image

Figure 12.18 Restoring the apple seeds

....

NOTE: You don't need to select Rework to erase parts of existing clones.

....

19. In the layer stack, select the layer "Silhouetted Apple."

20. In the Create menu, choose Image Clone. This new layer will be used to create clones of the apple.

21. Click on the Brush and select the Restore option. Then position the cursor over the Opple, as shown in figure 12.17. What you are seeing in the Size Circle is the apple image in the layer called "Silhouetting Apple."

     Restore actually creates a clone directly above the original image. In other words, it's a clone without a cloning vector.

22. Choose a small brush and brush in just the apple seeds, as shown in figure 12.18.

....

NOTE: If a composite contains only two image layers, you can achieve the same result by erasing parts of the top image. The underlying image becomes visible as you erase the top image. In the composite used in this exercise, however, there are two images and two clone layers on top of the "Silhouetted Apple" layer. So, it would be necessary to activate each of the four layers and erase the same area in each layer. This would be time consuming and imprecise. Hence the handiness of the Restore option. By using the Restore option, you can "burn a hole" through several layers with a single brush stroke.

....

CLONING LIVE PICTURE STYLE

Cloning in Live Picture differs from the rubber stamp tool available in Adobe Photoshop. Each tool presents advantages and disadvantages depending on what type of work you're doing.

In Live Picture, the clone you brush in is always based on the original IVUE image. For example, if you're retouching a face to remove blemishes, and you retouch a large area of skin, you cannot copy the cloned area to another area. So, you cannot clone a clone. You always copy the original image.

However, because you don't actually modify the original image, you can always delete Image Clone layers or erase some of the cloning. As with everything you do in Live Picture, you never lose the original.

To spot an image—that is, to remove scratches, spots, and dust marks—many current users tend to use the rubber stamp tool in Adobe Photoshop before inserting it in a Live Picture composite. Generally, you don't need to undo spotting, so editing the actual pixels is not a disadvantage here.

To clean up a small area of an inserted image, you can use the FastEdit/IVUE plug-in made by Total Integration, Inc. This plug-in enables you to select a small area of an image and open and edit it in Photoshop.

Live Picture cloning is especially useful and powerful when cloning large images. In figure 12.19, John Lund wanted to remove the pink coloring from the water. The image is 85 MB. But because Live Picture's brushes are unlimited in size, he zoomed to a comfortable level, took a large brush, and quickly cloned in some blue water from another part of the image (see figure 12.20).

The same point applies to small brushes. By zooming in, you can create brushes as small as you like. This enables you to clone with a very high level of precision.

In addition, because the brushes in Live Picture are very responsive to the pressure you apply to the stylus, you have full control to clone parts of an image at less than 100% opacity. This can be useful, for instance, when cloning to remove imperfections from facial skin.

Important: If you color-correct an image using the IVUE Correction command, existing clones are not color corrected, but clones created after the IVUE Correction are. Therefore, do IVUE Corrections before you clone! (See Chapter13, "Making Global Color Corrections.")

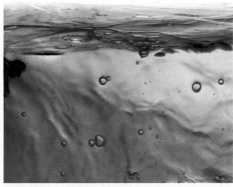

Figure 12.19　85 MB image before cloning

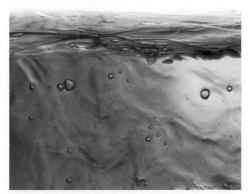

Figure 12.20　After cloning

MORE CLONING TIPS

Here are a few tips to maximize your cloning efficiency.

DON'T COUNT THE LAYERS!

Because you need to create a new layer if you want to clone to the same area, you might wind up with a large number of Image Clone layers. Don't count them! Create as many as you need. The FITS file used to create figure 12.6 contained 75 Image Clone layers! The large number of layers had relatively little effect on screen regeneration and build times, because each clone layer contained only a small piece of the image. On the other hand, it only took one layer to clone the water in figure 12.20.

GROUPING IMAGE CLONE LAYERS

If you find it confusing to see numerous Image Clone layers in the layer stack, just use the Group command to group them into one easy-to-handle layer bar.

INTERMEDIATE BUILDS

An intermediate build is probably the best solution for handling multiple Image Clone layers. To spot an image in Live Picture, insert the image in an Image Insertion layer, do all the cleaning you need, and then build out the image in IVUE format. The cleaned image is then ready to be reinserted into a single layer.

REPOSITIONING IMAGE CLONE LAYERS

Use the positioning tools to reposition an Image Clone layer. Figure 12.21 shows just the clone layer used to remove pink in figure 12.20. This area of water can be rotated, scaled, flipped, and so forth. By repositioning clones, you can sometimes avoid having to create additional Image Clone layers.

USING COLOR CORRECTION LAYERS

Use a Color Correction layer to selectively adjust the color of Image Clone layers. This can be helpful if the clone color doesn't quite match the area it's being brushed into. See Chapter 14, "Making Selective Color Corrections."

USING MASKS AND STENCILS

Because clones are in layers, you can use masks or stencils to define them. In figure 12.19, John Lund copied the stencil from the image layer onto the stencil of the clone layer. This kept the clone from appearing above the water line.

ZOOM FIRST, CLONE AFTER

If you clone and then zoom, the Prohibit cursor sometimes appears, making it impossible to perform additional cloning in that layer. It's best to zoom first to the level of magnification you need, and then to create the Image Clone layer.

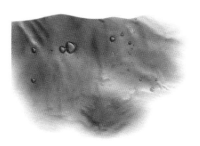

Figure 12.21   A clone layer by itself

CHAPTER **13**

MAKING GLOBAL COLOR CORRECTIONS

Global color corrections generally are used to modify the contrast or brightness of an image, or to remove or shift color casts. They're global because they affect the whole IVUE image in a given layer.

This chapter introduces you to the most commonly used global color corrections and tools. For additional information, read "Editing Photographic Tone and Color in Live Picture," an essay by nature photographer Joseph Holmes, contained on the CD. It provides an in-depth look into image color correction. Also see the Live Picture User Guide.

The three main reasons for making global color corrections are to do the following:

- Compensate for insufficient contrast, incorrect brightness, or color casts due to the way the image was scanned or shot

- Homogenize images used in the same composite but coming from different sources (different scanners, cameras, lighting conditions, and so on)

- Make creative changes to the colors in an image

Because global color corrections modify only a single IVUE image, they are called IVUE corrections, and the command is located in the Layer menu. The different types of IVUE corrections are available in the IVUE Correction submenu (figure 13.1).

When you make an IVUE correction, you do not create another layer. IVUE corrections are simply linked to the layer containing the IVUE image.

Figure 13.1 Layer menu with
IVUE Corrections submenu

Figure 13.2 "Tefal"

....

NOTE: Create a Color Correction layer to change the color of the entire composite, that is, all image layers and all non-image layers. There's also a trick to using IVUE Corrections on part of an image. For all this information, see Chapter 14, "Making Selective Color Corrections."

....

In this chapter, the composite "Tefal," created for the company of that name by Jean-Luc Michon, illustrates IVUE color correction (see figure 13.2). This composite contains 22 layers, including five different images. Each image is used to show a different IVUE Correction.

USING THE IVUE CORRECTION COMMAND

The procedure for making IVUE corrections is basically the same for all types of IVUE Corrections (except for the Invert and Presets commands, which do not have dialog boxes).

To make an IVUE correction, follow these steps:

1. In the layer stack, select the image layer you want to color-correct.

2. In the Layer menu, select IVUE Correction and choose a command from the submenu. A dialog box appears. (The Brightness/Contrast dialog box shown in figure 13.3 is used to illustrate IVUE Corrections in general.)

3. Make the IVUE corrections using the dialog box controls.

4. Click on OK to apply the corrections to the layer.

The Before image shows the IVUE before color correction. The After image shows the IVUE after color correction. To determine how the color correction fits in with the overall composite, click on the Preview button at the bottom of the dialog box. This updates the composite preview.

You can use the Zoom tool or the Pan tool to zoom or pan in the Before and After images, and in the Preview.

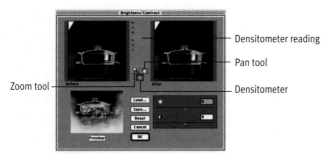

Zoom tool —
Densitometer reading
Pan tool
Densitometer

Figure 13.3   A typical IVUE Correction dialog box

To determine the Before and After color values of a specific point in the image, click on the densitometer and click on a point in the image. The densitometer reading shows the color values before and after the IVUE correction. A reading refers to the screen pixel clicked. Therefore, unless you are zoomed in, the reading represents the average of several image pixels. To obtain a CMYK reading, choose Color Mode/CMYK in the Edit menu.

Use the Save and Load buttons to save and reuse an IVUE color correction. This enables you to apply the same IVUE correction to several images in a composite, or to an image in another composite.

Use the Reset button to cancel the current color correction.

When you choose Invert or Presets, the IVUE correction is applied immediately because there is only one option for each command.

....
NOTE: IVUE Correction dialog box settings do not take previous IVUE corrections into account. For example, if you add 20 points in brightness to an image using the Brightness/Contrast dialog box, and then click on OK, the brightness is applied to the image. If you reopen the dialog box, the slider will be set at 0, not 20, although the image is brighter. Dragging the Brightness slider to 20 again is roughly equivalent to increasing the brightness of the original IVUE by 40 points.
....

Important: If you make IVUE corrections after creating an Image Clone layer, the cloned image does not contain the IVUE corrections. Therefore, make all IVUE corrections before you clone (see Chapter 12, "Cloning").

IMPROVING CONTRAST AND BRIGHTNESS

The three commands that control the brightness and contrast of an IVUE image are Brightness/Contrast, Color Levels, and Color Curves. They are described here in order of increasing complexity.

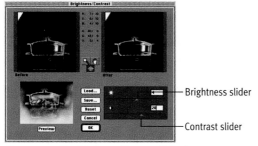

Figure 13.4   The Brightness/Contrast dialog box

Brightness slider

Contrast slider

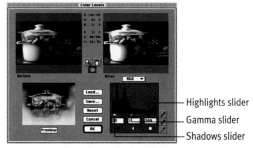

Figure 13.5   The Color Levels dialog box

Highlights slider

Gamma slider

Shadows slider

Using the Brightness/Contrast dialog box

Use the Brightness Contrast dialog box to globally modify the brightness and contrast of an image. In figure 13.4, the brightness was increased 4 points and the contrast 20 points.

Drag the sliders to the right to increase brightness or contrast, and to the left to decrease brightness or contrast.

Using the Color Levels dialog box

Use the Color Levels dialog box to control brightness, contrast, and gamma, which affect the midtones of an image.

The histogram describes the distribution of brightness values in an image. The darker values are to the left, the brighter values to the right. In figure 13.5, the darker values predominate in the image.

In figure 13.5, the Highlights slider was dragged from 255 to 209. This means that all values from 209 to 255 become white. The Shadows slider was dragged from 0 to 15. This means that all values from 0 to 15 become black.

The entire histogram of the image is then remapped based on these new black and white points, as shown in figure 13.6 (The histogram is not actually redrawn until you click on OK and reopen the Color Levels dialog box.) In the remapped image, the spectrum of colors is "stretched" out, thereby increasing the contrast.

To improve the contrast of any image that does not have an actual black or white in it (see figure 13.7), drag the Shadows slider to the darkest value in the image, and drag the Highlights slider to the lightest value in the image (see figure 13.8). The darkest and lightest values become black and white respectively. The values in between are remapped.

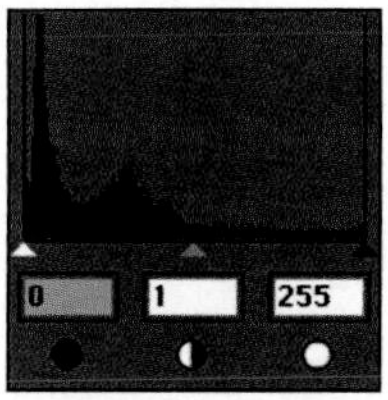

Figure 13.6   Histogram remapped based on new black and white points

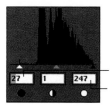

Figure 13.7   Image without black or white

This value will become 0

This value will become 255

Figure 13.8   Brightest color becomes white, darkest color becomes black

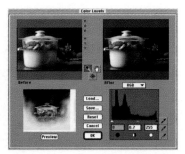

Figure 13.09 Darkens image, adds contrast to highlights

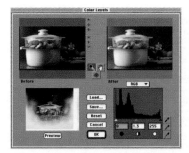

Figure 13.10 Lightens image, adds contrast to shadow

Also, use the Gamma slider to affect contrast and brightness. Dragging the slider to the right darkens the image and increases contrast in the highlights (see figure 13.9). Dragging the slider to the left brightens the image while increasing contrast in the shadows (see figure 13.10).

Using the Color Curves dialog box

The Color Curves dialog box enables you to adjust the brightness and contrast at any point on the brightness curve. The horizontal axis represents the Before value, and the vertical axis represents the After value.

Figure 13.11 shows an S-shaped curve, which increases the overall contrast of an image.

To adjust the curve, click on the Spline icon. Then click and drag the curve. Each time you click on the curve, you create an anchor point. You can create as many anchor points as you want. To remove an anchor point, drag it to the closest anchor point or the end of the curve.

Figures 13.12 and 13.13 show how to brighten and darken the overall image.

In figure 13.14, the highlights are brightened. An anchor point created toward the bottom of the curve "locks" the 1/4 tone values so they are not affected. In figure 13.15, the shadows are darkened, and the anchor point near the top of the curve preserves the highlights.

Spline tool —

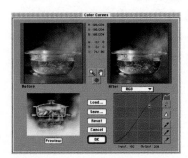

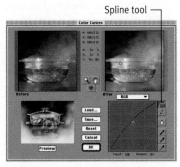

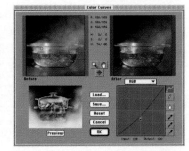

Figure 13.11 Increases contrast

Figure 13.12 Brightens the overall image

Figure 13.13 Darkens the overall image

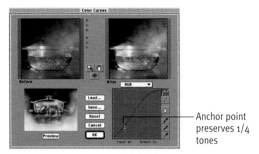

— Anchor point
preserves 1/4
tones

Figure 13.14 Brightens the highlights only

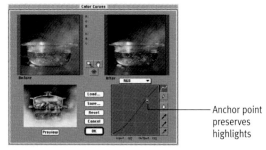

— Anchor point
preserves
highlights

Figure 13.15 Darkens the shadows only

REMOVING COLOR CASTS

Different types of scanners tend to produce different types of color cast in images. One of the most common ways to remove color casts is the Color Shift dialog box. In figure 13.16, blue was removed from the highlights. As you remove blue, you add yellow.

Drag the sliders to remove or create color casts. Each color shift is made to the highlights, midtones, or shadows. Click on the Highlights, Midtones, or Shadows buttons at the bottom of the dialog box to choose the range you want to affect.

HOMOGENIZING IMAGES FROM DIFFERENT SOURCES

In an ideal composite, all the images are taken with the composite in mind. However, in reality, your composite may contain images from different sources. If you're a photographer you may have shot one, another may come from a CD, and a third from an image bank. In this case, they may have different contrast, lighting, and color casts. For example, this can be due to the scanners used, the lighting conditions when the photograph was taken, or the cameras used. If you're a designer, your images may often come from different sources.

IVUE correction is the ideal tool for homogenizing images from different sources. In this case, though, the purpose is not necessarily to improve the color or dynamic range of an image, but rather to match image contrast and lighting so that your composite looks photorealistic.

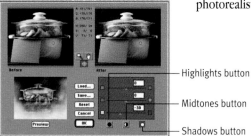

— Highlights button

— Midtones button

— Shadows button

Figure 13.16 The Color Shift dialog box

MAKING CREATIVE CHANGES TO IMAGE COLORS

IVUE Corrections can be used creatively. In the "Tefal" composite, the image of the boiling water was shot in black and white. It had good contrast and balance and was shot under the same lighting conditions as the other images. However, Jean-Luc Michon decided to add a bluish cast to the image, using the blue curve in the Color Curves dialog box. (In fact, this was the only IVUE Correction actually made to this composite.)

The presets can be used also to make creative changes. There are 10 different presets, available through the Presets command in the IVUE Correction submenu (see figure 13.18).

RGB pull-down menu ⌐

Figure 13.17 Blue curve dragged upwards to increase blue in image

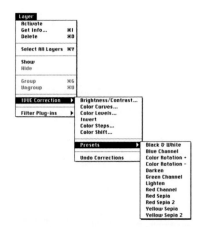

Figure 13.18 The Presets submenu

Figure 13.19 Black & White preset

Figure 13.20 Red Sepia 2 preset

Figure 13.21   Color Rotation + preset

You can select only one preset at a time. Selecting a new preset cancels out the current one. Presets cannot be modified in themselves. However, you can use a Color Correction layer to modify a preset. Figures 13.19 through 13.21 show how three different presets affect the boiling water image.

NOTE: If the presets do not appear in the Presets submenu, choose Preferences/Files & Folders in the Edit dialog box. Click on the Color Presets field and locate the Presets folder. It is located in your Live Picture folder. In the Select dialog box, click on Select "Presets." Then click on OK, quit Live Picture, and launch the application again.

UNDOING IVUE CORRECTIONS

As with everything in a FITS file, you are not modifying the original IVUE image when you make an IVUE correction. So IVUE corrections can be undone at any time.

To undo the IVUE corrections on an image, choose Undo Corrections in the IVUE Correction submenu.

Important: When you undo an IVUE correction, you undo all the IVUE corrections made to the image.

TIP

To undo just one IVUE correction, save each IVUE correction as you make it, using the Save command in each dialog box. Then choose Undo Corrections, and reload the ones you want to keep using the Load command.

CHAPTER 14

MAKING SELECTIVE COLOR CORRECTIONS

This chapter shows how to selectively modify the colors in your composite using a Color Correction layer. A step-by-step exercise features the full range of commonly used selective correction tools. Illustrations of corrected images and a number of special tips are also included.

Additionally, it is possible to make selective color corrections using a Colorize layer, or the IVUE Correction command. This is described at the end of the chapter.

For additional information on color correction, the CD includes an essay by photographer Joseph Holmes, entitled "Editing Photographic Tone and Color in Live Picture."

USING A COLOR CORRECTION LAYER

Selective color corrections are made using a Color Correction layer. So, to modify specific colors in your composite, first create a Color Correction layer.

A Color Correction layer affects only the layers beneath it. Furthermore, because each layer is a separate entity, the color correction remains separate from the image or images in the composite and can therefore be undone or modified at any time.

Color Correction layers also can be used without selectivity. So, you can make uniform color changes to an entire composite.

Introducing the interface

When you choose Color Correction in the Create menu, the new layer appears in the layer stack. The control bar is shown in figure 14.1.

The Before color represents the current color—the color you want to change. The After color represents the new color. When you change the Before color, you in fact change a more or less wide range of colors. The Before color is at the center of that range. The Tolerance control allows you to reduce or expand the range.

Selective Correction button ———

Figure 14.1 Control bar in a Color Correction layer

Select the color you want to change (Before color), and the color you want to change it to (After color).

Initially, the Before and After colors in the control bar represent only the hue of a color—its tone, such as red, orange, or purple. To modify more than the hue of a color, for instance its saturation or value, click on the Selective Correction button. The Selective Color Correction dialog box appears (see figure 14.2). This box offers the full range of selective color correction controls. For example, you can make the reds lighter or more saturated. You can also work in the RGB or CMYK color modes.

The Selective Color Correction dialog box is an expanded version of the control bar. The HSV sliders to the left represent the Before color, but they give you more control for selecting colors than the Before field in the control bar. Again, the Before color represents the color you want to change.

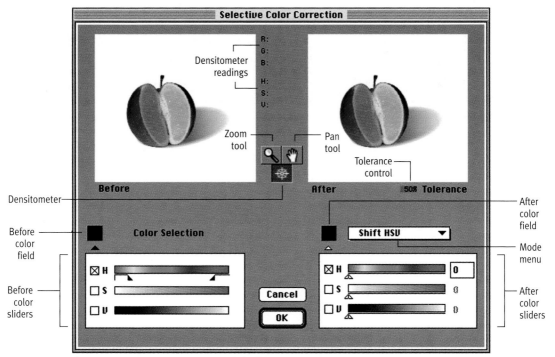

Figure 14.2 Selective Color Correction dialog box

The HSV sliders to the right represent the After color or new color. They give you more control for selecting new colors than the After field in the control bar. In addition, you can select colors using the RGB or CMYK modes.

The Before window shows the current composite. The After window shows a preview of what the composite would look like *if the color correction were applied at 100% opacity to the entire image.* Color corrections are actually applied using the creative tools (Brush, Marquee, and so forth).

Use the Tolerance control to fine-tune the color correction overall.

If you begin by making corrections with the control bar, and then switch to the Selective Color Correction dialog box for additional control, the colors and tolerance selected in the control bar are carried over to the Selective Color Correction dialog box.

Using a Color Correction layer

This exercise demonstrates a typical color correction. The FITS file used represents an early stage of an image created by British designer Helen Hann. The actual final image, "Choice Fruit 1," is shown in the Live Picture Gallery.

To modify a color selectively:

1. In the File menu, choose Open FITS. All other FITS files must be closed or the Open FITS command will not be available.

2. In the Open dialog box, select the FITS file "Opple 2" located on the CD in the Copy me to Hard Disk folder, and click on Open. The composite is displayed.

3. Press and hold the Option key and click on any layer toggle. All the layer panels open (see figure 14.3).

   We are going to color-correct the orange pulp inside the apple. (For an explanation of how this FITS file was created, see Chapter 12, "Cloning.")

4. In the Create menu, choose Color Correction. A new layer appears at the top of the layer stack. By default, it is called Modify Color, with a number.

5. In the control bar, click on the Before color field and drag the eyedropper to the right section of pulp, as shown in figure 14.4.

6. In the control bar, click on the After color field and drag to select an orange in the small color bar (see figure 14.5).

7. In the creative toolbar, click on the Brush. Brush in the color correction (see figure 14.6). Brush until all the pulp changes from yellow to orange.

   Notice that if you brush outside the orange pulp, other colors may also be modified. That's because we haven't worked on reducing the Before range to make the color correction more selective. We'll do that later in this exercise. For now, use the Eraser to remove any color change outside the orange pulp. Use a smaller brush if necessary, and brush carefully along the edges of the pulp.

The next series of steps (8 to 14) demonstrate the intuitive nature and flexibility of a Color Correction layer.

8. Click on the Eraser and erase bands of color correction, as shown in figure 14.7.

Figure 14.3   "Opple 2" with layer panels open

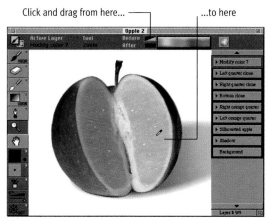

Figure 14.4   Selecting the Before color

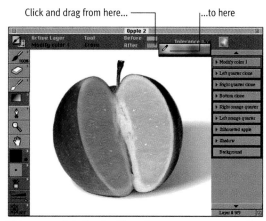

Figure 14.5   Selecting the After color

Figure 14.6 Brushing in a color correction

Figure 14.7 Erasing in bands

9. Click on the Palette Knife and choose the Diffuse option. Using the Palette Knife, blend the erased and non-erased areas partially. The idea is to produce something resembling a blood orange, with its slightly irregular pattern of red and orange (see figure 14.8). You can also try using the Palette Knife with the Push option.

10. Now click on the After color field once. The Live Picture Color Picker appears.

11. Drag the orange color in the Color Picker color box to the color palette to save the After color (see figure 14.9).

12. In the Color Picker mode menu, choose HSV (see figure 14.9). Then slide the H cursor slightly to the left, shifting the hue from orange to reddish-orange.

13. Click on OK. The color of the orange pulp automatically changes to the new color selected.

   Each time you select a new color, any existing color correction automatically changes to the new color. This means that once you create a mask using the creative tools (Brush, Eraser, and so forth), you can experiment with any number of new colors.

Figure 14.8 Using the Diffuse option to blend a color correction

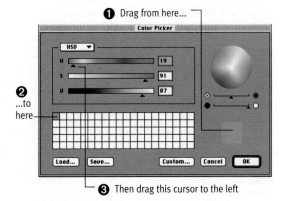

Figure 14.9 Modifying hue with the color picker

14. To recover the initial color, click on the After color field again. When the Live Picture Color Picker appears, click on the orange you placed in the color palette, and then click on OK. The initial color correction is reapplied.

    You have modified the color-corrected area using the Palette Knife and changed the hue by shifting the After color. To complete this exercise, you'll learn how to use the Selective Color Correction dialog box to change all the components of a color. You'll also learn how to be more selective when modifying colors.

15. In the control bar, click on the Color Correction button. The Selective Color Control dialog box appears. Notice how the Before and After colors you selected in the control bar are carried over to this dialog box (see figure 14.10).

    The preview shows what the FITS file would look like if you took the Marquee, selected the Fill option at 100% opacity, and dragged it over the entire composite. In actuality, in step 7 you used the Brush to color-correct only the orange pulp. That's why the After preview looks somewhat different from the image in your main document window. In addition, you used the Eraser and Palette Knife, so the color correction in your main document is not applied uniformly or at 100% opacity, differing from the preview.

16. Click on the S and V boxes next to the After sliders to activate the Saturation and Value sliders.

    Saturation refers to the amount of gray in a color. A red hue with 100% saturation produces bright red. A red hue with 0% saturation produces gray.

    Value refers to the luminance of a color. In visual terms, light colors have high value and dark colors have low value.

17. Slide the Saturation cursor slightly to the left. Then slide the Value cursor a bit to the right (see figure 14.11). Notice how the color in the After preview changes somewhat.

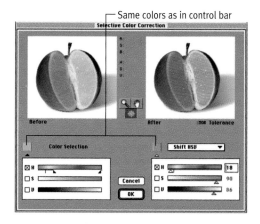

Figure 14.10 Colors chosen using the control bar are carried over

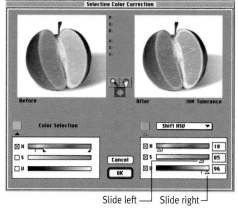

Figure 14.11 Modifying the saturation and value of the After color

You have changed the After color by using the Saturation and Value sliders. Initially, you simply shifted the hue of the pulp from yellow to orange. Now, you've made the yellow pulp not only more orange, but you've slightly desaturated and lightened it as well.

The vertical lines below each After slider indicate the hue, saturation, and value respectively of the Before color. Use these to determine whether the color correction is increasing or decreasing the original color component.

To make the color correction more selective let's examine the Before sliders. Currently, only the hue component is selected. The vertical line under the Hue slider shows the color selected in the main document using the eyedropper (see figure 14.4). The two triangles define a range of colors around the orange selected. This is the default range, but you can modify it by sliding the triangular Range cursors separately. When you select an orange, you are defining a more or less wide range of orange hues. So figure 14.11 shows how to selectively modify all yellow, orange, and red hues.

18. Click on the V box next to the Before slider. Two triangular Range cursors appear (see figure 14.12). These cursors indicate the Value range to be modified. Since the cursors are to the far right of the Value slider, they represent the lightest colors. By clicking on the V, you modify only those tones of yellow, orange, and red that are very light. Use this technique to be more selective.

Your V slider may not look exactly like the V slider in figure 14.12, because the color you selected in step 5 may have been brighter or darker than the color selected in the figure. Further, the vertical line representing the selected color may not be apparent (it may coincide with one of the Range cursors). Drag the triangular Range cursors so that the value range roughly resembles the value range in figure 14.12.

The After preview indicates that the left side of the orange is no longer color-corrected. That's because, in the original image, it is darker than the right side of the orange. In this case, clicking on the Value box prevents the darker colors from being modified. Remember, you are modifying only those tones of yellow, orange, and red that are very light.

19. Click again on the V box to cancel selectivity based on value. The left half of the orange is again color-corrected.

We made the Before color more selective by simply clicking on the V box. Sometimes this works, but in this case the value of the two halves of the orange is too different. We'll now use the densitometer to be more selective in our color correction.

20. Click on the densitometer and click on the top left side of the orange, as shown in figure 14.13. The HSV reading between the Before and After images indicates H38, S93, V62.

❶ Click here, then... ⌐
Before color change ⌐   ⌐ After color change

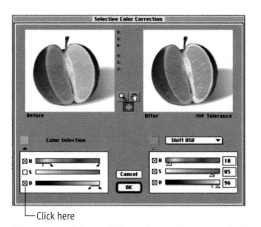

└─ Click here

Figure 14.12   Selecting Before color based on hue and value

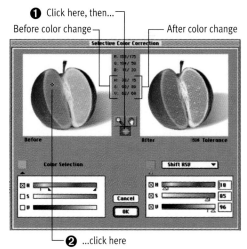

❷ ...click here

Figure 14.13   TSL reading of color to be changed

21. Repeat step 20, but this time take a reading on the edge of the apple. Use the Zoom tool to magnify the preview (see figure 14.14). The HSV reading indicates H34, S44, V76.

So far, we've remained selective by carefully brushing along the edges of the apple. Now, we'll increase selectivity, so that even if we brush the edges of the apple the color won't change.

The color difference between the orange pulp and the apple is quantified using the HSV readings, shown in table 14.1.

The greatest difference between the two colors is their saturation. The orange pulp is highly saturated (93/100), while the apple edge is only moderately saturated (44/100). So to change the color of the orange pulp without affecting the edge of the apple, we shall select only highly saturated colors.

22. Click on the Before S box. Two cursors appear on the saturation slider, defining the range of saturated colors to be corrected. In figure 14.15, the range already encompasses all highly saturated colors. This is normal, since the color originally selected in step 5 is highly saturated. If the range defined by the two cursors is too small, drag the left cursor slightly to the left to expand the range.

TABLE 14.1   HSV COLOR READINGS

	Orange pulp	Edge of apple
Hue	38	34
Saturation	93	44
Value	62	76

Take reading here

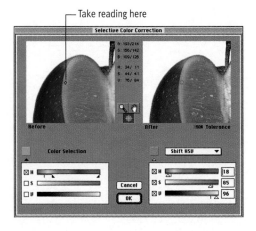

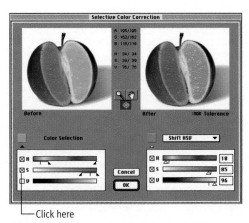

Click here

Figure 14.14 TSL reading of color to remain unchanged

Figure 14.15 Selecting color based on hue and saturation

By looking at the After preview, you can see how being selective with saturation affects the composite. Select and deselect the Saturation slider to get a better idea. If some of the apple's white edge is still affected by the color correction, drag the left Saturation cursor farther to the right to decrease the range of saturated colors affected.

To check whether a color is modified by the correction, click on the densitometer and click on the color in the Before or After image. In figure 14.15, the HSV reading to the left (Before) is the same as the HSV reading to the right (After): 34/34, 39/39, 76/76. This means the color selected won't be modified, even if you brush it. You can't always obtain perfect selectivity, but use this method to keep unwanted color changes to a minimum.

Click here and drag

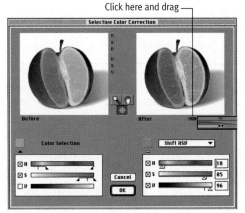

Figure 14.16 Using the Tolerance control to fine-tune selectivity

NOTE: Usually, the recommended method is to select the Saturation Range slider first without taking the densitometer readings, as we did in step 18 for the Value Range slider. Sometimes, however, the information obtained by making densitometer readings can help you better understand which HSV components you should use and how wide the ranges should be.

23. Click on the Tolerance control and drag out the cursor to approximately 25%, as shown in figure 14.16. Up to now, the red of the apple's skin was slightly color-corrected in the After preview. The red is now much less affected.

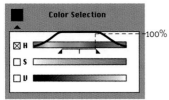

Figure 14.17   100% tolerance

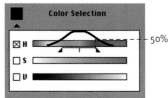

Figure 14.18   50% tolerance

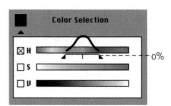

Figure 14.19   0% tolerance

By adjusting the tolerance, you affect the overall selectivity defined using the Before sliders. It is an additional tool for fine-tuning the selective intervals already defined. Monitor the After preview until you obtain the right selectivity.

NOTE: The tolerance value determines the percentage of the color correction at the ends of the interval. For example, a tolerance of 100% means the correction applies 100% inside the interval, and then drops off gradually (see figure 14.17). A tolerance of 50% means the color correction applies 100% to the middle of the interval, 50% at the ends, and then drops off (see figure 14.18). At 0%, the color correction applies 100% in the middle and 0% at the ends of the interval (see figure 14.19).

---

24. Set the tolerance to 25% and click on OK. The new selectivity defined in the Selective Color Correction dialog box is applied in the main document. Because you already brushed the mask, you don't need to brush again. The mask is automatically modified to reflect the new selectivity. If you hadn't brushed in the mask, you would do it now. In any case, remember that the After image is only a preview. You create the mask yourself using the creative tools.

Tips on defining the Before color

This section contains more methods and tips for defining the Before color and improving selectivity. Note that the Before color is always defined in the HSV color space.

STARTING WITH THE RIGHT BEFORE COLOR

When you select the Before color, try to choose a color as close to the average as possible. If you start by selecting the lightest or darkest color of an object, your interval will be built around that color and will be offset in relation to most of the colors to be corrected.

ADDING COLORS TO THE BEFORE RANGE

Use the Shift key to add colors to the interval as another method for selecting the range of Before colors.

TIP

Shift-clicking may create an interval which is too large, in other words, not selective enough. Reduce the interval by dragging the appropriate cursor inwards.

To add colors to the range of Before colors:

1. In the Selective Color Correction dialog box, click on the Before color field and drag to a color in the Before image. The Before field is framed in red (see figure 14.20).

2. Release the stylus. You have selected a Before color.

3. Now press and hold the Shift key, and click in the image to add colors to the interval (see figure 14.20). As you click, the HSV intervals defining the Before color range expand to include each new color clicked.

In figure 14.20, I clicked all over the orange pulp to include all the colors to be corrected. I clicked only on the orange pulp.

DON'T BE OVER-SELECTIVE

Remember, the After preview is only a preview! You apply the colors manually, in most cases with the Brush. Therefore, you don't need to be selective for colors which are not adjacent to the object you want to correct. Though all colors may be modified in the preview, you can simply avoid brushing non-adjacent colors in your composite.

By copying a mask or stencil to the stencil in a Color Correction layer, you can further constrain the area you color-correct. The preview does not take the stencil into account.

USING A COLOR CORRECTION LAYER WITHOUT SELECTIVITY

Use a Color Correction layer to modify all the colors in a composite. In this case, deselect the Before color sliders.

To color-correct an entire composite, follow these steps:

1. Deselect the three HSV Before sliders.

2. Choose a Before color. You can choose any color. It will be used as a reference.

3. Base the After color on the Before color. For more information, see "Basing After color on Before color" later in this chapter.

4. Modify the After sliders. For example, to darken the entire composite, drag the Value cursor to the left. You can apply this general darkening to your composite using the Marquee/Fill option, or you can apply it to areas using a brush. You can even apply it gradually using a gradient.

Tips on defining the After color

There are several ways to define the After color.

BASING AFTER COLOR ON BEFORE COLOR

This is probably the most common method used for color retouching. It allows you to make small modifications to an existing color.

❶ Click and drag from here... ⌐

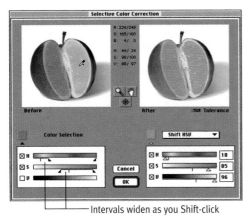 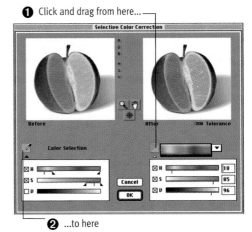

──────── Intervals widen as you Shift-click

❷ ...to here

Figure 14.20 Shift-clicking to expand the Before intervals

Figure 14.21 Basing After color on Before color

To base the After color on the Before color:

1. Select the Before color by dragging the eyedropper from the Before color field to a color in the Before preview.

2. Click on the After color and drag the eyedropper to the Before color field (see figure 14.21). Both colors are now the same.

3. Using the After sliders, modify the After color. For example, drag the Saturation cursor to the right to increase saturation.

TAKING AFTER COLOR FROM AN IMAGE

Use this method to make two different colors similar. For example, in the "Opple 2" image, you might want the left side of the orange to be as light as the right side of the orange. To do this, use the left side of the orange as the Before color and the right side of the orange as the After color. By brushing the left side, it will become as light as the right side.

MAKING YOUR OWN AFTER COLOR

You can define an After color using the color bar, Live Picture color picker, or Apple color picker. This method is illustrated in figure 14.5.

USING MORE THAN ONE COLOR COMPONENT

The various examples in this chapter illustrate the wide variety of color corrections possible with the Selective Color Correction dialog box. It all depends on which Before and After sliders are selected.

The following are examples of possible combinations.

- Saturate the reds

- Desaturate the dark greens

- Lighten the dark blues and shift them to green

> **TIP**
>
> When taking the After color from an image, make sure that all the After sliders are selected (checked), to account for the full color.

- Saturate and darken all blues, purples, and reds

- Saturate all desaturated colors

As noted earlier, the Before color is always defined in the HSV color space. The After color can be defined using the HSV, RGB, or CMYK colors spaces. For instance, you can decrease the green or increase the cyan in a given color. An explanation of the use of the RGB and CMYK color spaces follows.

Selective corrections in RGB and CMYK mode

So far, we've used the HSV mode to make color corrections. Other color correction modes are available. Press Shift HSV in the Color Correction dialog box for the mode pull-down menu (see figure 14.22).

```
Converge RGB
Shift RGB
Converge HSV
✓Shift HSV
Converge CMYK
Shift CMYK
```

Figure 14.22
The Mode pull-down menu

There are six possible color correction modes, with two in each of these modes: RGB, HSV, and CMYK. This section introduces Shift RGB, Shift HSV, and Shift CMYK. The difference between Shift and Converge is explained in the next section.

If you select Shift RGB, the After box displays a Red, Green, and Blue slider (see figure 14.23). Use these sliders to base your After color on the RGB color space.

If you select Shift CMYK, the After box displays a Cyan, Magenta, Yellow, and Black slider (see figure 14.24). Use these sliders to base your After color on the CMYK color space.

Important: When you slide one of the CMYK cursors or enter specific CMYK values next to the sliders, channels you have not modified may also be affected. For more information on working in CMYK, see Chapter 29, "Quality Color Separations in Less Than One Minute."

Shift and Converge modes

For each color mode, you can choose between two types of correction modes: Shift or Converge.

Selecting Shift causes the Before color to change to the After color. However, the other colors shift the same distance and in the same direction along the color wheel (see figure 14.25).

Selecting Converge causes the Before color to change to the After color, as in Shift mode. However, the other colors don't necessarily travel the same direction as the Before color. Rather, they take the shortest route to the After color. Furthermore, not all the colors travel the same distance along the color wheel: if they are closer to the After color than the Before color is, they stop at the After color (see figure 14.26). In other words, all colors converge toward—but don't necessarily reach—the After color.

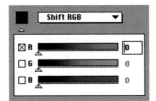

Figure 14.23 The RGB sliders

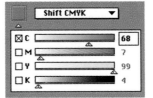

Figure 14.24 The CMYK sliders

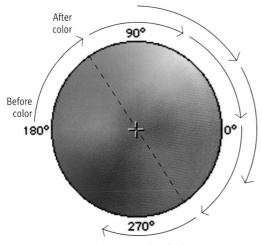

Figure 14.25 Shifting the entire color wheel

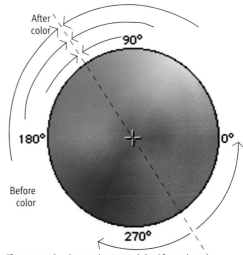

Figure 14.26 Converging toward the After color

Figures 14.27 and 14.28 show the effect of Shift and Converge using the same Before and After color. HSV is used here, but the same principle applies for RGB and CMYK.

1. The initial Before color (blue) is defined by clicking the eyedropper in the ocean.

2. The left Before Hue cursor is dragged further left to include the yellow hues of the continents.

3. The After Hue cursor is slid from blue to green.

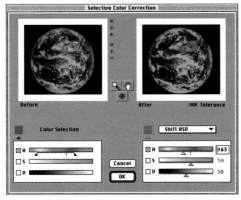

Figure 14.27 Blue shifts to green, yellow shifts to red

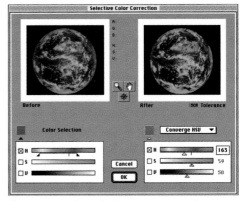

Figure 14.28 Blue and yellow converge toward green

In Figure 14.27, Shift HSV is used. The blue does indeed turn green, but the yellow-green shifts to a dark red. That's because the blue and the yellow shift the same distance and in the same direction along the color wheel.

In Figure 14.28, the same color correction is used, but this time Converge HSV mode is chosen. The blue changes to green, as in Shift HSV, but the yellow also changes to green. Blue and yellow travel the same distance along the color wheel, but they each take the most direct path to green. Blue and yellow converge toward the green from different directions (see figure 14.26).

In this example, to avoid the yellow converging toward green, drag the left Before Hue cursor back to the right. This excludes the yellow from the selection.

Choosing the right color correction mode

You can choose from the following two levels:

- Shift or Converge
- HSV, RGB, or CMYK

USING SHIFT OR CONVERGE

Shift has the advantage of maintaining the full range of colors in the original image. You shift the color wheel, but the difference between colors, in other words the contrast, is maintained. However, in some cases, you may wind up with unexpected colors (see figure 14.26).

Converge reduces the number of original colors, since many colors converge toward one. But it has the advantage of producing uniform colors and few surprises (see figure 14.27).

USING HSV, RGB, OR CMYK

There are no absolute rules for choosing a color mode. Often, you will work in the mode you are most comfortable with. Still, two points may prove helpful.

If you do not have a clear preference for one color mode, use HSV. More particularly, by shifting just the hue, you retain the original value and saturation of the color. Changes in hue don't modify the contrast or "texture" of an image.

Shifting and Converging in the RGB or CMYK color space generally results in flatter colors, where some color contrast is lost. Usually, it's best to begin in HSV mode. If the result is not fully satisfactory, try RGB and CMYK.

Recommended procedure for using the Selective Color Correction dialog box

The following recommended procedure is a summary designed to help you as you learn to make selective corrections. This is not the only order possible for making selective

TIP

Before you switch color correction modes, save your After color in the Live Picture color picker. Then select all the color components in the new mode (for example, C, M, Y, and K). Lastly, click on the After field and retrieve the saved After color from the color picker.

corrections. After you become familiar with the tools, you may prefer to follow a different order.

1. Select the Before color.

2. Select the After color.

3. Select a correction mode if you don't use Shift HSV.

4. To choose an After color based on more than one color component, click to activate the other After sliders.

5. To make the color change more selective, add color components by activating the S (saturation) and/or V (value) color sliders.

6. If necessary, try another color mode using the mode pull-down menu.

Getting around less-than-perfect selectivity

As you learn to make your color corrections more selective, you may find that the selectivity is not always perfect. The preview shows that parts of the image you don't want to modify will be modified if brushed. Here are several ways to get around less-than-perfect selectivity:

- Zoom in farther, use a small brush or minibrush, and brush carefully.

- Check that the Color Correction layer is as far down in the layer stack as possible. If you don't want to color-correct a particular image at all, there's no point in leaving the Color Correction layer above it. Drag the layer to a lower position in the layer stack.

- If a mask or stencil exists in another layer and would help constrain the color-corrected area, copy it to the stencil of the Color Correction layer.

- The Path tools are always available to create masks and stencils in a Color Correction layer.

- Lastly, if you don't have a mask or stencil, and if the Path tools are not appropriate, you can create a "selective mask." For more information, see Chapter 22, "Selective Masks Revealed."

More color correction tips

Once you've mastered the basics of using a Color Correction layer, the tips in this section may give you ideas on new ways to use this powerful and versatile tool.

CREATING MULTIPLE VERSIONS OF A COLOR CORRECTION

After you brush in a mask, you can change the Before and (more useful) After color. The change is applied immediately, allowing you to make several versions of a color correction.

The simplest way to store each version is to save the color in the color palette found in the Live Picture color picker. To view each version, just click on the different colors stored and click on OK in the color picker. Do the same to build an output file for each version.

Another method is to copy the Color Correction layer in the layer stack, open it and choose a new color. Then, using the Eye icon in the layer panel, show one layer at a time. This may seem simpler, but the screen refresh times will be slower than the first method, and your FITS file will be larger.

WORKING WITH THE FULL SCREEN

When you create a Color Correction layer, you are in HSV Shift mode and only the hue is affected. However, once you set your options in the Selective Color Correction dialog box and click on OK, the control bar takes the new parameters into account. From that point on, you can switch back and forth between the control bar and the Selective Color Correction dialog box.

If you prefer working with the full document window, use the Selective Color Correction dialog box to set the mode, select the sliders and color ranges, and use the Shift key to create the intervals, if needed. Then click on OK and return to the full document window. Using the control bar, you can still modify the Before and After colors, and use the Tolerance control. And you can always return to the dialog box by clicking on the Selective Correction button.

USING COLOR CORRECTION TO IMPROVE SILHOUETTED IMAGES

Use Color correction to removeany color remaining on the edges of silhouetted images. In the following example, I used three images (see figures 14.29, 14.30, and 14.31) to create a composite.

Figure 14.31 was silhouetted and inserted on top of the other two images. The image isn't very sharp, and the coconut leaves are quite fine, so some of the light blue from the original image remained around the leaves when the trees were inserted in their new, darker background (see figure 14.32).

Figure 14.29   Mountain torrent

Figure 14.30   Sunset

Figure 14.31   Coconut trees

Figure 14.32   Blue from original image still visible around leaves

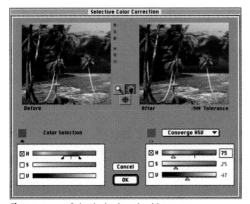

Figure 14.33   Selectively changing blue to green

Figure 14.34   Green color correction applied using stencil and Brush

To solve the problem, I created a Color Correction layer, zoomed in, and selected a blue from the edge of the leaves as the Before color. For the After color, I used the eyedropper to select a green near the edge of the leaves (see figure 14.33). The idea was to change the blue edge to green.

I used Converge HSV. I first attempted Shift HSV, but the green of the leaves shifted to orange. HSV ensured that both the green leaves and the blue edge would be green once corrected.

Finally, I copied the mask of the trees to the stencil of the Color Correction layer so that only the image of the trees was affected. I then applied the color correction to the leaves using the Brush. The color correction was also applied sparingly to the parts of the tree trunks which still retained a slight blue tint (see figure 14.34).

USING COLOR CORRECTION TO CREATE LAYERING EFFECTS

Use color correction to create a "fake" layering effect. In figure 14.35, the blues in the sky were shifted to orange.

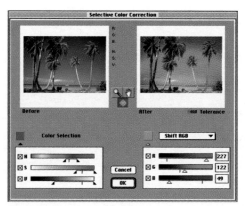

Figure 14.35   Blue sky shifted to orange

Figure 14.36   A text stencil and selectivity in a Color Correction layer

I created a text path ("Behind the Trees") and converted it to a stencil in a Color Correction layer. The stencil was then filled using the Marquee at 100% opacity (see figure 14.36). Since the color correction does not affect the trees and leaves, the text appears to run between the sky and the trees. In reality, it is positioned above a single image layer.

NOTE: For this effect to work, the selection interval had to be very precise. Due to this high selectivity, the After preview in figure 14.35 indicates that the orange gets faint as it approaches the horizon. I therefore made a copy of the Color Correction layer and modified the Before color in the second layer to affect the less saturated colors. "Behind the" is contained in the first layer, and "Trees" is contained in the second layer. I used RGB mode in both layers. It resulted in a flatter color than HSV, more compatible with text.

Figure 14.37   Original color image

MODIFYING THE PRESETS
The Presets are a set of ten color filters available in the IVUE Correction submenu. As their name indicates, they are preset and cannot be modified directly. However, you can use a Color Correction layer to modify a Preset.

The color image in figure 14.37 was inserted in an Image Insertion layer. It was then converted to black and white using the Black & White Preset (see figure 14.38).

A Color Correction layer was then created above the image (see figure 14.39). For the Before color, a white was selected from the black and white image. For the After color, the color picker was used to select a red. RGB mode was used because it provides best results when working with whites and other desaturated colors.

Figure 14.38   Black & White Preset applied to image

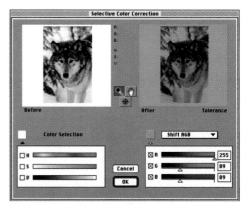

Figure 14.39   White shifted to red using Shift RGB

Figure 14.40   4-point gradient box

Figure 14.41   Color Correction gradient used to modify a Preset

After clicking on OK, a 4-point gradient was dragged around the image and four values were entered (see figure 14.40).

The white-to-red color correction was then applied. The different opacities at the four corners of the gradient resulted in varying intensities of red.

MAKING SELECTIVE CORRECTIONS USING A COLORIZE LAYER

In most cases, use a Color Correction layer to make selective corrections. However, in some cases a Colorize layer produces good results. Colorizing is generally best suited for the more creative color corrections.

Here are a few factors that could make you lean toward one or the other:

- An unlimited number of colors is available in a Colorize layer. In Color Correction layers, you need to create as many layers as there are color corrections.

- In a Colorize layer, there is no tool for creating selective intervals, in other words for defining a Before color range.

- Colorizing affects the saturation and value of colors in a way that is difficult to control. It increases color contrast. However, by colorizing in gray, you can increase just the contrast of an image, something a Color Correction layer cannot do.

- Colorizing affects colors unpredictably sometimes.

For more information on Colorize layers, see Chapter 4, "The Layers Revealed."

MAKING SELECTIVE CORRECTIONS USING IVUE CORRECTION

IVUE corrections are used to globally modify the colors in an IVUE image (see Chapter 13, "Making Global Color Corrections"). There is no ready-made way to use IVUE corrections on parts of an image. However, there is a trick to modify the contrast of an image or create color casts selectively.

To use IVUE corrections selectively, follow these steps:

1. Insert an image in an Image Insertion or Image Distortion layer.

2. Option-drag the layer to make a copy directly above the first layer.

3. Make the IVUE Corrections the top layer.

4. Click on the Marquee and use the Erase option to erase the entire top image.

5. Click on the Brush and brush back in parts of the image. The IVUE correction will appear where you brush. Use this to "brush in the IVUE correction" at the areas and the opacity of your choice.

   Variations on this method are possible. Figure 14.42 shows the original image inserted in an Image Insertion layer.

Figure 14.42 Original image

Figure 14.43 IVUE image color-corrected with Sepia 2, then lightened

The IVUE Correction Preset Sepia 2 was applied to the image. It affected the entire image, as in all IVUE corrections (see figure 14.43). Also, a Color Correction layer was created to lighten the Preset.

The Image Insertion layer was then copied, and the IVUE correction was undone on the top layer using the Undo Corrections command in the IVUE Correction submenu (at this point, the original, uncorrected image is visible). Finally, the background of the top layer was removed, leaving only the red ginger in its original colors (see figure 14.44).

NOTE: It would have been a lot of work to manually erase the background and leave just the red ginger. So, silhouetting was used to create a "selective mask." For more information, see Chapter 22, "Selective Masks Revealed."

Figure 14.44 Bottom layer with IVUE correction, top layer without IVUE correction

CHAPTER 15

PLAYING WITH COLOR AND LIGHT

This chapter describes some of the ways you can colorize images and create light and shadow. It also shows how to create backlighting for objects, and a glow effect for text. All these effects are illustrated using actual jobs.

COLORIZING IMAGES

In the strictest sense, to colorize an image is to add color to a black and white image. The Colorize layer in Live Picture allows you to do just that. However, with the Colorize layer, you can also color, brighten, darken, or add contrast to a color image.

You can also colorize images with a Color Correction layer. To colorize black and white images, use one of the RGB modes (Shift RGB or Converge RGB).

NOTE: IVUE Correction/Color Shift offers yet another way to colorize black and white images. For more information, see Chapter 13, "Making Global Color Corrections."

Using a Colorize layer

The image used to illustrate colorizing was created by Swedish designer Anders F. Rönnblom and photographer Mariann Eklund. Called "Sky Theatre and Metal Pizza Dreams # 1—Oh!," it was one of a series created for Sweden's 1994 Mac World Expo.

Two images were used as the background for this composite. Figure 15.1 was created using a mixture of KPT Bryce, KPT Gradient Designer, and the pinch and twirl distortion filters in Adobe Photoshop. Figure 15.2 represents a Milanese church wall. Before being composited, the relief of the church wall was emphasized using the Gallery Effects "Craquelure" filter.

Figure 15.1   KPT background

Figure 15.2   Milan church wall

Figure 15.3   Sara

Figure 15.4   Three images composited

Figure 15.5   Colorizing in blue

Figure 15.6   Final image

The image in figure 15.3 was composited with its alpha channel, created in Photoshop. The result is shown in figure 15.4.

At this point, a Colorize layer was created. A light blue was selected and brushed into the image. This deepened the existing colors, and added a blue tint where the stone wall was brushed (see figure 15.5).

In the final image (see figure 15.6), another figure was added, along with a piece of metallic-looking text created using Pixar Typestry. The images used to create this composite total 101 MB.

Using a Color Correction layer

In "Florence," Jean-Luc Michon used color correction layers to colorize a black and white image. The original image is shown in figure 15.7.

Three successive color correction layers were created. Figures 15.8, 15.9, and 15.10 show what was done in each layer. The color bars show what colors were selected, and what new color was chosen. The previews show the image before and after the color correction.

In figure 15.8, blue and a bit of red were added to the shadows of the image. In figure 15.9, green was removed from the light grays in the image, creating a magenta hue. In figure 15.10, the bluish shadows resulting from figure 15.9 were shifted to brown, creating a sepia effect.

Notice that all color corrections were made using the RGB modes (Shift and Converge). Figure 15.11 shows how the color correction settings in 15.10 were brushed in locally. Remember, the After preview is only a preview. Color corrections are actually applied with the creative tools.

Figure 15.7   Original B&W image

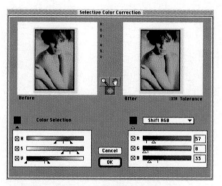

Figure 15.10   Third color correction layer

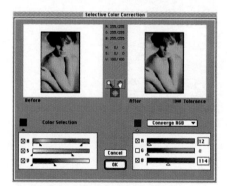

Figure 15.8   First color correction layer

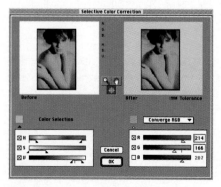

Figure 15.9   Second color correction layer

Figure 15.11   Color-corrected image

CREATING LIGHT AND SHADOW

Shadow and light can be applied using a color correction layer or a Colorize layer.

Using a color correction layer

To selectively lighten and darken the watch shown in figure 15.12, Jean-Luc Michon created two color correction layers. The first was used to darken the shadows, midtones and quarter tones of the image, with little effect on the highlights (see figure 15.13). The second was used to lighten the highlights and midtones of the image (see figure 15.14).

The overall result is an increase in contrast (see figure 15.15).

Jean-Luc could have used IVUE Correction/Curves to increase the contrast of the image, but he would have lost the freedom the Brush affords to modify areas selectively. Furthermore, by varying the opacity and pressure, he could apply the changes in light at varying intensities wherever he wished.

Figure 15.12   Original image

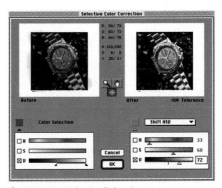

Figure 15.14   Selective lightening

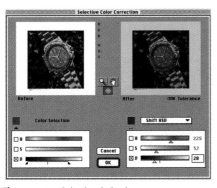

Figure 15.13   Selective darkening

Figure 15.15   Watch after selective lightening and darkening

Figure 15.16
Brush options in a
Colorize layer

Using a Colorize layer

Colorize layers contain two Brush options in addition to Paint. They are lighten and darken (see figure 15.16).

When you lighten or darken in a colorize layer, you are in fact colorizing with white and black respectively. Therefore, as with all colorizing, you increase the contrast in the image. In particular, for most colors you increase the saturation.

Lighten and darken are very easy to use. Lighten is particularly effective for recreating sunlight and other types of lighting. Unlike color correction layers, there is no selectivity.

In "Colorizing images" earlier in this chapter, we saw how Jean-Luc Michon colorized the black and white image shown in figure 15.7 (and colorized in figure 15.11). After the colorization, he created a layer of Sharpen/Blur and blurred the edges of the image (see figure 15.17).

To complete the image, he created a Colorize layer and used the Lighten and Darken options to further emphasize the play of shadow and light on Florence (see figure 15.18).

BACKLIGHTING AND GLOWS

Various backlighting and glow effects can be obtained using the Path tools. Thierry Petillot's "Information Superhighway 1" is used to illustrate these effects.

Figure 15.17   Florence after a blur

Figure 15.18   Final image

Backlighting

Three images are used in this composite. They are shown in figures 15.19, 15.20, and 15.21. The "Horizon" image was silhouetted and the "Satellite" image was cut out using the Path tools. They were both composited onto a starry backdrop (see figure 15.22).

To create a backlit effect for the satellite, Thierry first used the Path tools to draw a path around the satellite (see figure 15.23).

He then:

1. Created a Monocolor layer.

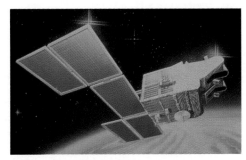

Figure 15.21   Satellite

Figure 15.19   Stars

Figure 15.20   Horizon

Figure 15.22   The three images composited

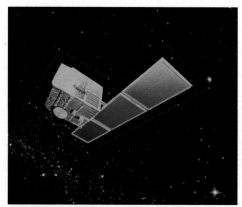

Figure 15.23   Path drawn around satellite

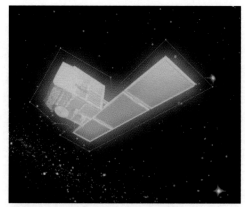

Figure 15.24   Wide-feather stencil filled with bluish-green paint

TIP

Another method would be to retrieve the path used to cut out the satellite (Stencil –> Path command) and enlarge it using the positioning tools.

2. Selected a pale bluish-green from the color bar.

3. Used the Marquee tool to create a 65% fill larger than the path.

4. Converted the path to a stencil in the Monocolor layer, using a 40-pixel feather, to obtain a glow-like effect (see figure 15.24).

To switch from frontal lighting to backlighting, Thierry dragged the Monocolor layer from above the satellite to directly beneath it in the layer stack. The light filters out along the edges of the satellite, giving the impression it's coming from behind (see figure 15.25).

At any time, Thierry can change the color of the light, as well as the size and feather of the stencil.

Glow effects

We'll continue with the image used in the previous section to illustrate glow effects on type. To create the glow effect, Thierry used the Brush Along Path command (for information on using type, see Chapter 16, "Creating Type").

Starting with the image in figure 15.25, Thierry used the Type tool to obtain a path in the shape of numbers. Then he created a Monocolor layer and converted the path to a mask of pale blue paint (see figure 15.26).

Thierry then:

1. Created another Monocolor layer, using the same light blue.

2. Retrieved the path used to create the type using the Path –>Mask command.

3. Pressed Command-A to select the entire path.

4. Clicked on the Brush.

5. In the Mask menu, chose Brush Along Path (see figure 15.27).

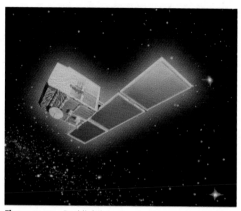

Figure 15.25   Backlighting

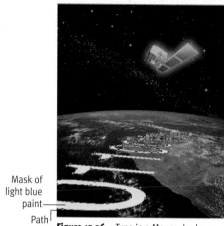

Mask of
light blue
paint
Path

Figure 15.26   Type in a Monocolor layer

Figure 15.27
The Brush Along
Path command

When you choose this command, the Brush automatically paints along the path. Figure 15.28 shows the result. The layer of type is hidden so that you can see the blue paint following the path.

To obtain a strong brush stroke, increase the Pressure control setting in the creative toolbar, or press a higher digit on your numeric keypad. To add to the existing brush stroke, choose the Brush Along Path command again.

To obtain a softer brush stroke, decrease the pressure setting or press a lower digit on your numeric keypad. You can also decrease brush opacity. To remove the stroke, select the Eraser and choose Brush Along Path. The stroke is partially or completed erased.

To complete the glow effect, Thierry moved the "glow" layer beneath the layer of type (note that both are Monocolor layers) in the layer stack. He then added the lines of light in Photoshop—hard lines are easier to create in pixel-based applications (see figure 15.29).

Paint
brushed
along path

Figure 15.28   Painting along a path

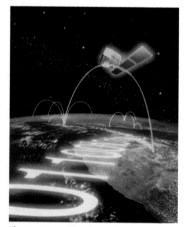

Figure 15.29   Glow beneath type

CHAPTER 16

CREATING TYPE

You can directly create type in Live Picture. Type can be letters, numbers, or anything you have a font for. This chapter explains how to create type and modify it.

NOTE: This chapter does not deal with text imported from other applications. See "Layer for importing EPS files" in Chapter 4, "The Layers Revealed."

ABOUT TYPE

Live Picture enables you to create type using TrueType and PostScript Type 1 fonts. When you create the type, it is vectorized directly in your document, in the form of a path.

NOTE: A few PostScript Type 1 fonts do not provide their path information. These fonts are not available in Live Picture.

Type is a path just like any path created using the Path tools. Therefore, it can be used in any layer. To fill type with paint, create a Monocolor or Multicolor layer. To fill it with an image, create an image layer. You can even create colorized type, color correction type, or sharpened or blurred type.

Figure 16.1 Beginning of composite

Figure 16.2 Type displayed as a path

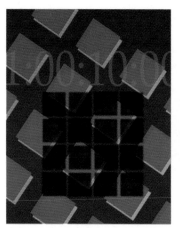

Figure 16.3   Type filled with paint   **Figure 16.4**   Numbers created in Live Picture

David Bishop used a Monocolor layer in "Sybex Multi-Media Textbook" to create ghosted numbers. Figure 16.1 shows the composite before he added the type.

After creating a Monocolor layer, he created the type using Palatino (which he later deformed slightly using the positioning tools). The type appears as a path (see figure 16.2).

The path was converted into a hard-edged stencil. To fill the stencil, David chose a light blue, and used the Marquee/Fill option at an opacity of 25% (see figure 16.3).

Figure 16.4 shows the type and all the layers created above it.

CREATING TYPE

This section provides the step-by-step procedure for creating type. We'll first create an Image Insertion layer, and then create a Multicolor layer for the type.

To create type, follow these steps:

1. In the Create menu, choose Image Insertion.

2. If the Auto Insert option is not selected, click on it to select it. Then select the image on the CD called "Cheetah Lying" and open it. The image is located in the IVUE folder.

3. In the Create menu, choose Multicolor.

4. In the creative toolbar, click on the Path tool and drag out the Path tool palette. Select the Type tool (see figure 16.5).

Figure 16.5   Type tool in Path tool palette

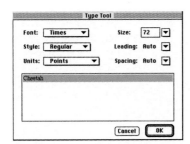

Figure 16.6 Type Tool dialog box

Figure 16.7 Text appears where you click

5. In the composite, click a few inches above the Cheetah's head, in the sky (see figure 16.7). The Type Tool dialog box appears.

6. In the Type Tool dialog box, select Times from the font pop-down menu and enter "Cheetah" in the Type box.

   The size field allows you to select a font size in points. You can leave the default setting, unless you require a specific font size, since you can quickly scale the font within your composite (see step 8).

7. Click on OK. The text appears in vector form. The bottom of the type begins where you clicked in step 5.

NOTE: Your text may not appear the same size on your screen. Type size depends on the resolution of your document.

8. To scale the text path, click on the mode toggle to switch to the creative tools. Make sure that none of the layers or layer elements are selected. If a layer is selected, it will also be scaled. To deselect a selected layer or layer element, click on the Background layer.

9. Drag a corner handle, as shown in figure 16.8. The text path is enlarged and the proportions are maintained.

   To change the proportions, drag a middle handle.

   You can center the text path by positioning the cursor inside the positioning box and dragging.

10. In the creative toolbar, click on the color selector and drag out the color bar. Choose orange or any other color you want.

11. In the creative toolbar, click on the Marquee and choose the Fill option. Then drag a rectangle around the text path and release your stylus (see figure 16.9).

12. In the layer stack, select the Multicolor layer you created earlier.

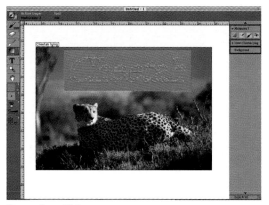

Figure 16.8   Path scaled

Figure 16.9   Fill for text

Figure 16.10   Stencil filled with paint

13. Press Command-A to select all the points in the path.

14. In the Mask menu, choose Path –>Stencil.

15. In the dialog box, click on the Create Hard Edge option. Then click on OK. The path is transformed into a stencil, which is filled with paint (see figure 16.10).

NOTE: To create text with a very hard edge, use the Extra Precision option. This guarantees the highest quality text. However, this option requires additional RAM, and generates much larger FITS files.

You've just created type in a composite. The next section shows you how to modify the type.

MODIFYING TYPE

Modifying type is easy—and possible at all times. (You can use the same procedure to modify any path, whether or not it is type.) In this section we'll reposition the type, soften the edge, modify one of the letters, and add new color. This exercise is a continuation of the previous exercise.

Repositioning

The text is now part of the Multicolor layer. You reposition the text by repositioning that layer.

To reposition the text, follow these steps:

1. In the layer stack, select the Multicolor layer.

2. Click on the mode toggle to switch to positioning mode.

Figure 16.11 Text modified with Perspective tool

3. Drag out a middle side handle so the text covers most of the width of the image. This changes the proportion of the text. (To maintain the proportions using a middle handle, press and hold the Shift key.)

4. In the positioning toolbar, click on the Perspective tool.

5. Drag the bottom middle handle downward. Your text should be similar to figure 16.11.

Changing the edge of the text

Originally, we converted the path into a hard-edged stencil. Now we're going to make the edge softer.

To change the text edge, follow these steps:

1. In the layer stack, select the Multicolor layer.

2. In the Mask menu, choose Stencil –>Path.

3. In the Compute Path dialog box, click on Retrieve Original Path (see figure 16.12).

4. Click on OK. The path you used to create the stencil is displayed.

5. In the Mask menu, choose Path –>Stencil. In the Convert Path dialog box, enter 4 in the Feathering field.

6. Click on OK. The stencil is recalculated with a softer, more gradual edge.

   Retrieve the path and modify the hardness of the edge until the text looks just right on your image (see figure 16.13).

Modifying the path

You can modify just part of a text path. For instance, you can select a single anchor point, or all the anchor points of a letter, as we'll do next.

Figure 16.12 Compute Path dialog box

Figure 16.13 Modifying edge hardness

To modify one letter, follow these steps:

1. In the layer stack, select the Multicolor layer.

2. In the Mask menu, choose Stencil −>Path.

3. In the Compute Path dialog box, click on Retrieve Original Path.

4. Click on OK. The path is displayed, and all the anchor points are selected.

5. Click on the Path tool in the creative toolbar.

6. To deselect the path, press and hold the Command key, and click anywhere outside the path. The anchor points disappear.

7. To select just the first letter, press and hold Command + (plus) Option, and click on the C path (see figure 16.14).

8. To scale the letter C, click on the mode toggle to switch to the creative tools. Remember, all layers and layer elements must be deselected or they will be repositioned as well. (Click on the Background layer bar to deselect.)

9. Drag the X-point from the center of the positioning box to the bottom middle anchor point. It snaps into place (see figure 16.15).

10. Drag the top middle anchor point upwards (see figure 16.15).

    The bottom of the C stays in place because you snapped the X-point into a bottom handle.

11. Toggle to Creative mode.

12. Now press Command-A to select the entire text path.

13. In the Mask menu, choose Path −> Stencil. In the Convert Path dialog box, enter 4 in the Feathering field.

┌─ Command + Option-click here   ┌─ Drag this point up

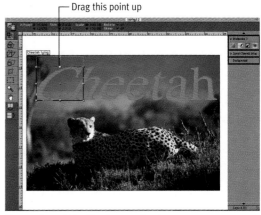

Figure 16.14   Text path with "C" selected   **Figure 16.15**   Using X-point to scale a letter

Figure 16.16 New stencil computed from modified path

14. Click on OK. The previous stencil is replaced with the new stencil. The C is enlarged (see figure 16.16).

. . . .
NOTE: If the top of the C is not filled with orange, use the Brush or Marquee to fill it.
. . . .

Changing the color

You can change the color of type at any time. If this were a Monocolor layer, you could choose a new color and the type would automatically change to that color. In a Multicolor layer, you have the possibility of using several colors.

To add a color, follow these steps:

1. Click the color selector and choose black.

2. In the creative toolbar, click on the Tool Size control and drag to select the smallest brush.

3. Press and hold the Control key. Then drag out a vector at an angle of roughly 45° (see figure 16.17).

   This keyboard shortcut for Direction control constrains the direction of a brush stroke to an angle.

4. Brush the letters at a 45° angle.

You can use any number of colors, any opacity, and any brush size to add colors. Try using the Palette Knife with the Push option. Also, you can fill the letters with a Multicolor gradient (see Chapter 17, "Creating Gradients").

To create glow effects, see Chapter 15, "Playing with Color and Light." To learn how to make a shadow for type, see Chapter 19, "Creating Drop Shadows."

Figure 16.17 Setting brush direction

Figure 16.18 Adding colors to the text

CREATING GRADIENTS

You can create gradients in any layer type. The source of the layer determines the type of gradient you create. For instance, in paint layers, you create a color gradient, in image layers you create a transparency gradient, and so on. This chapter illustrates the different types of gradients.

Very little banding, if any, occurs in the gradients, and rounding errors are eliminated, because Live Picture works internally in 48-bit color and all masks are resolution-independent.

RECTANGULAR GRADIENTS

The Marquee tool in the creative toolbar offers a Gradient option in every layer except Image Clone. That Gradient option in turn features a submenu with three sub-options: Horizontal, Vertical, and 4 points (see figure 17.1).

Horizontal creates a gradient running along the horizontal axis and Vertical creates a gradient running along the vertical axis. A 4-point gradient combines a vertical and horizontal gradient—the gradient merges toward the center.

Creating rectangular gradients

The procedure is basically the same for all rectangular gradients.

To create a gradient, follow these steps:

1. Create a layer.

Figure 17.1
The Gradient option
and sub-options

2. In the creative toolbar, click on the Marquee and choose the Gradient option and a sub-option.

3. In your document, drag open the gradient. Depending on what type of layer is active and which sub-option you choose, the gradient box will look slightly different.

TIP

The gradient box is dotted if the box is too small. In this case, zoom in and redraw the gradient box.

The gradient boxes are the same in the following layers: Monocolor, Artwork, Image Insertion, Image Distortion, and Color Correction (see figures 17.2, 17.3, and 17.4).

In Multicolor and Colorize layers, the gradient boxes also include a color control for selecting more than one color. Figure 17.5 shows a 4-point gradient box for these layers.

Finally, figure 17.6 shows a 4-point gradient box in a Sharpen/Blur layer.

4. To set the opacity, click on the opacity control and enter a number. You can also drag out the Opacity slider (see figure 17.7).

5. To select a color in layers with several colors, click on the color control and drag out the color bar (see figure 17.8).

   You can also click once or twice to use the Live Picture color picker or the Apple color picker respectively, or you can drag from the color control to select any color on your screen. For more information on selecting colors, see Chapter 3, "The Tools Revealed."

6. To create a blur gradient, click on the Sharpen/Blur control (see figure 17.9). The control is set on Sharpen by default.

7. Click inside the gradient box to preview the gradient.

   You can modify any of the gradient settings and click again inside the gradient box to preview the new settings. This can be repeated as many times as necessary.

8. Once you are satisfied, click outside the gradient box to create the gradient.

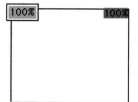

Figure 17.2 Horizontal gradient box

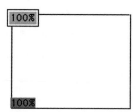

Figure 17.3 Vertical gradient box

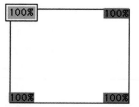

Figure 17.4 4-point gradient box

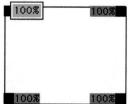

Figure 17.5 4-point gradient box with color controls

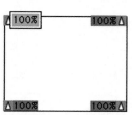

Figure 17.6 4-point gradient box for sharpening and blurring

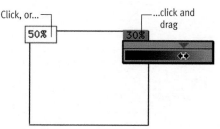

Figure 17.7 Setting the opacity of a gradient

Click here and drag

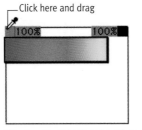

Figure 17.8 Selecting the colors of a gradient

Click to toggle between Sharpen and Blur

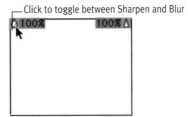

Figure 17.9 Setting a Sharpen/Blur gradient

Creating color gradients

This section describes different uses of gradients in Monocolor, Multicolor, Colorize, and Artwork layers.

CREATING A MONOCOLOR GRADIENT

This exercise shows how to create a white gradient. The gradient is of a single color, but the opacity changes. Gradients of this type can be used to highlight text created in a page layout program, such as QuarkXpress or Pagemaker.

To create a white gradient, follow these steps:

1. In the Create menu, choose Image Insertion.

2. If the Auto Insert option is not selected, click on it to select it. Then open the image on the CD called "Moorea," located in the IVUE folder.

3. In the Create menu, choose Monocolor.

4. In the creative toolbar, click on the color selector and drag to choose white from the gradient strip.

5. Click on the Marquee and choose the Gradient/Vertical option.

6. Drag open the gradient box as shown in figure 17.10.

7. Enter 70% in the top opacity control, tab to the bottom opacity control, and enter 40%.

8. Click inside the gradient box to preview the gradient (see figure 17.11).

   You can change the opacities of the gradient using the opacity controls.

9. Click outside the gradient to create it.

Figure 17.10 Gradient box

Click here

Rectangle tool

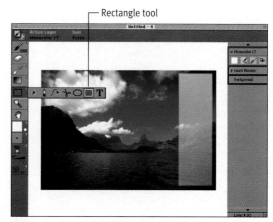

Figure 17.11   Previewing the gradient

Figure 17.12   Selecting the Rectangle tool

10. The edges of the gradient are soft. To create a hard-edged gradient, click on the Path tools in the creative toolbar and drag out the Rectangle tool (see figure 17.12).

11. Drag open a rectangle slightly smaller than the white gradient, as shown in figure 17.13.

12. In the Mask menu, choose Path –> Stencil.

13. In the Convert Path dialog box, click on Create Hard Edge. Then click on OK. The gradient takes on a hard edge (see figure 17.14).

Now we'll learn how to reposition the gradient and change its color.

14. In the layer bar, click on the Monocolor layer to select it.

15. Click on the mode toggle to switch to the positioning toolbar.

16. To move the gradient, position the cursor inside the positioning box and drag it to another location.

Rectangular path

Figure 17.13   Creating a Rectangular path

Figure 17.14   Creating a hard-edged gradient

Position cursor here

Drag to reduce size of gradient

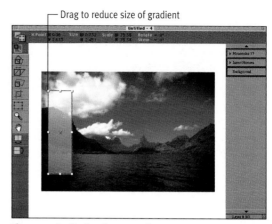

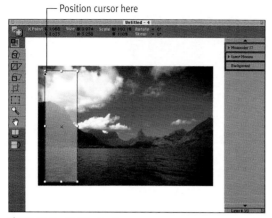

Figure 17.15   Positioning the cursor

Figure 17.16   Scaling down a gradient

17. To scale the gradient, position the cursor on one of the corner handles of the positioning box, as shown in figure 17.15. Then drag the handle inwards (see figure 17.16).

18. Click on the mode toggle to switch to the creative toolbar.

19. In the creative toolbar, click on the color selector and drag to choose an orange from the color bar. The gradient changes color automatically (see figure 17.17).

CREATING A MULTICOLOR GRADIENT

In "Sybex Multi-Media Textbook," David Bishop created a Multicolor gradient in two shades of blue. He then drew a set of square paths using the Rectangle tool (see figure 17.18).

Click and drag here

Square paths

Multicolor gradient

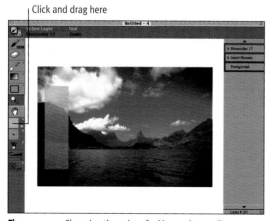

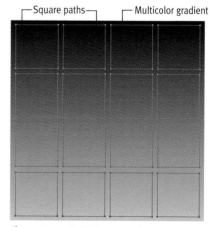

Figure 17.17   Changing the color of a Monocolor gradient

Figure 17.18   Multicolor gradient with square paths

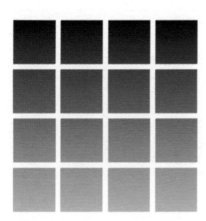

Figure 17.19   Paths converted to a stencil

Figure 17.20   Multicolor layer and underlying layers

David converted the paths to a stencil to create the tiles (figure 17.19). Figure 17.20 shows the tiles, and the underlying layers he had created prior to making the gradient.

The completed image is shown in Chapter 8, "Isolating Images from their Background" (see figure 8.16).

CREATING A GRADIENT WITH MORE THAN FOUR COLORS
A Multicolor gradient allows you to create gradients with up to four different colors. To create gradients with more than four colors, use several gradient boxes.

To create a "rainbow" gradient, follow these steps:

TIP

To use the exact same green, save the green of the first gradient in the color palette and reuse it for the second gradient.

1. In the Create menu, choose Multicolor.

2. In the creative toolbar, click on the Marquee and choose the Gradient/Horizontal option.

3. Drag open a gradient box and create a gradient as shown in figures 17.21 to 17.23.

4. To create the second gradient, position the cursor on the top right part of the gradient box (see figure 17.24). Be as precise as possible, to make the transition between the two gradients smooth.

Figure 17.21   Selecting the first color

Figure 17.22   Selecting the second color

Figure 17.23   Previewing the gradient

Position cursor here

Figure 17.24   Positioning the second gradient

Figure 17.25 Selecting the second color field

Figure 17.26 Selecting the right color field

Figure 17.27 Hard-edged Multicolor gradient

TIP

If the gradient edge is not straight, use the Marquee/Erase option to even it out.

5. Now drag open the second gradient. Make it basically the size of the first gradient.

6. To select the left color, click the color field and drag to select the green from the first gradient.

7. For the right color field, select a blue (see figure 17.25).

8. Follow the same procedure for the third gradient, but choose blue for the left color field and red for the right color field (see figure 17.26).

9. Preview the last gradient. Then click outside to create it.

10. To create a hard-edged gradient, create a stencil using the Rectangle tool. This process is described in "Creating a Monocolor gradient," steps 10 to 13, earlier in this chapter.

If you want more colors in your gradient, use more gradient boxes.

CREATING A COLORIZE GRADIENT

While Colorize gradients can be used on any type of image, they are particularly effective on images where grays predominate. With colorize gradients, there's always a bit of trial and error. It's difficult to predict just how a gradient will affect all the colors in your image.

To create a Colorize gradient, follow these steps:

1. In the Create menu, choose Image Insertion.

2. If the Auto Insert option is not selected, click on it to select it. Then open the image on the CD called "Pillows," located in the IVUE folder.

3. In the Create menu, choose Colorize.

4. In the creative toolbar, click on the Marquee and choose the Gradient/4 Points option.

gradient box—
slightly
larger than
image

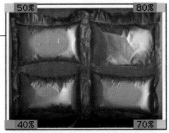

Figure 17.28 Defining a Colorize gradient   **Figure 17.29** Colorize gradient

5. Drag open the gradient box so that it's slightly larger than the image. Then select the opacities and colors so that they approximate those in figure 17.28.

6. Click inside the gradient box to preview the gradient.

   Experiment with the opacities values and colors.

7. Click outside the gradient box to create the gradient (see figure 17.29).

CREATING AN ARTWORK GRADIENT

Artwork gradients create some pretty stunning patterns. It's good to experiment with Artwork gradients because they often are unpredictable. Remember that Artwork patterns are often partially transparent. This means they are affected by the layers beneath them, or the color of the background if the Artwork layer is at the bottom of the layer stack.

To create an Artwork gradient, follow these steps:

1. If the background color is not white, click the color selector and drag out the color bar. Choose something close to white in the gradient strip.

2. In the Create menu, choose Artwork.

3. Using the color selector, choose a blue.

4. In the creative toolbar, click on the Marquee and choose the Gradient/4 Points option.

5. Drag open the gradient and enter the values shown in figure 17.30.

6. Click inside the gradient box. It should be similar to figure 17.31.

7. In the control bar, click on the Patterns control and select Radio Waves from the Patterns palette (see figure 17.32).

   A new pattern appears inside the gradient box (see figure 17.33).

Figure 17.30 Defining an Artwork gradient

In figure 17.34, the gradient was obtained using the same opacity values as above, a black background, purple in the Artwork layer, and the Tree Rings pattern.

Figure 17.31 Previewing an Artwork gradient

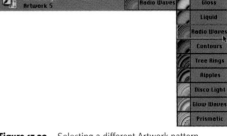

Figure 17.32 Selecting a different Artwork pattern

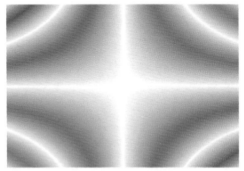

Figure 17.33 Previewing the new pattern

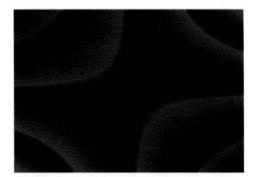

Figure 17.34 Purple "tree rings" gradient

Figure 17.35 shows the same gradient after running the Palette Knife across it in all directions. First the Push option was used to disrupt the regular lines, and then the Diffuse option was used to soften the lines.

Figure 17.36 is the same as 17.35, except that the pattern selected this time was Prismatic.

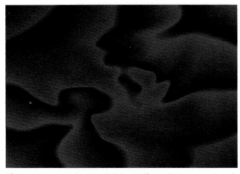

Figure 17.35 Using the Palette Knife to distort an artwork gradient

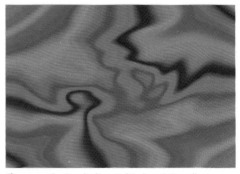

Figure 17.36 Purple distorted "prismatic" gradient

Creating an image gradient

An image gradient means that you are gradually varying the opacity of an image. Image gradients can be used to blend an image into a solid background. They can also be used to blend one image into another, as illustrated in the image below, created by Helen Hann.

The two images used in "Choice Fruit 2" are shown in figures 17.37 and 17.38. Helen first silhouetted the apple to remove its gray background. She then created a Monocolor layer and re-created a drop shadow, shown in figure 17.39 (for more information, see Chapter 19, "Creating Drop Shadows").

Helen then inserted the orange above the apple. To ensure that no orange appeared outside the form of the apple, she copied the silhouetted mask of the apple to the stencil of the orange (see Chapter 10, "Sources, Masks, and Stencils Revealed").

After erasing the entire orange, Helen reinserted the bottom of the orange at 100%. She then dragged open a vertical gradient, as shown in figure 17.40.

By using the values 100% and 0%, the orange changes smoothly from completely opaque to completely transparent. As the orange becomes transparent, the underlying apple shows through, merging the two fruits and creating, in Helen's words, an "Opple"(see figure 17.41)!

Figure 17.37 Apple

Figure 17.38 Orange

Figure 17.39 Apple silhouetted, with drop shadow

Figure 17.40 Vertical gradient

Figure 17.41 "Choice Fruit 2"

Creating Sharpen/Blur gradients

Use Sharpen/Blur gradients to create gradual increases or decreases in image sharpness. You can enter either sharpness or blur values, or you can combine the two, as shown in the following example.

To create a Sharpen/Blur gradient, follow these steps:

1. In the Create menu, choose Image Insertion.

2. If the Auto Insert option is not selected, click on it to select it. Then open the image on the CD called "Coconut Trees," located in the IVUE folder.

3. In the Create menu, choose Sharpen/Blur.

4. In the creative toolbar, click on the Marquee and choose the Gradient/Vertical option.

5. Drag open the gradient box so that it's slightly larger than the image.

6. In the top opacity field, enter 50%. Then tab to the bottom opacity field and enter 70%.

7. At the top left of the gradient box, click on the Sharpen/Blur control. The Sharpen icon switches to a Blur icon (see figure 17.42).

8. Click inside the gradient box to preview the gradient. The top of the image is blurred, and gradually sharpens towards the bottom, giving the impression that the coconut leaves are rustling in the wind (see figure 17.43).

TIP

For every kind of gradient, you can modify areas locally with the Brush and Eraser.

You can remove the blur from the tree trunks by selecting a small tool size and using the Eraser.

Sharpen/Blur gradients can emphasize perspective in an image. Use sharpening to make one side of the image look closer, and blur to make the other side appear more distant. Sharpen/Blur gradients can emphasize the main subject of an image also.

Figure 17.42   Selecting Sharpen or Blur

Figure 17.43   Vertical Sharpen/Blur gradient

❶ Click and drag from here...

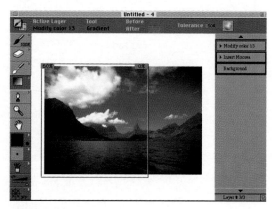

❷ ...to here

Figure 17.44 Choosing the Before color

Figure 17.45

Creating color correction gradients

Use color correction gradients to apply a gradually changing color to an object. By applying color changes to objects at a decreasing opacity, you can create shadow and light effects.

To create a color correction gradient, follow these steps:

1. In the Create menu, choose Image Insertion.

2. If the Auto Insert option is not selected, click on it to select it. Then open the image on the CD called "Moorea," located in the IVUE folder.

3. In the Create menu, choose color correction. A new color correction layer is created.

4. In the control bar, click on the Before color control and drag the eyedropper onto the sky. Select a blue (see figure 17.44).

5. In the control bar, click on the After color control and drag to choose a purple from the color bar.

6. In the creative toolbar, click on the Marquee and choose the Gradient/Horizontal option.

7. Drag open the gradient box as shown in figure 17.45. Enter 60% and 0% in the opacity controls.

8. Click inside the gradient box to preview the gradient (see figure 17.46).

9. Experiment with other opacity values. Use the After color control to try other colors.

Figure 17.46 Previewing a color correction gradient

OTHER GRADIENT SHAPES

There are several ways to create non-rectangular gradients. You can combine rectangular gradients, use the Path tools, or use the Brush.

TIP

Use the Diffuse option in the Palette Knife to smooth the gradient edges if any breaks or unevenness occur between the gradients.

Combining gradients

To create a gradient with more than four points, you can combine several gradients. In the previous example, we used the image "Moorea" and a color correction layer to create a single horizontal gradient. Figures 17.47 to 17.50 demonstrate how to create a gradient that emanates from the center of the image using the Gradient/4 Points option.

Each time you drag open a new gradient box, line it up along the edge of the previous gradient box. This avoids breaks in the gradient. The completed gradient is shown in figure 17.51.

Second gradient starts where first gradient ends

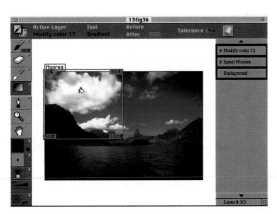

Figure 17.47   Creating the first gradient

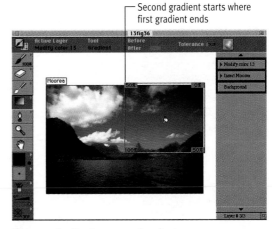

Figure 17.48   Creating a second gradient

Figure 17.49   Creating a third gradient

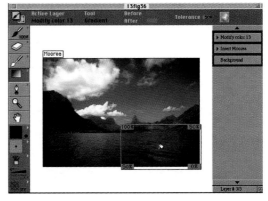

Figure 17.50   Creating a fourth gradient

Figure 17.51   Gradient emanating from center of image

Using the Path tools

Use the Path tools to create gradients in any number of shapes. Thierry Petillot needed to create a series of floodlights for his image "Information Superhighway 2." He first created a Monocolor layer to create a 4-point gradient in bluish white (see figure 17.52).

Then, using the Path tools, he drew four cone-like shapes (see figure 17.53).

The paths were then converted into a single stencil, so that the gradient appeared only within the paths (see figure 17.54).

The Monocolor gradient is the top layer of "Information Superhighway 2" (see figure 17.55).

To complete the image, Thierry used the Eraser to remove parts of the gradient on the arm.

Figure 17.52   Monocolor gradient

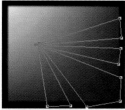

Figure 17.53   Defining paths for the gradient

Figure 17.54   Gradient constrained inside stencil

Figure 17.55   "Information Superhighway 2" completed

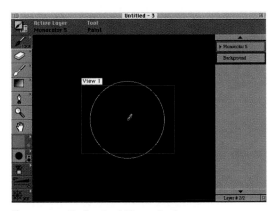

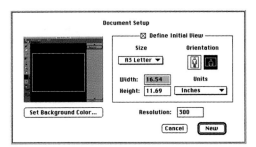

Figure 17.56 Defining a black two-page spread

Figure 17.57 Finding the right zoom level

Using the Brush

Use the Brush to create a circular gradient.

To create a circular gradient for a two-page spread, follow these steps:

1. In the File menu, choose Document Setup. All documents must be closed or the command is grayed out.

2. In the Document Setup dialog box, click on Define Initial View. In the Size pop-down menu, choose A3 Letter. Under Orientation, click on the landscape icon. In the Resolution field, enter 300. Then click on the Set Background Color field and choose black from the Apple color picker. The dialog box should look like Figure 17.56.

3. Click on New. The document opens with a view of a black two-page spread.

4. In the Create menu, choose Monocolor.

5. Using the color selector, choose a pink or some other color.

6. Select the largest tool size.

7. In the creative toolbar, click on the Brush.

8. Zoom out (Option-zoom) so that you can easily fill the view with the brush (see figure 17.57). After zooming, click on the Brush again to reactive it.

9. Apply pressure to the Brush while generating a slight circular motion with the stylus. Brush until you have a circle similar to figure 17.58. Depending on the settings of your digitizing tablet, you may need to press fairly hard for the paint to fill the Size Circle.

Figure 17.58 Creating a one-color circular gradient

Figure 17.59 Creating a two-color circular gradient

10. To use another color, create another Monocolor layer and choose another color. Apply the paint at the center of the first gradient, but don't press as hard, so the paint doesn't quite fill the circle (see figure 17.59). You can also try this with a slightly smaller brush.

You have just created a circular gradient for a double-page. This image was built out to create a 1.5 MB file for this book, but since the paint is resolution-independent, you could use the same FITS file to build the 68 MB file needed for the 300-dpi double spread. The time it took to create the gradient and the smoothness of the gradient is the same.

By using two Monocolor layers, you can change the color of either circle at any time. You can also change the relative size of the circles by scaling one Monocolor layer.

CHAPTER 18

USING FILTER PLUG-INS

This chapter shows how to use Photoshop-compatible filter plug-ins in Live Picture. Filters can be applied to a single IVUE image, or to an entire composite.

ABOUT FILTER PLUG-INS IN LIVE PICTURE

Live Picture supports the plug-in architecture for third-party Photoshop-compatible filter plug-ins. These plug-ins include such products as Kai's Power Tools (KPT) and Xaos Tools.

You can apply a filter to a single IVUE image, or to the entire FITS file. In addition, you can apply a filter to a view, or to a selection.

Using Photoshop-compatible filters in Live Picture is a mixed blessing. These filter plug-ins use pixel-editing technology—they actually modify the entire pixel image. Therefore, you don't benefit from the speed and resolution-independence usually associated with the FITS technology. With these plug-ins, the larger the image, the longer it takes to apply the filter. This process will probably seem very slow compared to other operations performed in Live Picture.

Before you can use a filter plug-in, Live Picture needs to know where the plug-in is located.

To locate the plug-in, follow these steps:

1. In the Edit menu, choose Preferences/Files & Folders.

2. In the Files & Folders Preferences dialog box, click on the Plug-ins field, and locate the folder containing the filter plug-ins.

3. Select the folder and click on "Select ....." (name of folder).

4. Click on OK. Then quit Live Picture and launch the application again.

If you use Adobe Photoshop, you can avoid creating two copies of the plug-ins by using the same plug-in folder for Live Picture and Photoshop. Furthermore, Live Picture uses a single plug-ins folder for the filter plug-ins and the import/export plug-ins (EPS/DCS, Photoshop 3.0, and Scitex 3.0). Place all plugs-ins in the same folder.

....

NOTE: You cannot use the filters that ship with Photoshop. These are protected and are only available in Photoshop. Also, certain third-party filters are Adobe-specific and only work with Photoshop. A list of working plug-ins is provided with the full version of Live Picture.

....

Plug-ins require 2 to 4 MB of additional RAM. This means that to run the filter plug-ins, you need a bit more than the 18 MB minimum RAM requirement.

APPLYING A FILTER TO AN IVUE FILE

You can apply a filter to an IVUE file inserted in a composite. This creates a new IVUE file, which is automatically substituted for the original in the FITS file. To stay true to the IVUE/FITS approach to digital imaging, the original remains untouched. You can substitute it again at any time.

To filter a single IVUE image, follow these steps:

1. In the layer stack, select the image layer you want to filter. In figure 18.1, the top layer is selected.

2. In the Layer menu, choose Filter Plug-ins, and choose a filter from the submenu (see figure 18.2).

    After a few seconds, the Filter dialog box appears (see figure 18.3).

3. Select Apply to One Image Layer if the option is not already selected.

4. To take opacity into account, click on Use Selected Layer. This option creates an alpha channel based on the visible area of the layer (in other words, a combination of the mask and the stencil).

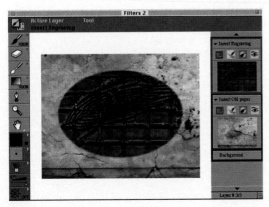

Figure 18.1   Selecting the image to filter

Figure 18.2   Selecting a filter plug-in

Figure 18.3   Filter dialog box

Figure 18.4   KPT Spheroid Designer dialog box

Filtered IVUE automatically replaces original IVUE ——

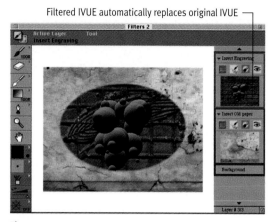

Figure 18.5   New IVUE with filter applied to selection

5. Click on OK. The Save dialog box appears.

6. Enter a name for the new filtered IVUE and click on Save. The third-party plug-in dialog box appears (see figure 18.4).

7. Select or create your filter. Then click on OK (for more information, see the documentation provided with the filter plug-in). A new filtered IVUE file is created and automatically substituted for the original IVUE in the FITS file. In figure 18.5, Use Selected Layer was selected, so the filter is only applied to the stencil.

   To reuse the original IVUE, use the Substitute Image button in the Get Info dialog box (see Chapter 5, "Handling Layers").

   ....

   NOTE: If you apply a filter plug-in to a compressed IVUE file, the file is decompressed to apply the filter, and recompressed after the new IVUE is created. When you build your final output, the IVUE is again decompressed. This means that the IVUE goes through the compression/decompression cycle twice, so some quality loss is possible on some types of images. However, in many cases filter effects will probably "mask" any noticeable quality loss.

   ....

APPLYING A FILTER TO AN ENTIRE COMPOSITE

You can apply a filter to an entire FITS file, or to part of a FITS file using a view. You can also use the opacity information from an image layer or a Monocolor layer as a selection. In this case, the filter is only applied to the visible area of the layer selected, at the opacity of the layer.

Photoshop-compatible filters are designed for work on pixel images. They cannot be applied directly to FITS files. Therefore, to apply a filter to a FITS file, the view selected is first built into an IVUE at document resolution. The filter is then applied to the new IVUE, which is inserted above the active layer, in an Image Distortion layer. The original IVUEs and other layers remain unchanged.

NOTE: Filters are applied only to layers that are visible when you choose the Filter Plug-ins command. Hidden layers and layers above the active layer (in other words, layers not currently visible) are not taken into account when the new IVUE is built. This allows certain layers to remain unaffected by the filter.

To filter a composite, follow these steps:

1. In the layer stack, select an image layer or a Monocolor layer if you want to use a layer as a selection.

2. In the Layer menu, choose Filter Plug-ins, and choose a filter from the submenu.

   After a few seconds, the filter dialog box appears.

3. Select Apply to Entire Composite if the option is not already selected.

4. Select a view in the View pop-down menu. This view will be built into a new IVUE file. (To apply a filter, the FITS file must contain a view.)

5. To take opacity into account, click Use Selected Layer. This option creates an alpha channel based on the visible area of the layer selected in step 1.

6. Click on OK. The Save dialog box appears.

7. Enter a name for the filtered IVUE that will be built and click on Save. Live Picture builds an IVUE file at document resolution. (You can set the resolution of the IVUE before beginning this procedure by choosing Document Resolution in the Edit menu.)

   When the IVUE is built, the plug-in dialog box appears.

8. Select or create your filter. Then click on OK. The IVUE is filtered and inserted in an Image Distortion layer, above the active layer. Existing layers remain unchanged (see figure 18.6).

   The Distortion tools allow you to distort the filtered image.

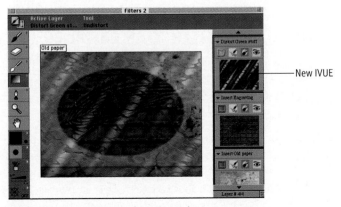

Figure 18.6   New IVUE inserted at 40% opacity

FILTER TIPS

A few tips on using filter plug-ins in Live Picture.

Filters and IVUE correction

If an IVUE file has been color-corrected using IVUE correction, the IVUE correction is not visualized in the filter plug-in preview. This is because the filter plug-in reads the original IVUE directly from disk. When the new filtered IVUE is actually created, the IVUE corrections are included.

If you have made significant IVUE corrections to the image layer, such as conversion to black and white, inversion, or a complete shift in color balance, previewing the filter image with the IVUE corrections is important. The trick is to apply the filter to the FITS file using the Apply to Entire Composite option. First, hide all layers except the image layer you want to filter. (When the filter is applied to the FITS file, it affects only visible layers.) Once the new IVUE is inserted in the layer stack, delete the layer containing the original IVUE.

Filters and transparency

Obtain interesting effects and gain added control over filtered images by playing with transparency. For filters applied to FITS files, gently erase parts of the new filtered image, or use an opacity gradient—the unfiltered layers below show through. For filters applied to IVUE files, reinsert the original, unfiltered IVUE in a new layer, and play with transparency to blend it with the new, filtered image. See "Mixing two similar images" in Chapter 20, "One Image, Two Layers."

Using filter plug-ins in Photoshop

The Live Picture™ IVUE plug-in supplied with Live Picture enables you to open IVUE files directly in Photoshop (the plug-in must be placed in the Photoshop plug-ins folder) and save images to IVUE. Therefore, filter plug-ins can be applied directly in Photoshop.

In favor of using Photoshop:

- It's somewhat faster to apply filter plug-ins to IVUE files directly in Photoshop. That's because in Photoshop the entire image is already loaded into RAM, whereas in Live Picture, IVUE files are disk-based.

- You can use all Photoshop filters shipped with the software, and all filter plug-ins.

In favor of using Live Picture:

- No need to jump from one application to another, especially if you allocate all your RAM to one application at a time.

- A new file is created automatically. The filtered IVUE is substituted seamlessly for the original IVUE. If you filter an entire composite, the resulting IVUE is reinserted in the composite and positioned properly. No need to reposition.

PART iv

COMBINING SKILLS

CREATING DROP SHADOWS

This chapter explains how to create drop shadows for objects. Learn the basic procedure for creating drop shadows in "Drop shadows 101: an introduction." Learn alternate procedures in "Drop shadows 201: advanced skills and variations," where several variations are described, including how to make shadows for text.

DROP SHADOWS 101: AN INTRODUCTION

The exercise in this section takes you step-by-step through the basic procedure for creating a drop shadow. The procedure is summarized here:

1. Silhouette an image.

2. Create a black Monocolor layer.

3. Copy the silhouetted mask to the Monocolor mask.

4. Soften the edge of the Monocolor mask.

5. Copy the Monocolor mask to the Monocolor stencil.

6. Modify the opacity of the mask.

7. Reposition the shadow.

8. Move the shadow behind the silhouetted image.

In the following exercise, a drop shadow is created for a silhouetted image. Drop shadows can also be created for images cut out using the Path tools.

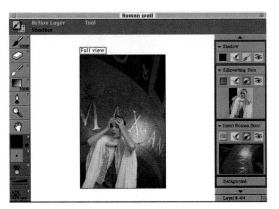

Figure 19.1 "Roman Wall" FITS file

To create a drop shadow, follow these steps:

1. In the File menu, choose Open FITS.

2. Select the FITS file "Roman Wall" in the Copy me to Hard Drive folder, and click on Open.

3. Option-click on the layer toggle to open the layer panels. Your screen should look like figure 19.1. If your screen is larger than 13", you can drag open the Live Picture window to fill your entire screen.

   "Roman Wall" contains two layers. The bottom layer, "Insert Roman floor," is an Image Insertion layer. It contains the image "Roman Floor." The top layer, "Silhouetting Sara," is an Image Silhouette layer. It contains the image "Sara."

   Both images were color-corrected using the Brightness/Contrast dialog box to make their contrast and brightness more uniform.

   Both layers contain a stencil. The stencil in the "Insert Roman floor" layer is the default stencil. The stencil in the "Silhouetting Sara" layer was created by copying the silhouetted mask to the stencil.

4. In the Create menu, choose Monocolor. A new Monocolor layer appears in the layer stack. Press Command-I, and change the name of the layer to "Shadow" (see figure 19.2). This layer will contain the drop shadow.

5. If the current color is not black, use the color selector to choose black.

6. Copy (Option-drag) the mask in the "Silhouetting Sara" layer to the mask in the "Shadow" layer. A black mask, the shape of the silhouette, is created in the Monocolor layer (see figure 19.3).

7. Using the Zoom tool, zoom so that the image on your screen approximates figure 19.4.

Figure 19.2 Black Monocolor layer named "Shadow"

Figure 19.3　Black mask in a Monocolor layer

Figure 19.4　Selecting the Diffuse option

TIP

If the edge of the mask becomes jagged, zoom in and diffuse again.

8. In the creative toolbar, select the Palette Knife and choose the Diffuse option. Then set the Pressure control at the lowest setting (far left), and select the smallest tool size (see figure 19.4).

9. Soften the edge of the black mask by running the Palette Knife lightly over the edge (see figure 19.5). Press softly on the stylus at the bottom of the shadow, and increase the pressure as you move toward the top. When you reposition the shadow, the top will be farther away from the person than the bottom, so the top of the shadow should be more diffused.

10. In the "Shadow" layer bar, copy the mask to the stencil (see figure 19.6). This "freezes" the edge of the shadow, but allows you to modify the shadow's opacity.

11. In the creative toolbar, click on the Marquee and choose the Gradient/Vertical option.

12. Drag open the gradient box and enter 40% and 55% in the opacity fields, as shown in figure 19.7.

— Softer edge

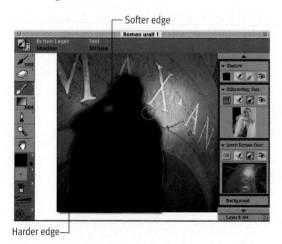

Harder edge—

Figure 19.5　Selecting the Diffuse option

Figure 19.6 Stencil created in the Monocolor layer

13. Click inside the gradient box to preview the gradient, then click outside. The opaque black fill (100% opacity) becomes more transparent (40% to 55% opacity gradient).

14. Select the layer named "Shadow" and toggle to the positioning toolbar.

15. Click on the Positioning Box tool and drag open a new Positioning box. Begin the new box at the bottom left corner of Sara's shawl, drag to the bottom right corner of the shawl, and then drag upward (see figure 19.9). The idea is to position the bottom handles at the lower extremes of the image.

16. Click on the Skew tool.

17. Drag the X-point from the center of the Positioning Box to the bottom right handle (see figure 19.10). When the shadow is skewed, that point will not move.

18. Drag the top right handle to the right (see figure 19.10).

Figure 19.7 Setting up the shadow gradient

Figure 19.8 Creating a transparent shadow

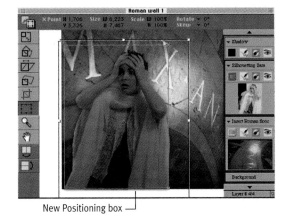

New Positioning box ⌐

Figure 19.9 Creating a new Positioning box

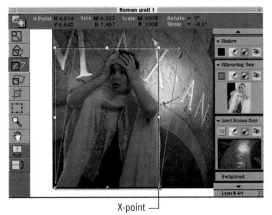

X-point ⌐

Figure 19.10 Skewing the shadow

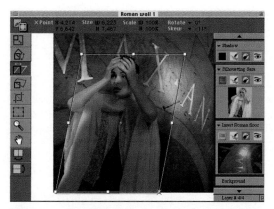

Figure 19.11   Skewed shadow

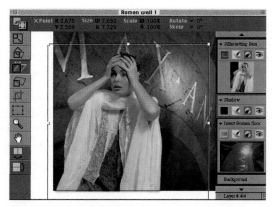

Figure 19.12   Reordering the layers

Figure 19.13   Completed exercise with drop shadow

Once skewed, the shadow should be similar to figure 19.11.

19. In the layer stack, drag the layer named "Shadow" beneath the layer named "Silhouetting Sara." In the composite, the shadow moves behind Sara (see figure 19.12).

20. Toggle back to creative mode. In the View menu, choose Go To Full View. Your completed image should resemble figure 19.13.

NOTE: Some of the steps in this exercise can be performed in a different order. For example, you can reposition the Monocolor layer before you use the Palette Knife to soften the shadow edge.

DROP SHADOWS 201: ADVANCED SKILLS AND VARIATIONS

There are many possible variations to the exercise described in "Drop shadows 101: An Introduction." Several of them are described in this section.

Using the Path tools to soften the edge

In "Drop shadows 101: An Introduction," you used the Palette Knife to soften the edge of the image. You can also use the Path tools to create a soft edge. The Path tools offer greater flexibility for experimenting with edge diffusion, or softness. In addition, soft edges computed using the Path tools are calculated automatically, and are therefore even. However, the same amount of diffusion is applied to the entire shadow edge.

Aside from the use of the Path tools, the procedure is roughly the same as the "basic" procedure, though the order is slightly different.

1. Silhouette an image.

2. Create a black Monocolor layer.

3. Copy the silhouetted mask to the monocolor stencil.

4. Modify the opacity of the shadow.

5. Reposition the shadow.

6. Move the shadow behind the silhouetted image.

7. Convert the shadow to a path.

8. Convert the path to a soft-edged stencil.

To create a drop shadow using the Path tools, follow these steps:

1. Repeat steps 1 to 5 in the exercise "To create a drop shadow," described in "Drop shadows 101: an introduction" earlier in this chapter.

2. Copy the mask in the "Silhouetting Sara" layer to the stencil of the "Shadow" layer (see figure 19.14). Because there is just a stencil, but no mask, no visible change occurs in the composite.

3. Zoom into the image, so your screen approximates figure 19.15.

4. In the creative toolbar, click on the Marquee and choose the Gradient/Vertical option.

5. Drag open the gradient box and enter 40% and 55% in the opacity fields. Then click inside the gradient box to preview and outside the gradient box to create the gradient (see figure 19.15).

6. Select the layer named "Shadow" and toggle to the positioning toolbar.

Figure 19.14   Copying the mask to the stencil

Figure 19.15   Creating a transparent shadow

TIP

The higher the toler-ance, the faster the mask is computed, but the lower the precision. If you are going to use the Path to create a soft edge, you can use a high tolerance, because high precision isn't required.

7. Using the Skew tool, skew the shadow as shown in figure 19.16. For more infor-mation, see steps 15 to 18 in the exercise "To create a drop shadow," described in "Drop shadows 101: An Introduction" earlier in this chapter.

8. In the layer stack, drag the layer named "Shadow" beneath the layer named "Sil-houetting Sara" (see figure 19.17).

    The edge of the shadow is relatively hard because it was created from the silhouet-ted mask, which is also relatively hard-edged. We are now going to soften the edge of the shadow. First we'll convert the Monocolor stencil to a path, and then we'll con-vert the path back to a stencil. This procedure enables us to feather the stencil edge.

9. In the layer stack, select the layer named "Shadow."

10. In the Mask menu, choose Stencil –>Path. The Compute Path dialog box appears (see figure 19.18). Enter a tolerance of 5 pixels.

NOTE: We convert the *stencil* to a path, because the silhouetted mask was copied to the stencil. The stencil determines the outline of the shadow, whereas the *mask* determines its opacity.

---

11. Click on OK. The Compute Path progress bar appears. When the path is comput-ed, it appears in your document (see figure 19.19).

    Now we'll convert the computed path back to a stencil.

12. In the Mask menu, choose Path –>Stencil. The Convert Path dialog box appears (see figure 19.20).

13. Enter a value of 80 pixels. This relatively high value will create a feather of 40 pix-els (80/2) on either side of the path. The higher the value, the wider the feather.

14. Click on OK. The new shadow has a softer edge than the original (see figure 19.21).

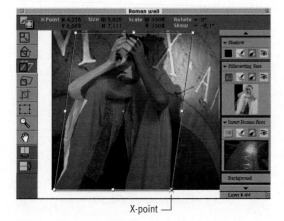

X-point ⌐

Figure 19.16   Skewed shadow

Figure 19.17   Reordering the layers

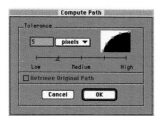

Figure 19.18   Compute Path dialog box

Figure 19.19   Path computed from stencil

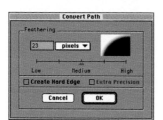

Figure 19.20   Convert Path dialog box

Figure 19.21   New softer-edged shadow

15. To modify edge softness again, choose Stencil –>Path in the Mask menu, and click on Retrieve Original Path in the Compute Path dialog box. Then choose Path –>Stencil in the Mask menu, enter a different tolerance, and click on OK. This procedure enables you to modify edge softness at any time.

Using different positioning tools

In the previous exercises in this chapter, the Skew tool was used to reposition the shadow. You can use any positioning tool to reposition a shadow. The appropriate tool will depend on the image and the shadow.

Use the Perspective tool to create more complex kinds of perspective. For example, use it if the base of the silhouetted object rests on a surface. Examples are a person standing, a perfume bottle, a box, and other such objects.

Drag this handle upward

Option
-drag
from
here...

... to here

Figure 19.22 Defining stationary points

Figure 19.23 Creating vertical perspective

To reposition a drop shadow using the Perspective tool:

1. Click on the Perspective tool.

2. Option-drag the bottom left handle to the left base of the silhouetted image (see figure 19.22). Then Option-drag the bottom right handle to the right base of the image.

   If the image is a person standing, Option-drag the handles to the feet. If the image is a bottle, Option-drag the handles to the two lower extremes of the bottle. The idea is to define two points of the shadow that will not move when you apply perspective to the shadow.

3. Drag the top middle handle upward (see figure 19.23). A perspective effect is created for the shadow. The bottom of the shadow does not move.

   Always define the stationary points on the side opposite the perspective. For example, to create horizontal perspective, Option-drag the handles to the side opposite the perspective (see figure 19.24). Those handles will remain stationary (see figure 19.25).

Option-
drag
handles
to here
and
here

Drag this handle

Figure 19.24 Setting the stationary points for horizontal perspective

Figure 19.25 Creating horizontal perspective

Figure 19.26   Dragging the top right handle   **Figure 19.27**   Dragging the top left handle

4. To create "free" perspective, set the stationary points at the base of the image (Option-drag). Next drag one top corner handle, and then the other (see figures 19.26 and 19.27).

This type of repositioning is useful for laying the shadow of a standing object flat on the ground.

Using a Color Correction layer

You can use a layer type other than Monocolor to create a drop shadow. Figure 19.28 shows the dialog box of a Color Correction layer used to create a shadow.

- The Before color bars are deselected, because no selectivity is required. The color correction used to create the shadow will only be applied within the stencil.

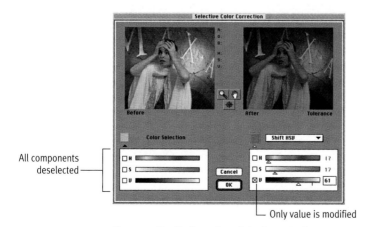

All components deselected

Only value is modified

Figure 19.28   Shadow using a Color Correction layer

- The Before color is taken from the shawl. The After color is based on the Before color.

- On the After color sliders, only V is selected. By decreasing the value (or luminance), the image is darkened in the preview, creating a shadow. Again, in the actual composite, the stencil will constrain the darkening to the shape of the shadow.

For more information, see Chapter 14, "Making Selective Color Corrections."

You can also use Colorize or Multicolor layers to create shadows. And you can combine layers. For instance, to create a shadow with a bluish cast, you can darken using a Color Correction layer and add blue using a Colorize layer.

Creating shadows for type

Creating a shadow for type follows the same basic procedure as other objects.

1. Create type using the Type tool. In figure 19.29, type was created using a Multicolor layer. For more information, see Chapter 16, "Creating Type."

2. In the Create menu, choose Monocolor. Using the color selector, choose black.

3. In the creative toolbar, click on the Marquee and choose Fill.

4. Drag the Marquee at 100% opacity around the type to fill the area with black (see figure 19.30).

5. Copy (Option-drag) the stencil from the Multicolor layer to the stencil in the Monocolor layer (see figure 19.31).

6. Select the Monocolor layer and toggle to the positioning tools.

TIP

Group the text and the shadow to facilitate any future repositioning or hiding of layers.

Figure 19.29   Type in a Multicolor layer

Figure 19.30   Creating a black fill over type

Figure 19.31 Constraining black to the stencil

Figure 19.32 Nudging the shadow

Figure 19.33 Moving the shadow behind the text

7. Use the arrow keys on your keyboard to nudge the shadow three or four pixels to the right (see figure 19.32).

NOTE: To use the nudge keys, all fields in the control bar must be deselected. You can deselect all fields by clicking on the Rotate, Skew, or Perspective tool.

8. In the layer bar, drag the Monocolor layer (shadow) under the Multicolor layer (type) (see figure 19.33).

Shadows on more than one plane

A shadow in a single layer lies on a single plane. To create a shadow on more than one plane, create more than one layer. Use the following procedure, for example, to make a shadow run along the ground and up a wall.

To create a shadow on two planes, follow these steps:

1. Create the shadow in a single layer.

2. Position it so that the shadow runs along the ground.

3. Make a copy of the layer (Option-drag).

4. Reposition the second layer so that the top half of the shadow runs up the wall.

5. In the first layer, erase any parts of the shadow on the wall.

6. In the second layer, erase any parts of the shadow on the ground.

CHAPTER 20

ONE IMAGE, TWO LAYERS

An image opened in a composite is inserted in one layer. However, it is sometimes useful to insert a single image in two layers. This chapter describes when you should insert an image in two layers, and how to do it.

REASONS FOR INSERTING AN IMAGE IN TWO LAYERS

There are several reasons for inserting one image in two layers. The most common ones are listed here:

- To break down an image into background and foreground. This enables you to insert an object (a third layer) between the elements in an image. An example is described in "Breaking down an image into background and foreground" in this chapter.

- To reposition part of an image. If an image is inserted in a single layer, you must reposition the entire image. The procedure is illustrated in "Repositioning part of an image" in this chapter.

- To color correct part of an image, especially when using IVUE correction. Because the example also makes use of a selective mask, see "Using selective masks" in Chapter 22, "Selective Masks Revealed."

NOTE: Some effects require that you break a non-image layer into two layers. See "Shadows on more than one plane" in Chapter 19, "Creating Drop Shadows."

BREAKING DOWN AN IMAGE INTO BACKGROUND AND FOREGROUND

The purpose of this exercise is to insert an island in between the trees and the sky of the image shown in figure 20.1.

There are several ways you could do this. The most direct is to insert the island on top of the trees and erase the island where the tree trunks stand. The tree trunks appear, creating the impression that the island is behind the trees. The problem with this approach is lack of precision. You have to zoom and erase the island carefully. While feasible, this is time-consuming.

A similar approach is to create an Image Clone layer of figure 20.1, and use the Restore option to reveal the trees in front of the island. This can be as time-consuming as the first approach.

You could use the Path tools to create a stencil containing just the portions of the island you want to show. The trees would appear between the stencil. This method is more effective, and could be used here, where the lines of the tree trunks are clear-cut. However, if the objects were complex, this approach would be less effective and more time-consuming.

This exercise shows another approach. The island is broken down into two layers. One layer contains the background, and the other the foreground. Images can then easily be inserted between the two layers.

To break down an image into background and foreground, follow these steps:

1. In the Create menu, choose Image Insertion.

2. Select the image called "Coconut Trees," located on the CD in the IVUE folder.

3. Check that Auto Insert is deselected, and click on Open. The image fills your document window.

4. In the control bar, scale the image to 100% (see figure 20.1). You may need to zoom out first, or the image will scale outside the document window.

5. Click the mode toggle to switch to Creative mode.

6. In the layer stack, select the layer. Then press Command-I. The Get Info dialog box appears (see figure 20.2).

Figure 20.1 Scaling to 100%

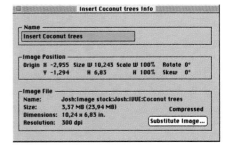

Figure 20.2 Get Info dialog box

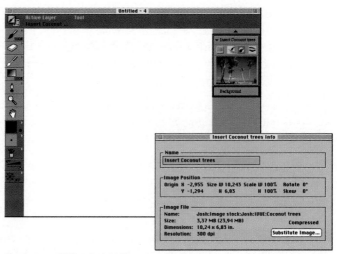

Figure 20.3 Hiding the initial image

7. Drag the Get Info dialog box slightly to the side so that the middle of the document window is uncluttered. Then click on the Eye icon in the layer stack to hide the image (see figure 20.3).

We are now going to reinsert the same image in an Image Silhouette layer. To insert the image exactly on top of the image already inserted, we are going to use the Image Position information contained in the Get Info dialog box.

By hiding the initial image, it won't interfere when we check the silhouette preview.

8. In the Create menu, choose Image Silhouette. Select and open the image "Coconut Trees" on the CD again. Do not use the Auto Insert option.

9. Drag the X-point from the center of the image to the upper left handle of the Positioning Box (see figure 20.4).

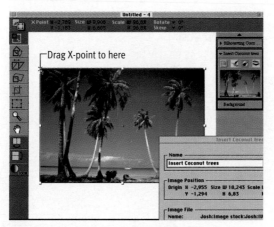

Figure 20.4 Using the X-point to define the origin

The Origin coordinates in the Get Info dialog box refer to the top left corner of the IVUE image. By dragging the X-point to the top left handle, you can position the image at the same Origin coordinates as the initial image.

NOTE: The Origin coordinates in the Get Info box always refer to the original IVUE. They do not take repositioning into account. For example, if the IVUE image was rotated 90°, the top left corner of the original IVUE becomes the top right corner in the composite. The Origin coordinates then refer to top right corner of the image. In this case, drag the X-point to the top right corner of the image you are inserting. Origin coordinates do not take cropping into account either. They refer to origin of the uncropped image.

10. In the control bar, enter the Origin and Size (W and H) indicated in the Get Info dialog box (see figure 20.5). Then click on OK. The newly inserted image moves to the same position and scale as the initial image.

    If an image is rotated or skewed, enter the Rotate and Skew values in the control bar.

NOTE: The values in your Get Info dialog box may be different from those indicated in figure 20.2. Use the values in *your* Get Info dialog box.

11. Toggle to the creative tools and create the Inside and Outside selections (see figure 20.6). The Inside selection is the trees, the Outside selection is the sky.

12. Click on the Compute Mask icon in the control bar.

13. In the Compute Mask Options dialog box, choose Medium from the Edge Precision pop-down menu. Leave all other default values and click on Preview. Your image should approximate figure 20.7.

TIP

In this image, it is easier to begin with the Outside selection.

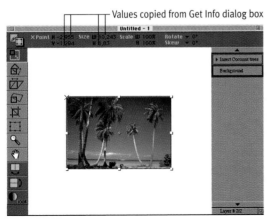

Figure 20.5   Copying Origin and Size from Get Info dialog box to control bar

Figure 20.6   Creating the Inside and Outside selections

Figure 20.7 Silhouetting preview

Figure 20.8 Improving the mask using Retouch

For more information on silhouetting images, see Chapter 9, "The Great Silhouetting Lab."

14. Click on Retouch, click on the Brush and use the Retouch option to make transparent areas more opaque. If you have a large screen, you will be able to do a fair amount of retouching. Figure 20.8 shows a slight improvement in the mask after retouching.

15. Click on Compute. The mask is computed.

16. In the layer stack, click on the Eye icon to show the bottom layer (see figure 20.9).

The composite now contains two image layers. The bottom layer (Insert Coconut trees) contains the entire image, and the top layer (Silhouetting Coco...) contains just the foreground and trees. We are now going to insert a new image between the foreground and the background.

Visually, the composite appears to have just one layer, because the top layer is lined up exactly with the bottom layer.

Figure 20.9 One image in two layers

Figure 20.10 Activating the bottom layer

17. In the layer stack, activate the bottom layer by double-clicking (see figure 20.10). When you create a new layer, it is inserted above the active layer. This enables us to insert a new layer between the two existing layers.

18. In the Create menu, choose Image Insertion.

19. Select the image "Turquoise Pool," located on the CD in the IVUE folder. Check that Auto Insert is deselected, and click on Open. The image fills the screen. In the layer stack, the layer appears above the active layer (see figure 20.11).

20. In the toolbar, click on the Crop tool.

21. Crop the image by dragging the middle handles of the positioning bar. Crop all areas except the island (see figure 20.12).

22. Click on the Scale tool. Position the cursor inside the Positioning Box and drag the image so that the bottom of the island lines up with the horizon in the background image (see figure 20.13).

Figure 20.11 Inserting "Turquoise Pool"

Figure 20.12 Cropping the sky and water

Figure 20.13 Positioning the island

Figure 20.14 Brushing in the island

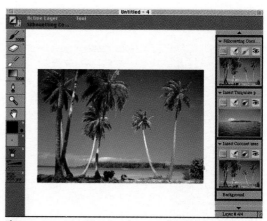

Figure 20.15 Island between foreground and background

TIP

If you know in advance that you want to insert the island, you can avoid inserting "Coconut trees" twice by silhouetting "Coconut trees" first. Then duplicate the layer and use the Marquee tool to reveal the entire image in the bottom layer.

23. In the toolbar, click on the Opacity control and drag the Opacity slider to 0%. The image disappears.

24. Toggle to the creative tools. Select the smallest tool size, and click on the Brush. Reveal just the island (see figure 20.14).

    You can zoom to increase your precision. You can also toggle back to the positioning tools and reposition the island. For instance, you can rotate the island slightly to line it up exactly with the horizon.

25. In the layer stack, activate the top layer. The foreground reappears. The island is behind the trees and in front of the sky (see figure 20.5).

There are several possible variations to this procedure. For example, to increase precision, you could silhouette the island instead of brushing it in.

The important point is that you broke down a layer into background and foreground. This breakdown facilitates other operations. For instance, by inserting a Sharpen/Blur layer directly under the layer named "Silhouetting Coco...," you can easily blur the background without affecting the foreground. Likewise, you can use the silhouetted mask of the trees to constrain the effects of Color Correction layers to the foreground.

REPOSITIONING PART OF AN IMAGE

For "Raychem Cable" (see figure 20.16), John Lund needed to re-create the magnifying effect that water has on objects. As long as the image was in a single layer, he had no way of enlarging part of the cable. To solve the problem, he broke the image down into two layers.

In the exercise "Breaking down an image into background and foreground," the image was reinserted because the new layer and the original layer were of different types (Image Insertion and Image Silhouette). In this image, both layers are Image Distortion layers, so duplicating the layer was sufficient. This avoids having to position the new layer.

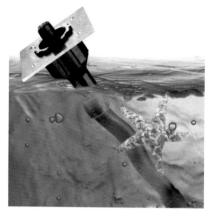

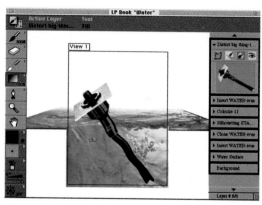

Figure 20.16   "Raychem Cable," with enlarged
underwater cable

Figure 20.17   Cable inserted and distorted

The image of the cable was inserted after the rest of the composite was created. It was inserted in an Image Distortion layer with its alpha channel, created in Photoshop. John distorted the image using the Freehand option (see figure 20.17).

The section of cable beneath the water line was erased. John then duplicated the image. At this point, there are two layers, each with the same section of cable showing above the water. However, the different names of the cable layers ("ABOVE WATER" and "UNDER WATER") indicate that each one will be used for a different section of cable (see figure 20.18).

The layer named "UNDER WATER" is activated. This is where the layers begin to differentiate. John erased the section of cable above the water, and inserted the section below the water at an opacity of 80% (see figure 20.19). Each layer now contains a different section of cable.

The slight transparency (80%) allows the water behind the cable to be just barely visible in front, giving the impression that the cable is surrounded by water.

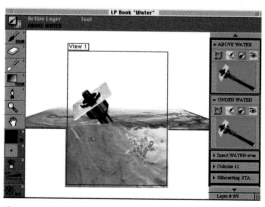

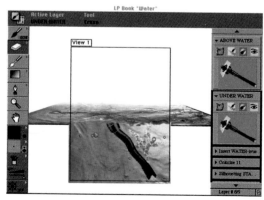

Figure 20.18   Duplicating the cable layer

Figure 20.19   Erasing the top and inserting the bottom of the cable

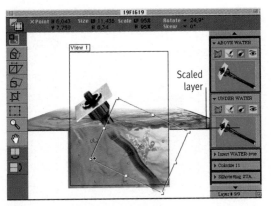

Figure 20.20 Enlarging part of an image

Figure 20.21 Reordering the layers

John activated the top layer to have both visible. He then selected the layer named "UNDER WATER" and enlarged it slightly using the Scale tool (see figure 20.20).

By separating the image in two layers, John was able to enlarge just part of the image.

Finally, John dragged the layer named "UNDER WATER" below the layer with the starfish (see figure 20.21). The starfish now appears on top of the cable.

MIXING TWO SIMILAR IMAGES

The example shown in this section differs from the others in this chapter. Two different images are inserted in two different layers. This is nothing special, but in this case, the images are almost the same.

Jean-Luc Michon began with an IVUE file of a boot (see figure 20.22). Using the Live Picture™ IVUE plug-in supplied with Live Picture, he opened the IVUE file in Photoshop (Acquire command). He then used the motion blur filter to create an impression of movement. After applying the filter, Jean-Luc saved the blurred image as an IVUE (Export command), under a different name, using the same plug-in (see figure 20.23).

Jean-Luc inserted the blurred boot in an Image Insertion layer. He then inserted the original boot exactly on top of it, and set the opacity at 0% using the Opacity control. Then, by brushing in parts of the original boot (the side and the Paraboot trademark), he emphasized certain areas, leaving the rest of the boot in a relative blur (see figure 20.24). The layer containing the original boot is featured alone in figure 20.25. It shows which parts of the original boot were revealed.

Figure 20.22   Original boot

Figure 20.23   Boot blurred in Photoshop

Figure 20.24   Mix of two images

Figure 20.25   Boot brushed in, shown alone

To complete the image "Paraboot," Jean-Luc added a layer of white paint and a Color Correction layer (see figure 20.26). This example is interesting because it shows how transparency lets you selectively use effects created with other software, or with filter plug-ins.

NOTE: Total Integration, Inc. has developed FASTedit™/IVUE, a third-party Adobe Photoshop plug-in that enables you to select part of an IVUE file in Photoshop, open it, edit it, and save it back to IVUE. This plug-in can save a lot of time when opening large files in Photoshop.

Figure 20.26   "Paraboot" completed

CHAPTER 21

SIMULATING MOVEMENT

This chapter describes various methods and tricks for simulating movement in composites. In the following sections, movement is simulated using paint tools, the Smudge option, and transparency. The effects are illustrated using both actual jobs and images created for this chapter.

USING PAINT

In "IBM Anti-Virus Package" (see figure 21.1), David Bishop wanted his red and gray computer-generated bugs to zoom around.

David first created a Multicolor layer. For the bug in figure 21.2, David used the Direction tool to define the direction of the speed trail (Control-drag) (see figure 21.3).

He then took a small brush and painted gradually fading lines (see figure 21.4). The lines are constrained to the direction set. Each color was taken from the bug using the eyedropper. For the middle of the bug, David switched to a larger brush.

David used the same method for the blue bug in figure 21.5, but he created two Multicolor layers. Each layer contains a different part of the trail. In figure 21.6, the first Multicolor layer was positioned beneath the bug, to avoid coloring the bug itself. In figure

Figure 21.1 Hovering bugs

Figure 21.2 Hovering red bug

Figure 21.3 Setting the direction of the trail

21.7, the second Multicolor layer was inserted above the bug, and contains the blues and grays of the bug.

Another advantage to creating the trail in two layers is that David can add to one layer without the risk of modifying what he's already done. Figure 21.8 shows both completed bugs.

Alternatives to using the Brush: For two colors use a Multicolor gradient, for one color use a Monocolor gradient. Reduce the opacity as the colors trail off. Then set the Direction control and erase the excess paint. Erasing with the Pastel style selected works quite nicely—the streaks are softer.

Figure 21.4　Bug on the move　　　　　　　　　　　**Figure 21.5**　Hovering blue bug

Figure 21.6　Multicolor layer beneath bug　　　　**Figure 21.7**　Multicolor layer above bug

Figure 21.8　Completed speed effect

✓Smudge
Blend
Push
Diffuse

Figure 21.9   Smudge option

THE SMUDGE OPTION

The Smudge option is located in Sharpen/Blur layers, in the Palette Knife pull-out menu (see figure 21.9). This option smudges all colors in all underlying layers. In this section, we'll use the Smudge option on the gray bug.

A Sharpen/Blur layer is created above the bug. Then the Smudge option is selected. The size of the tool should be slightly larger than the object to be smudged (see figure 21.10). Also, the smudge should begin toward the front of the object so that all colors are smudged.

Figure 21.11 shows the object after smudging. Notice the white on the edge of the trail. It occurs because all colors are smudged, including the white background.

To diminish the smudge, click the Brush and select the Blur option. Set brush opacity at roughly 30% (see figure 21.12).

Run the blur brush gently over the areas where you want to reduce the smudge. Especially, run it over the object itself (see figure 21.13). By using the Blur tool instead of the Eraser, you diminish the smudge without making the object look stationary.

Another type of trail can be obtained by moving the Sharpen/Blur layer beneath the object after it has been smudged. The object is unaffected by the smudge, but the trail has the colors of the object (see figure 21.14).

Figure 21.10   Preparing the smudge

Figure 21.11   Smudging the bug

Figure 21.12
Selecting a 30% blur

Figure 21.13   Diminishing the smudge

Figure 21.14   Moving the Sharpen/Blur layer behind the bug

NOTE: If you change an underlying image after creating the Sharpen/Blur layer, the smudge will contain the colors of the original image.

USING TRANSPARENCY

Transparency in images can be used to simulate different types of motion. Two cases are dealt with in this section: transparency and repositioning, and transparency and distortion.

Transparency and repositioning

To create motion using transparency, follow these three basic steps:

1. Duplicate the image.

2. Reposition the duplicate.

3. Erase parts of the duplicate or lower its opacity.

To make the watch look as if it's ticking, Jean-Luc Michon began by duplicating the image shown in figure 21.15. The duplicate was slightly rotated in relation to the original. Next the entire duplicate image was erased. Then just the second and minute hands were brushed in (see figure 21.16).

In the following exercise, you'll simulate a spinning motion for the earth.

To simulate a spinning motion, follow these steps:

1. In the File menu, choose Open FITS. Open the FITS file called "Earth Silhouetted" located in the Copy me to Hard Drive folder.

2. Open the layer panel and copy the mask to the stencil (Option-drag) (see figure 21.17). This will allow you to modify mask opacity without losing the shape of the earth.

Figure 21.15   Motionless watch   **Figure 21.16**   Ticking watch

Figure 21.17   Copying the mask to the stencil

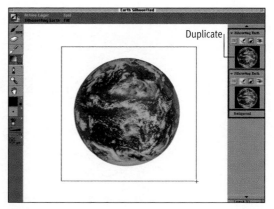

Figure 21.18   Duplicated earth at 50% opacity

3. Duplicate the layer (Option-drag).

4. In the creative toolbar, select the Marquee and choose the Fill option.

5. Set the opacity at 50% and drag the Marquee around the earth (see figure 21.18). For the moment, no change is visible, because the duplicated layer is positioned directly above the original.

    We are now going to reposition the top earth layer.

6. Select the top layer and toggle to the positioning tools.

7. Drag the X-point to the edge of the earth, as shown in figure 21.19. Then enter 1 in the Rotate field in the control bar.

8. Press Return. The earth rotates 1 degree. The top layer is semi-transparent, so the bottom layer is partially visible underneath. Because the two layers are offset in relation to each other, this creates a motion blur (see figure 21.20).

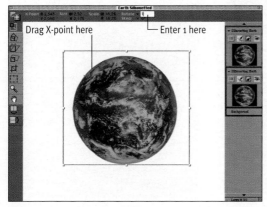

Figure 21.19   Defining the axis of rotation

Figure 21.20   Creating a motion blur

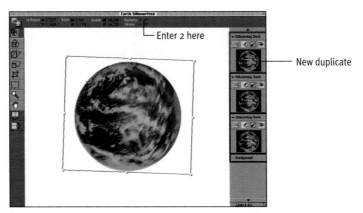

Enter 2 here

New duplicate

Figure 21.21   Accelerating the spin

9. Duplicate the top layer and repeat steps 7 and 8, but this time use 2 as the rotation value. The blur is increased (see figure 21.21).

Each time you duplicate a new layer, you increase the blur, giving the impression that the spin is accelerating.

Transparency and distortion

This method follows the same principle as using transparency and repositioning, except that distortion is used instead of repositioning.

The image shown in figure 21.22 is inserted in an Image Distortion layer.

The layer is duplicated, and the opacity is reduced to 50% using the Marquee with the Fill option. Using the Brush with the Freehand option, the top image is distorted. The non-distorted image remains partially visible underneath. Figures 21.23, 21.24, and 21.25 show three levels of distortion.

CREATING DIFFERENTIAL SHARPNESS

In some types of images, you can use a Sharpen/Blur gradient to give an impression of movement. Figures 17.42 and 17.43 in Chapter 17, "Creating Gradients," illustrate this point.

Figure 21.22 Paris

Figure 21.23 "Tremors"

Figure 21.24 "Windy day"

Figure 21.25 "One glass too many"

CHAPTER 22

SELECTIVE MASKS REVEALED

This chapter explains what is meant by the term selective mask as well as how to create them, and when to use them. It begins with the description of an image which uses a selective mask. This is followed by an exercise showing you how to create selective masks.

LIVE PICTURE, OR "WORKING WITHOUT SELECTIONS"

For most operations in Live Picture, you do not need to create selections. The soft-edged, pressure-sensitive brushes allow you to do high quality work by brushing. By zooming, the brushes can be made as small as you need for precise work on detail. And the unlimited undo using the Eraser allows you to correct any mistakes.

So the basic philosophy behind Live Picture is to brush directly onto your image. This makes the software friendly and easy to use.

However, using selective masks can allow for more precisely detailed work on intricate objects. They can also save you time.

USING SELECTIVE MASKS

A selective mask is a mask created in an Image Silhouette layer, which is designed to constrain modifications to part of an image.

The key term here is *modifications*. In most cases, you create an Image Silhouette layer to isolate part of an image from its background. A selective mask has a different purpose. It allows you to *modify* part of an image using a mask. In that sense, it resembles the *selection* used in Photoshop and other pixel-based applications.

The use of selective masks is illustrated in "Sacred Datura, Escalante, Utah 1976" by American photographer Joseph Holmes. The starting point of this retouching job was an image shot and scanned at 250 MB.

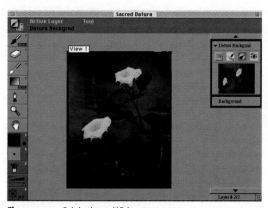

Figure 22.1   Original 250 MB image

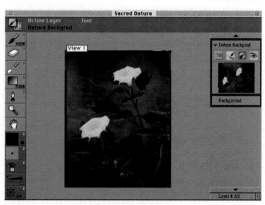

Figure 22.2   Image after IVUE correction

In figure 22.1, Joseph inserted the image in an Image Insertion layer. He then used IVUE Correction to color-correct the entire image. With this color correction, he increased the contrast of the leaves and brought out the green in them. However, because IVUE correction is global, it affected the flowers negatively—they lost their contrast and became greenish (see figure 22.2).

To solve this problem, Joseph reinserted the original image in an Image Silhouette layer, which he named "Flowers Silhouette." He positioned this layer exactly on top of the bottom layer, which he named "Datura Backgrnd," and silhouetted just the flowers. Figure 22.3 shows the silhouetted flowers alone. The "Datura Backgrnd" layer is hidden. In figure 22.4, both layers are visible.

Joseph then used IVUE correction to color-correct the "Flower Silhouette" layer (see figure 22.5). The selective mask allowed him to work on the contrast and color balance of the flowers without affecting the rest of the composite. Notice the thumbnail image in the layer panel—the IVUE correction is "forced" to the point where the background becomes black. But the black does not appear in the composite, since the flowers are silhouetted.

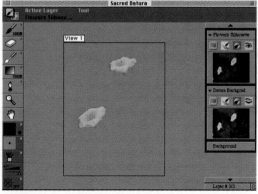

Figure 22.3   Silhouetted flowers alone

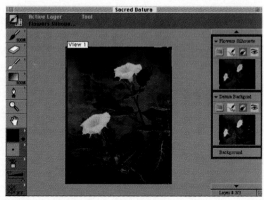

Figure 22.4   Silhouetted flowers and original image

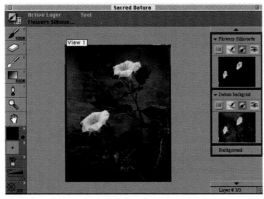

Figure 22.5   Silhouetted flowers after IVUE correction

Figure 22.6   Final image

Several finer color corrections were made to complete the image, shown in figure 22.6.

Instead of silhouetting, Joseph could have duplicated the layer, used IVUE correction, and erased all parts except the flowers. However, by silhouetting the flowers, he obtained a more precise mask than he could have with the Brush and Eraser. In addition, he saved time, since the strong contrast between the flowers and their background made silhouetting quick and easy.

CREATING SELECTIVE MASKS

In this section, a step-by-step exercise demonstrates how to create a selective mask for a watch. The mask will be used to make the watch glow in the dark.

This exercise takes the use of selective masks a step further than "Using selective masks" earlier in this chapter. In the example in that section, the selective mask was used in the Image Silhouette layer it was created in. In this exercise, the selective mask is copied from an Image Silhouette layer and used in other layer types. Namely, it allows us to selectively colorize and sharpen small details. This would be painstaking and time-consuming with a brush. With a selective mask, it's quick and simple.

To create a selective mask, follow these steps:

1. Open your document window to maximum screen size. This will make it easier to do detailed silhouetting.

2. In the Create menu, choose Image Insertion, and select the image named "Watch" located on the CD, in the IVUE folder.

3. Select Auto Insert, and click on Open. The image fills your document window.

4. Click on the color selector and drag out the color bar to select a bright red.

TIP

Deselecting the Cursor icon makes it easier to select precise points during silhouetting.

5. In the Edit menu, choose Set Background. The background changes to red (see figure 22.7).

6. Click on the Visibility icon to hide the layer.

7. In the Edit menu, choose Preferences/General. In the dialog box, deselect the Cursor icon and click on OK.

8. In the Create menu, choose Image Silhouette, and select the image "Watch" again. This silhouetting job is fairly intricate. It helps to have some experience with the silhouetting tools.

9. Deselect Auto Insert and click on Open. The image is inserted exactly on top of the first layer, which is currently hidden.

NOTE: If you zoomed or panned after creating the bottom layer, use the Get Info dialog box to obtain identical positioning for both images. For more information, see Chapter 20, "One Image, Two Layers."

10. Zoom into the image so that the clock face fills your work space (see figure 22.8). This gives you the largest screen display for silhouetting.

11. Toggle to the creative tools.

12. In the creative toolbar, click on the Brush. We'll use the Auto option to create the Inside selection (Auto and Inside are selected by default when you toggle to the creative tools).

13. Drag the Brush along the button of the second hand, as shown in figure 22.9.

    The Inside selection should resemble figure 12.10.

14. Click once on the bottom right-hand part of the 0 in "150," as shown in figure 22.11.

Figure 22.7 Setting the background color

Figure 22.8 Zooming before silhouetting

Drag here

Figure 22.9   Selecting colors using Auto

Figure 22.10   Inside selection

— Click here

Figure 22.11   Clicking using Auto

Figure 22.12   Selection expanded

The selection should now resemble figure 22.12. If other parts of the clock face are selected, press Command-Z to undo the click, and try again until the selection is satisfactory. If the red selection is too restrained, click again to expand it.

NOTE: At this point, you can use the smallest brush and the Selective option to select areas not selected with the Auto option.

15. Click on the Eraser and select the Selective option.

16. Click in the light gray area of each 5-minute increment and drag to erase the selection in the gray. Figure 22.13 shows the cursor being clicked in the light gray area of the increment representing the "4" (20 past the hour).

Clean up these gray areas

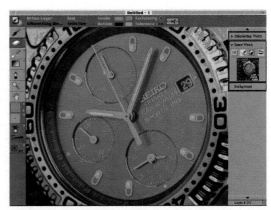

Figure 22.13   Erasing bits of red selection

Figure 22.14   Red selection cleaned up using the Eraser

Figure 22.14 shows the gray areas after being cleaned up.

17. Using the Remove options with either the Marquee, the Eraser, or both, erase parts of the Inside selection so that your image looks like figure 22.15.

18. In the control bar, click on the Outside control.

19. Click on the Marquee and choose the Fill option. Then draw a rectangle over the entire image. This creates the Outside selection (see figure 22.16).

20. In the control bar, click on the Compute Mask icon. The Compute Mask Options dialog box appears.

21. In the dialog box, choose Standard computing mode, High Edge precision, and click on Hard Edge (see figure 22.17).

22. Click on Preview. Your image should resemble figure 22.17.

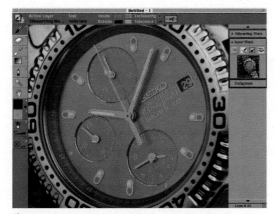

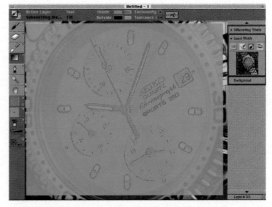

Figure 22.15   Erasing unwanted selection manually

Figure 22.16   Creating the Outside selection

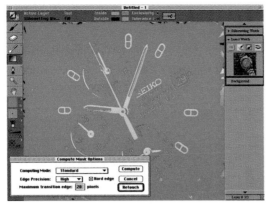

Figure 22.17 Checking the preview

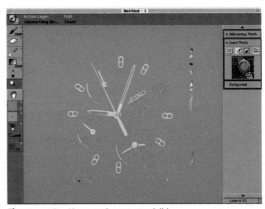

Figure 22.18 Unwanted areas are visible

NOTE: If you had not hidden the bottom layer before silhouetting (step 6), you would not be able to judge the preview, since the same image would appear directly beneath it. The red background created in step 5, chosen to contrast with the colors of the watch hands, also makes it easier to check the preview.

23. Click on Compute. The mask is calculated.

24. Zoom out so that your screen approximates figure 22.18. Bits of unwanted areas remain.

25. Click on the Marquee or Eraser, and choose the Remove option. Then remove the unwanted areas along the edge, taking care to not erase the parts you want to keep (see figure 22.19). When you are finished, your image should resemble figure 22.20.

For the purpose of this exercise, we shall leave the mask in its present state. However, you can zoom in and perfect the mask using the Insert and Outline options. For more information, see Chapter 9, "The Great Silhouetting Lab."

Hide this layer | Show this layer

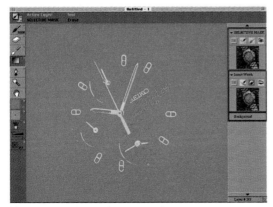

Figure 22.19 Unwanted areas erased

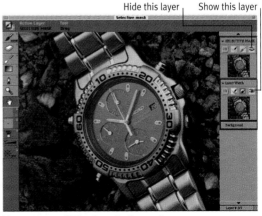

Figure 22.20 Hiding the selective mask

TIP

Remember, you can always erase parts of the mask used to fill the stencil.

26. Select the top layer and press Command-I. In the Get Info dialog box, name the layer "SELECTIVE MASK."

27. Click on the Eye icon to hide the "SELECTIVE MASK" layer and show the "Insert Watch" layer (see figure 22.20). The "SELECTIVE MASK" layer was created solely to make a mask and use it in other layers. The layer itself should be hidden.

We are now going to use the selective mask in other layers.

28. In the Create menu, choose Colorize.

29. Click once on the color selector. In the Live Picture color picker, create a greenish-blue. You can use the following RGB values: R=4, G=207, B=154.

30. In the layer stack, copy the mask from the "SELECTIVE MASK" layer to the stencil of the Colorize layer.

31. Click on the Marquee and choose the Fill option. Then drag a rectangle around the entire image. The stencil constrains the colorization to the parts of the watch that were silhouetted (see figure 22.21).

32. In the Create menu, choose Sharpen/Blur.

33. Copy the mask from the "SELECTIVE MASK" layer to the stencil of the Sharpen/Blur layer.

34. Click on the Marquee and choose the Sharpen Fill option. Drag a rectangle around the entire image. The area defined by the stencil is sharpened (see figure 22.22).

In this exercise, you used a selective mask to selectively colorize and sharpen an image. You can use a selective mask in any layer type as a means of being selective. Even Color Correction layers, which have their own system for defining selectivity, are not as precise as the silhouetting tools when it comes to being selective. So for color corrections requiring a high degree of precision, you can create a selective mask and use it in a Color Correction layer.

Figure 22.21 Using the selective mask in a Colorize layer

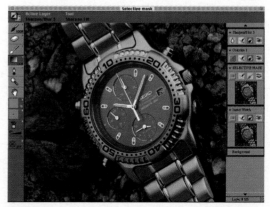

Figure 22.22 Using the selective mask in a Sharpen/Blur layer

CHAPTER 23

Luminance Masks and Texture Revealed

Luminance masks are probably one of the lesser known tools of Live Picture. This chapter explains what luminance masks are, and how you can use them. Several composites are used to illustrate this chapter, and an exercise at the end shows how to re-create texture using luminance masks.

ABOUT LUMINANCE MASKS

A luminance mask is based on the luminance values in an image. In other words, the opacity at each point in the mask is determined by the luminance of the image at that point. This allows you to emphasize the highlights or shadow in an image in interesting ways.

For example, to emphasize the darker areas in an image, create a luminance mask where the shadows have a high opacity and the highlights have a low opacity. The dark areas will become opaque, and the light areas will become more or less transparent. You control the opacity of the mask by means of a histogram.

Figure 23.1 shows "Roman Floor" with a 100% opacity mask. Figures 23.2 and 23.3 show the image after applying two different types of luminance masks. In figure 23.2, the mask is more opaque on light values and more transparent on darker values. In figure 23.3, the opposite is true.

Figure 23.4 shows the luminance mask setting used to obtain figure 23.2. The histogram represents the luminance values of the image. The white cursor represents the luminance value masked at 100% opacity. It is called the Opacity cursor because it represents full opacity. The Opacity box indicates that luminance value.

The black cursor represents the luminance value masked at 0% opacity. It is called the Transparency cursor because it represents transparency. The Transparency box indicates the luminance value which will be transparent. Opacity decreases gradually from the value in the Opacity box to the value in the Transparency box.

Figure 23.1 100% opacity mask

Figure 23.2 Lightest values are opaque

Figure 23.3 Darkest values are opaque

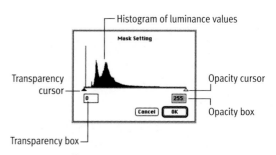

Figure 23.4 Mask setting for figure 23.2

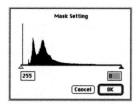

Figure 23.5 Mask setting for figure 23.3

(The use of white to represent opacity and black to represent transparency is indeed a bit confusing.)

In this example, 255 (the lightest possible value) is opaque, and 0 (the darkest possible value) is transparent. If you look at figure 23.2, this is the case. The lightest gold areas on the letters are opaque, and the darkest areas are transparent. The white background shows through the darkest values of the image.

Figure 23.5 shows the luminance mask setting used to create figure 23.3. Compared to figure 23.4, the opacity settings are switched. The Opacity cursor is set at 0, and the Transparency cursor is set at 255. So the darkest value is opaque, and the lightest value is transparent. In figure 23.3, the lightest gold areas are transparent: you can see the white background showing through.

You can position the cursors anywhere on the histogram. In figure 23.6, the Opacity cursor is set at 190. This means that all values from 255 to 190 will be opaque. In fact, the histogram shows that 190 is the lightest value contained in the image. The transparency cursor is moved slightly beyond the darkest value in the image, to 24. This means that all values from 0 to 24 will be transparent. Because the opacity will fall from 100% to 0% over a smaller interval than in figure 23.4, the mask will have greater contrast. The resulting luminance mask is shown in figure 23.7. Compare with figure 23.2.

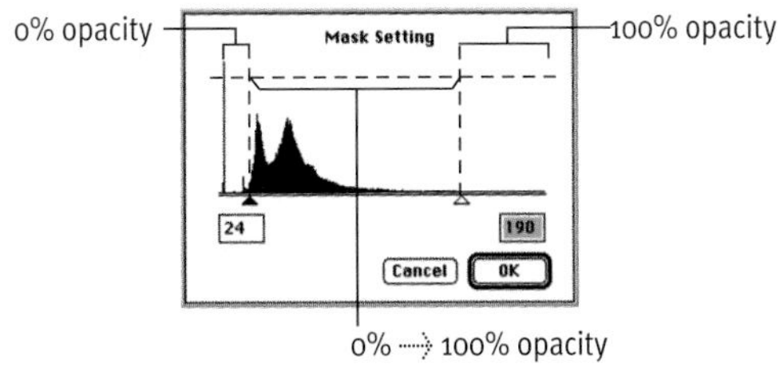

0% opacity

100% opacity

Mask Setting

24

190

Cancel   OK

0% ⋯⋯⋗ 100% opacity

Figure 23.6 Mask setting for figure 23.7

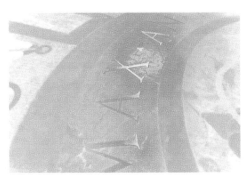

Figure 23.7   Increasing contrast in a luminance mask

For the mask setting shown in figure 23.8, opacity will fall from 100% to 0% over an even smaller range of luminance values (39 to 72). It results in an opacity mask with high contrast. The mask is shown in figure 23.9.

Remember that often in these figures, what appears to be white is not white, but transparent. That's because all the images up to now were set on a white background. Figure 23.10 shows what happens if you change the background in figure 23.9 from white to yellow.

The following section describes the procedure for creating luminance masks.

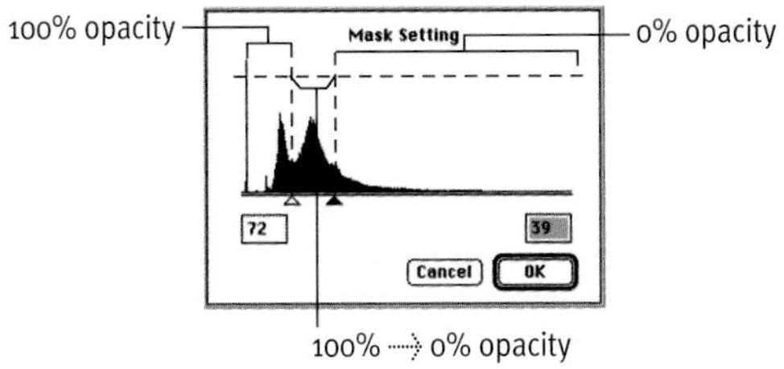

100% opacity

0% opacity

Mask Setting

72

39

Cancel   OK

100% ⋯⋯⋗ 0% opacity

Figure 23.8   Mask setting for figure 23.9

Figure 23.9   Luminance mask with high contrast

Figure 23.10   Figure 23.9 with yellow background

CREATING LUMINANCE MASKS

Luminance masks are created in Image Silhouette layers. In the previous section, the luminance masks were created for the entire image. However, you can create luminance masks for part of an image. In this case, create an Inside Selection and an Outside selection, as you would to silhouette any image. The luminance mask will be applied only to the Inside selection.

To create a luminance mask, follow these steps:

1. Create an Image Silhouette layer and insert an image.

2. Create an Inside and Outside selection (see figure 23.11), and click on the Compute Mask button. The luminance mask will be created for the Inside selection.

   If you click directly on the Compute Mask button without creating Inside and Outside selections, Live Picture considers that the entire image is the Inside selection. In this case, a luminance mask is created for the entire image.

3. Click on the Compute Mask button. The Compute Mask Options dialog box appears.

4. In the Computing Mode pop-down menu, choose Luminance (see figure 23.12).

5. Click on Preview. The Mask Settings dialog box appears.

   The histogram represents the distribution of luminance values in the Inside selection. If you did not create a selection, it represents the luminance values for the entire image.

6. Set the cursors as desired. Then click on OK. The luminance mask is previewed.

7. To modify the luminance mask, click on Luminance in the Computing Mode pop-down menu. Then click on Preview, move the cursors and click on OK again. Preview and modify the luminance mask as many times as needed.

8. To create the luminance mask, click on Compute.

NOTE: Images built with luminance masks have a slightly soft, blurred quality in the output file.

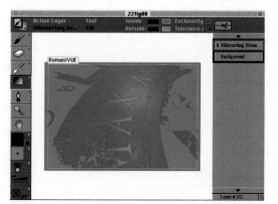

Figure 23.11 Luminance mask created for the Inside selection

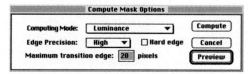

Figure 23.12 Selecting Luminance

APPLICATIONS

After you become familiar with luminance masks, you'll probably find many interesting and creative ways to use them. The following sections describe a few possible applications.

Using luminance masks to emphasize shadow or highlight

Luminance masks can be used to "knock out" the shadows or highlights in an image. In this example, French Photographer François Marquet used a luminance mask to make the highlights almost transparent in "Julie," a close-up shot of a face (see figure 23.13).

François began by creating a luminance mask. In the Mask Settings dialog box, he set the cursors so that the darker colors would remain fully opaque, but the lighter areas (skin) would become more or less transparent (see figure 23.14).

François then reinserted the image in an Image Silhouette layer above the luminance mask. However, this time he silhouetted just the lips using Color Compensation mode. At 100% opacity, the lips were emphasized in relation to the rest of the face. A Multicolor layer was also added to paint the lips a fuller red (see figure 23.15).

Then François created a peach Monocolor layer, named "Peachy luminance." Next, he copied the mask from the "Luminance mask" layer to the stencil of the "Peachy luminance" layer. He then used the Marquee tool to fill the stencil. Figure 23.16 shows the layer "Peachy luminance." All other layers are hidden.

....

NOTE: By using a luminance mask in a Monocolor layer, a virtual image is created made entirely of paint. This image contains no pixels and has no resolution. While the image is too "soft" to be used in place of a pixel image, it's an interesting concept, rich in creative possibilities.

....

Finally, François dragged the "Peachy luminance" layer below the "Luminance mask" layer. In figure 23.17, the peach color shows through the mask, giving it a peachy coloring. Since "Peachy luminance" is a Monocolor layer, François could change the skin coloring simply by changing the color of the layer, as in figure 23.18.

Figure 23.13   Original image

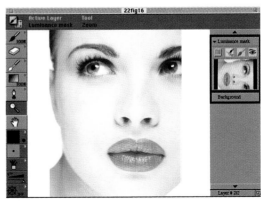

Figure 23.14   Julie inserted with luminance mask

Just mouth ⌐ Darkened lips ⌐

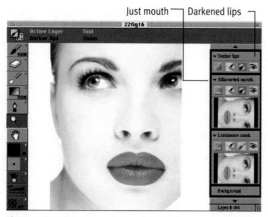

Figure 23.15 Lips silhouetted and painted

Mask copied... ⌐ ...to stencil ⌐

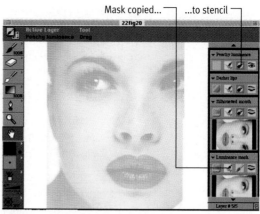

Figure 23.16 Monocolor layer using Luminance mask

Monocolor layer dragged
to bottom of layer stack ⌐

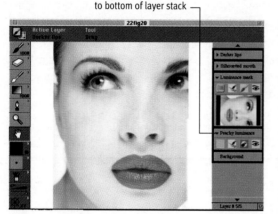

Figure 23.17 Peachy skin

New color ⌐

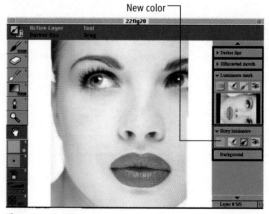

Figure 23.18 Rosy skin

The Monocolor layer mostly affects the light areas of the skin, because it shows through in areas where the "Luminance mask" layer is more or less transparent.

Using luminance masks to generate selective masks

In the following illustration, American digital artist Terri J. Wolf used luminance masks to selectively repaint her own painting. First she scanned her original painting of Edith Sitwell to IVUE (see figure 23.19).

Terri then inserted the image in an Image Insertion layer, and cropped it. Next, she reinserted the same image in an Image Silhouette layer, and created a luminance mask where the lighter values have high opacity, and the darker values are transparent. In figure 23.20, the bottom layer is hidden to show just the luminance mask. The hair and clothes of the figures appear in white. In fact, they are transparent—the white is the background showing through.

Figure 23.19   Original scanned painting

Terri then created a Monocolor layer and copied the luminance mask to the Monocolor stencil. She then filled the stencil with paint. In figure 23.21, all other layers are hidden to show the Monocolor layer.

Figure 23.22 shows the original image and the Monocolor layer. The layer containing the luminance mask has been deleted. It only served to create the stencil in the Monocolor layer. Through the stencil, the paint is applied only to the light parts of the image (compare with original painting).

Terri then used IVUE Correction to shift the original image to sepia. The sepia coloring appears delicately through the luminance mask (see figure 23.23).

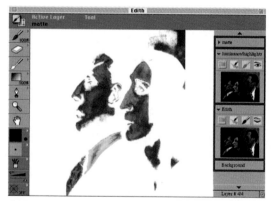

Figure 23.20   Luminance mask revealing highlights

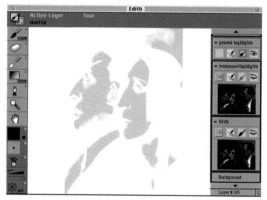

Figure 23.21   Luminance mask copied to Monocolor stencil

Figure 23.22   Image painted selectively

Figure 23.23   Bottom layer shifted to sepia

Figure 23.24 "Edith 2"

By the time the image was completed, Terri had created four different types of luminance masks for the original image, and copied them to nine different Artwork and Monocolor layers. The final image, "Edith 2," is shown in figure 23.24.

Using luminance masks on textures

Another interesting application of luminance masks is for textures. In the following exercise, we're going to apply a pattern to a solid-colored fabric while retaining the texture of the fabric.

To retain texture, follow these steps:

1. In the File menu, choose Open FITS.

2. Choose "Roman wall" from the Copy me to Hard Drive folder and click on Open.

3. Zoom and pan so that your document window approximates figure 23.25.

4. In the Create menu, choose Image Insertion.

5. Check that Auto Insert is deselected. Then Open the image called "Red etching," located on the CD in the IVUE folder.

6. Using the Opacity control, set the opacity to 60%. Then drag the image to the position shown in figure 23.26. It should entirely cover Sara's clothes.

7. Copy the mask from "Silhouetting Sara" to the stencil of "Red etching (Option-drag). The etching now appears only within "Sara's" mask.

8. Select a small tool size and click on the Eraser/Erase option.

Figure 23.25 Roman wall

Figure 23.26 Positioning "Red etching"

Figure 23.27   Manually erasing excess etching

9. Carefully erase the etching from Sara's arms, and from her clothes, except on the white scarf (see figure 23.27).

The "Red etching" image is partially transparent, so you can see the creases of the white scarf underneath. However, the transparency is insufficient, and is not necessarily in the right places. We're going to create a luminance mask to make the pattern change credible.

10. Select the layer "Silhouetting Sara" and press Command-I. The Get Info dialog box appears. Drag the dialog box to the side of the screen. You'll need it to position the next image inserted.

11. In the Create menu, choose Image Silhouette, and open the image called "Sara," located on the CD in the IVUE folder.

12. Position "Sara" directly above the "Sara" image already inserted. For more information on exact positioning, see "Breaking down an image into background and foreground" in Chapter 20, "One Image, Two Layers."

13. Create an Inside selection and an Outside selection, to isolate Sara from the gray background. Then click on the Compute Mask button.

14. In the Compute Mask Options dialog box, click on Luminance, and click on Preview. The Mask Settings dialog box appears.

15. In the Mask Settings dialog box, set the cursors as shown in figure 23.28.

16. Click on OK. A luminance mask is created. The pattern ("Red etching") is "sandwiched" between two images of Sara. The luminance mask in the top layer re-creates the texture of the scarf (see figure 23.29).

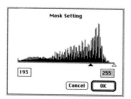

Figure 23.28   Mask Settings

Figure 23.29   Re-creating texture using a luminance mask

By clicking again on Luminance and Preview, you can change the mask settings to modify the luminance mask.

17. Click on Compute to create the mask.

You've modified the pattern of a textured scarf. Now you're going to modify the pattern color.

18. In the layer bar, select the "Insert Red etching" layer.

19. In the Layer menu, choose IVUE Correction/ Color Shift.

20. In the Color Shift dialog box, click on the Highlights button. Shift the highlights to red and green by 40 points. Then click on OK (see figure 23.30).

Because the pattern is contained in its own separate layer, you can use IVUE Correction to modify it whenever you like. You can also use the positioning tools to scale, rotate, move, and generally reposition the pattern without affecting the rest of the composite.

Figure 23.30 Shifting pattern colors

In this exercise, we *maintained* or *re-created* texture. To *create* texture, you don't necessarily need a luminance mask. Figure 23.31 shows an image with a tile texture. In figure 23.32, the tiles were inserted above the image "Roman floor." The opacity of the tiles was set at roughly 50%. The tiles were then converted to black and white using the Black & White Preset. This removes the color of the texture, keeping just the form.

Figure 23.31 Tile texture

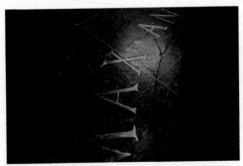

Figure 23.32 Tile texture applied to "Roman floor"

CHAPTER 24

HOW TO BE SELECTIVE

This chapter summarizes the different ways you can apply color, opacity masks, effects, filter plug-ins, or repositioning to certain parts of a composite without affecting others. All the material is covered in earlier chapters. The purpose of this chapter is to group all the methods together. Use it as a reference.

The image "Information Superhighway 4," created by French photographer Thierry Petillot, is used to illustrate this chapter. The actual image is shown in figure 24.1. All other images in this chapter are my modifications, made solely to illustrate the art of being selective.

MANUAL BRUSHING AND ERASING

The most direct and intuitive way to apply something to part of a composite is to brush it in. You can then switch back and forth between brush and eraser.

In figure 24.2, a colorization layer was created. The section of earth inside the TV screen was colorized in blue using the Brush. By zooming and using a small brush and eraser, the result was obtained quickly and intuitively.

Figure 24.1 Information Superhighway 4

Figure 24.2 Using the Brush and Eraser to be selective

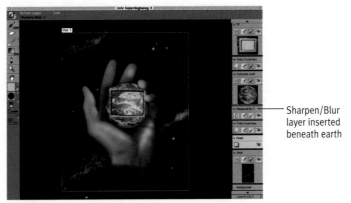

Sharpen/Blur
layer inserted
beneath earth

Figure 24.3   Using layer order to be selective

LAYER ORDERING

Layers affect only the layers beneath them in the layer stack. To avoid affecting a layer, insert the new layer beneath it in the layer stack. You can also change the order of already inserted layers.

In figure 24.3, a Sharpen/Blur layer was inserted beneath all the layers used to create the earth. A Blur fill was applied to the entire view, but it only affected the underlying layers, in other words the hand and the background.

For more information, see Chapter 5, "Handling Layers."

Path tools

The Path tools allow you to create masks and stencils for constraining effects. In figure 24.4, a path was drawn around the earth. The path was converted to a stencil in a Mono-color layer. White paint was then applied at a low opacity. The paint is only visible within the stencil.

For more information, see Chapter 8, "Isolating Images from their Background."

Copying masks and stencils

Existing masks and stencils can be copied and used in other layers. In figure 24.5, a silhouetting mask was created for the hand when it was inserted in the composite. By copying the mask in the "Hand" layer to the stencil of the "Insert Starburst" layer, the image of the starburst only appears within the hand. In addition, the opacity of the starburst was set at 30% to allow the hand to show through.

Figure 24.4   Using the Path tools to be selective

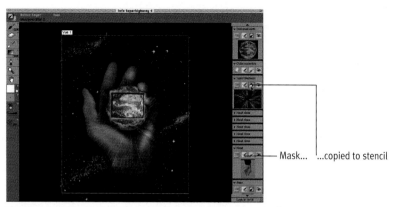

— Mask...   ...copied to stencil

Figure 24.5   Using masks and stencils from other layers to be selective

For more information, see Chapter 10, "Sources, Masks, and Stencils Revealed."

IVUE CORRECTIONS

IVUE corrections allow you to modify an entire image layer without affecting any other layers in the composite. In figure 24.6, the Color Shift command was used to shift the colors of the "Earth inside TV" layer. Notice that the same image is used in another layer ("Deformed earth"). The image in that layer is not affected by the IVUE correction.

For more information, see Chapter 13, "Making Global Color Corrections."

SELECTIVE COLOR CORRECTION

In a Color Correction layer, the tools allow you to color-correct selectively. In figure 24.7, the hand is shifted to green, but the background is barely affected because the range of colors to be modified was defined using the Selective Color Correction dialog box.

Color Correction layer ⌐

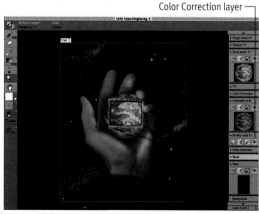

Figure 24.6   Using IVUE Corrections to be selective

Figure 24.7   Using a Color Correction layer to be selective

NOTE: Combine several selective methods when possible. In figure 24.7, the Color Correction layer was inserted below the earth in the layer stack, to avoid affecting the earth. Also, the stars are slightly affected by the color correction. To avoid affecting the stars altogether, the Brush could have been used to color-correct the hand rather than the Marquee/Fill option.

For more information, see Chapter 14, "Making Selective Color Corrections."

ONE IMAGE, TWO LAYERS

To reposition part of an image, you can insert the same image in two layers. In figure 24.8, the "Hand" layer was duplicated, and the top of the two hand layers was distorted using the Perspective tool. To use just the index and middle finger of the distorted hand, the top layer was erased, except for the two enlarged fingers (see figure 24.9).

In figure 24.10, the bottom layer is activated, so you don't see the layer above it. Two fingers are erased so that they don't interfere with the distorted fingers in the top hand layer. The full composite is shown in figure 24.11, with parts of both hands being used.

For more information, see Chapter 20, "One Image, Two Layers."

SELECTIVE MASKS

If you want a high degree of precision to modify part of an already inserted image, you can create a selective mask by silhouetting part of the image.

Layer with distorted hand —

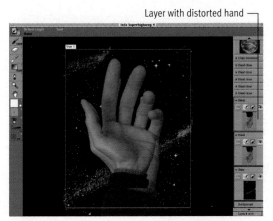

Figure 24.8 Breaking down an image into two layers

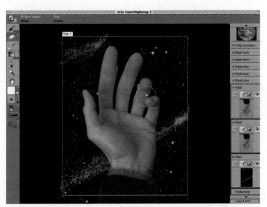

Figure 24.9 Erasing part of one layer

Active layer being erased —

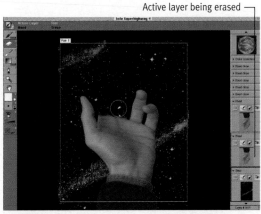

Figure 24.10 Erasing part of the bottom hand layer

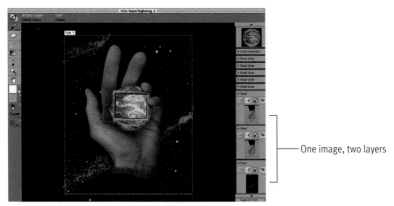

— One image, two layers

Figure 24.11 Using two layers to reposition part of an image

In figure 24.12, the hand is inserted a second time and positioned exactly on top of the original hand. Then the shirt sleeve is silhouetted. The silhouette is shown alone in figure 24.13.

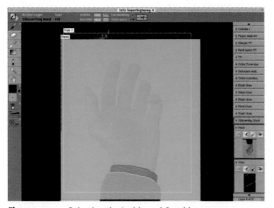

Figure 24.12 Selecting the Inside and Outside

After silhouetting, the original hand is shown, and the shirt sleeve is hidden. Then the mask of the shirt sleeve is copied to the stencil of a Colorize layer. In the Colorize layer, the stencil is used to colorize the shirt sleeve quickly with complete precision (see figure 24.14). At this point, you can delete the layer with the silhouetted shirt sleeve.

For more information, see Chapter 22, "Selective Masks Revealed."

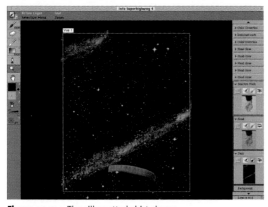

Figure 24.13 The silhouetted shirt sleeve

Figure 24.14 Using a selective mask to be selective

Figure 24.15 Applying filter plug-ins to a single layer

SELECTIONS FOR FILTER PLUG-INS

There are several ways to apply filter plug-ins selectively. You can apply a filter to an entire IVUE image, or to a selection (the visible part of the image). You can also apply a filter to an entire FITS file, to a view in a FITS file, or to a selection (the visible part of a layer).

In figure 24.15, Paint Alchemy was used to apply a filter to the layer "Deformed earth."

For more information, see Chapter 18, "Using Filter Plug-ins."

ALPHA CHANNELS

The Use as Alpha Channel command in the mask menu allows you to output the visible area of a layer as an alpha channel. By itself, this does not allow you to be selective in Live Picture. However, if you build an output file using an alpha channel, that alpha channel can be reused in Live Picture as an alpha channel, mask or stencil, or in Photoshop as a selection.

Alpha channels are particularly useful for applying brush distortion in Live Picture. For more information, see Chapter 11, "Distorting Images."

CHAPTER 25

EMBOSSING

This chapter shows you how to emboss images. The exercise leads you through the standard embossing procedure, and then shows a few variations.

To emboss an image, follow these steps:

1. In the Create menu, choose Image Insertion.

2. With Auto Insert selected, select the image called "Clock Face," located on the CD in the IVUE folder.

3. Click on Open. The image fills the document window.

4. In the layer stack, copy the layer by Option-dragging it upward. You now have two identical images, positioned one on top of the other (see figure 25.1).

5. With the top layer selected, choose IVUE Correction in the Layer menu, and Invert in the submenu. The color values of the top layer are inverted, producing a negative (see figure 25.2).

Figure 25.1 Duplicating the layer

Figure 25.2 Inverting the top layer

To nudge, all fields must be deselected

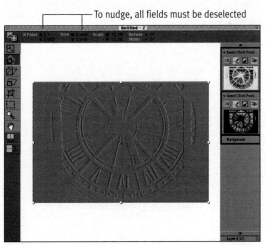

Figure 25.3 Setting opacity at 50%

Figure 25.4 Embossing an image

6. Click on the Marquee and drag the Opacity slider to 50%. Then drag the Marquee around the image. The image turns to a solid gray (see figure 25.3).

NOTE: When you invert an image, you invert each color value in the image. For example, white becomes black. When you set the opacity of the top image at 50%, you are mixing the original image and the inverted image. In our example, by mixing white with black, you get gray. The same logic applies to all the other colors.

7. With the top layer selected, toggle to the positioning tools.

8. Use the keyboard arrows to nudge the top image one pixel to the right. (To use the arrows, click the Rotate tool to deselect the control bar fields.) This embosses the image (see figure 25.4).

The rest of this exercise combines embossing skills with other skills. In the following steps, we will create and modify embossed text.

9. In the layer stack, select both layers (Command-Shift).

10. Duplicate the two layers (Option-drag), dragging them above the existing layers (see figure 25.5).

11. Rename the top layer "Inverted text" (Command-I). Rename the next layer down "Text" (see figure 25.6).

12. With both layers selected, click the Rotate tool and rotate both layers, roughly as shown in figure 25.6.

13. Select the Type tool and click anywhere in your composite. In the Type dialog box, type the word EMBOSSING. Use Geneva or another font.

14. Click on OK. The path appears.

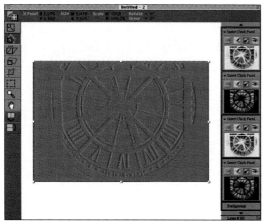

Figure 25.5 Duplicating two layers

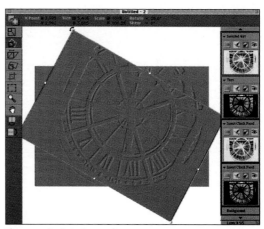

Figure 25.6 Rotating two layers

15. Deselect all layers in the layer stack by clicking on the "Background" layer bar. Then reposition the text paths, as shown in figure 25.7.

16. Select the layer named "Inverted text."

17. In the Mask menu, choose Path –> Stencil (the paths must be selected for the command to available).

18. Click on Create Hard Edge and click on OK. A text stencil is created in the top layer (see figure 25.8).

19. Copy the stencil in the "Inverted Text" layer to the stencil of the "Text" layer (remember to first deselect the layer, or you will copy the entire layer). The text stencil now exists in both layers. The embossing effect is recreated on the text (see figure 25.9).

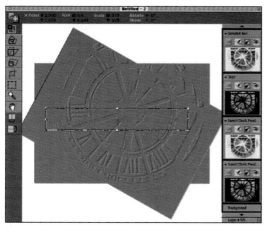

Figure 25.7 Repositioning the text paths

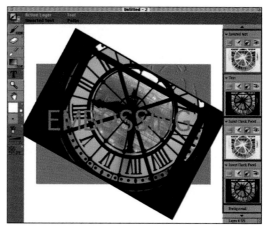

Figure 25.8 Creating a text stencil

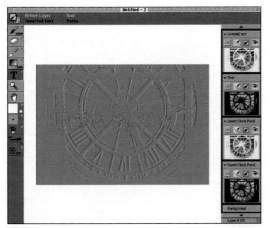

Figure 25.9 Copying the text stencil

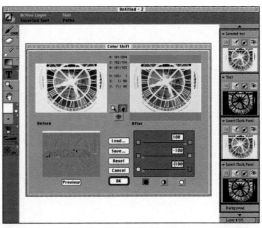

Figure 25.10 Using the Color Shift dialog box

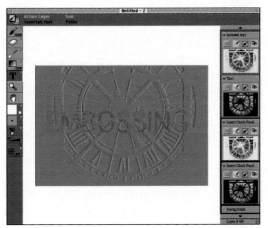

Figure 25.11 Shifting text color

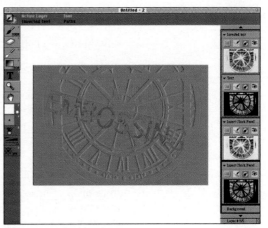

Figure 25.12 Rotating the text

20. Select the layer named "Inverted stencil."

21. In the Layer menu, choose IVUE Correction, and choose Shift from the submenu. The Color Shift dialog box appears. We'll use this color correction to differentiate the text from its gray background.

22. Click on the Shadows button. Drag the cursors to red (100), magenta (-100) and yellow (-100) as shown in figure 25.10.

23. Click on OK. The color of the text shifts (see figure 25.11).

24. Select the two top layers and rotate them, as shown in figure 25.12.

CHAPTER 26

THE PALETTE KNIFE: MOST UNDERRATED TOOL

This chapter is devoted to the Palette Knife, and in particular to the Push and Diffuse options. While not the most important tool, it is the easiest one to overlook. The exercise will give you an immediate feel for this tool and how it can be useful.

As with every tool, each layer has different Palette Knife options. However, there are two Palette Knife options common to almost every layer: Push and Diffuse (see figure 26.1).

The Push option pushes the mask. And because you see everything in Live Picture through a mask, you can push everything: a spot of blur, a color correction, an opacity mask, or anything else. Figures 26.2 and 26.3 show a Multicolor layer before and after using the Push option.

The Diffuse option diffuses or redistributes the opacities in a mask. Along the edge of a mask, the opacity drops relatively quickly from 100% to 0%. By diffusing the edge, you make it more gradual. However, if your mask is 100% opaque and you try to diffuse the center, nothing will happen because you are redistributing 100% to 100%.

Figure 26.1
The Push and Diffuse options

Figure 26.4 shows a pair of silhouetted lips placed on a white background. In figure 26.5, François Marquet used the diffuse option to diffuse the edge of the mask.

Figure 26.2   Three spots of paint

Figure 26.3   Paint after using the Push option.

Figure 26.4   Silhouetted lips   **Figure 26.5**   Lips after using the Diffuse option

....

NOTE: To blend the edges of a silhouetted image into a background image, you can use the Palette Knife/Blend option, available in a Sharpen/Blur layer.

....

The following exercise allows you to experiment with the Push and Diffuse options.

To use the Push and Diffuse options, follow these steps:

1. In the Create menu, choose Image Insertion.

2. With Auto Insert selected, select the image named "Earth Horizon" located on the CD in the IVUE folder, and click on Open (see figure 26.6).

3. With Auto Insert selected, select the image named "Roman Floor" located on the CD in the IVUE folder, and click on Open. The image opens directly on top of the image "Earth Horizon" (see figure 26.7).

4. Click on the Marquee and choose the Erase option. Then erase the entire image "Roman Floor."

5. Using a small brush, reveal part of the image, as shown in figure 26.8. Do not brush right up to the edge of the continent.

6. Click on the Palette Knife and choose the Push option.

7. Set the Pressure control at the lowest setting.

Figure 26.6   "Earth Horizon"

Figure 26.7   "Roman Floor"

Figure 26.8 Brushing in part of an image

Figure 26.9 Roman floor ghosted into earth

8. Push from the center of the image toward the edge of the continent. The image should gradually reappear toward the edge. Then push from the edge of the continent towards the center. The image gradually disappears. The idea is to blend the image into the continent. Use the Push option until your image resembles figure 26.9.

NOTE: You can use the Eraser and Brush to obtain a similar effect. However, the sensitivity and way of working with the Push option is different.

---

9. In the Create menu, choose Color Correction.

10. In the control bar, click on the Before control and drag the eyedropper to select a yellowish color from the Roman floor (see figure 26.10).

11. Then click on the After control and drag to select a reddish-brown color from the earth (see figure 26.10).

12. Copy the mask in the "Roman Floor" layer to the stencil of the color correction layer. This ensures that the earth will not be color-corrected.

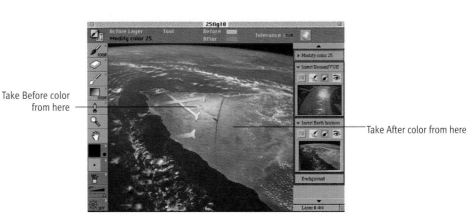

Take Before color from here

Take After color from here

Figure 26.10 Selecting the Before and After colors

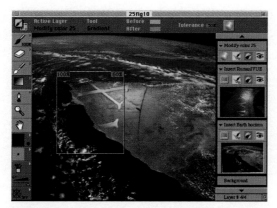

Figure 26.11   Setting the color correction opacities

13. Click on the Marquee and choose the Gradient/Horizontal option.

14. Drag open the gradient, tab to the right opacity field and enter 60% (see figure 26.11).

15. Click inside the gradient box to preview, and click outside the box to create the gradient (see figure 26.12).

16. Click on the Palette Knife and choose the Diffuse option.

17. Brush the Palette Knife along the right edge of the gradient. This diffuses the break between a color correction at 60% (the edge of the gradient) and 0% (no color correction).

Figure 26.12   Color correction gradient

Figure 26.13   Diffusing the edge of the gradient

CHAPTER 27

THE MOST FLEXIBLE SOFTWARE YOU'VE EVER SEEN

This chapter summarizes one of the most important aspects of Live Picture: its flexibility. The points addressed in this chapter have been dealt with separately earlier in the book. The aim here is to bring them together, to show how you can use this flexibility.

UNLIMITED UNDO

In Live Picture, anything can be undone at any time. There are several types of undo:

- Command-Z, or Undo in the Edit menu. Use this command to undo the last action. If you are brushing with the stylus, the last action begins when you apply pressure to the stylus.

....

NOTE: Some actions, such as copying masks to stencils, cannot be undone with this command.

....

- Command-Option-Z undoes everything done in a layer since you activated it, or since the screen was regenerated (in other words, since you zoomed, panned, repositioned, and so on).

- For the rest of your undoing, use the Eraser. This is the most flexible tool. You can undo partially or completely. The Eraser affects only the active layer. In some layers, you can undo selectively. For instance, in an Image Distortion layer, you can undo the distortion without erasing the image.

MODIFYING YOUR COMPOSITE AT ANY TIME

All aspects of the composite can be modified at any time. For example, you can change the softness of a stencil edge, darken a shadow, change a color correction, increase or decrease an angle of rotation, substitute one image for another, and much more.

UNLIMITED EXPERIMENTATION

Live Picture is the ultimate tool for experimenting with images. Because you are not actually modifying the IVUE file, you can skew, distort and color-correct as many times as you want, undo and redo, and never have to worry about image quality loss. In addition, you rarely have to wait long to see the result on the screen.

MULTIPLE VERSIONS IN ONE DOCUMENT

With a single compact FITS file, you can create more versions than you could with multiple pixel-based versions. Here's how.

Displaying multiple versions on your monitor

By clicking on the Eye icon, you can hide or show one or several layers. The layer bar in figure 27.1 contains five layers, but the top four are hidden, showing just the original image.

Figures 27.2 and 27.3 show the original image with green eyes and blue eyes. Only one Color Correction layer is shown at a time.

Layer shown ⌐

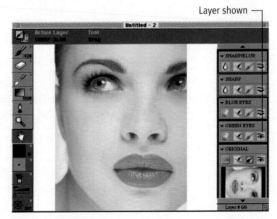

Figure 27.1   Four top layers hidden

Figure 27.2   Green eyes

Layer shown

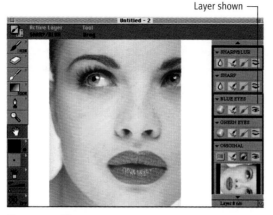

Figure 27.3   Blue eyes

Figure 27.4   Blues eyes plus sharpening

Figure 27.5   Blues eyes plus sharpening/blur

Figure 27.4 shows the original image, plus blue eyes and sharpening on the eyes and mouth. In figure 27.5, the top Sharpen/Blur layer is shown. It contains the same sharpening, but blur was also added around the nose and cheeks to further soften the lines.

Use the Eye icon to quickly view different versions of an image on the screen. You and your client can then choose one of the versions without having to save and load several files.

Outputting multiple versions

When you build an output file, only the visible layers will appear in the output. For instance, you can create an output file for each version shown in figures 27.1 to 27.5.

NOTE: If you use the Batch command, you need to save a separate FITS file for each version.

Outputting at multiple resolutions

With the same FITS file, you can build several outputs at 72 dpi for screen viewing or a multimedia job. You can then build a 200 dpi output for a dye sublimation printer, and a 300 dpi file for four-color printing. When you build, you don't modify the resolution of the original images.

The resolution of the images must be sufficient for the output resolution, but even there, it is usually safe to interpolate up to roughly 200%. For instance, you can output most 300 dpi images up to 600 dpi without any noticeable quality loss.

Outputting multiple views

Chapter 6, "Using Views," showed that you can output any number of views. Each view can be of a different size and proportion, and show a different part of the image. This allows you to create several "frames" for a FITS file without actually cropping parts of the document.

CREATING MULTIPLE FITS FILES

For the following images, Thierry Petillot used the Save FITS As command to save several versions of a composite. He began by creating an A4 page (see figure 27.6) for the French publisher Hachette, for use in their catalog for Millia, a French multimedia show held in Cannes.

After the image was delivered, Hachette asked for a 3' x 8' poster for the show. Thierry created a view for the poster. He then repositioned several of the composited elements to fill the view (see figure 27.7), and saved the FITS file under a different name.

The output file was 130 MB. Thierry likes to take advantage of Live Picture's flexibility and speed, so he had scanned the hand and both CD-ROMs at 45 MB each, even though he only needed an A4 originally. With images this size, creating a larger output didn't pose a problem. And the time it took to create the new image was almost insignificant.

Later on, the same image was modified yet again, saved under another name, and used for the design of a mouse pad (see figure 27.8).

Figure 27.6   Original A4 image

Figure 27.7   3' x 8' poster

Figure 27.8   Mouse pad design

FITS files are generally quite small. Even composites containing hundreds of megabytes worth of image files are usually described by a FITS file of a few megabytes.

FITS files can also be used to store different versions of the same IVUE file. For example, you can scan five or six high-resolution images. Then modify each image: silhouette, convert to black and white, color-correct, colorize, create a luminance mask. Store each version in a separate FITS file. From five or six scans, you can obtain a library of some 25 to 30 compact FITS files, each representing a different image or version of an image, ready to be merged into a composite at any time.

To summarize, Live Picture allows unlimited undo and unlimited experimentation. A single FITS file allows you to create multiple versions, at multiple resolutions, and with multiple frames. You can also use the Save FITS As command to save several versions of a composite: FITS files are very small. Add to that the capability to substitute one image for another, and you've got the most flexible software ever seen.

CHAPTER 28

BUILDING OUTPUTS AND PRINTING

This chapter explains how to build output files and print them. The Build command is available in the full version of Live Picture. It is disabled in the demo software provided with this book.

BUILDING AN OUTPUT FILE

When you complete an image, you need to build it before it can be opened in another application or printed. To build an output means to take the original IVUE files used in the composite and build a new image based on the FITS file.

NOTE: You don't need Live Picture to open an output file. For example, if you build a TIFF file, it can be opened with Photoshop or any other application that reads TIFF files. It's an industry-standard TIFF. The same holds true for any other file format (except IVUE).

You can build your output files one-by-one, or you can use the Batch command to queue several builds. Batching the builds is useful when you have several files to output.

Note that when you build an output file, the IVUE files and the FITS file with all its layers remain intact. For more information on building, see Chapter 2, "An Overview" and Chapter 6, "Using Views."

To build an output file, follow these steps:

1. In the File menu, choose Build. The Build dialog box appears (see figure 28.1).

NOTE: The composite must contain at least one view for the Build command to be available.

2. In the View pop-down menu, select a view.

3. To change the size of the view, enter different values in the Output Size fields, or change the scaling percentage. In both cases, view proportions remain unchanged.

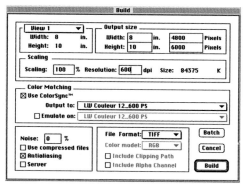

Figure 28.1   The Build dialog box

Figure 28.2   Output file types

4. To change the resolution, enter another value. The default value is document resolution.

5. In the Export To pop-down menu (see figure 28.2), choose a file type.

6. Choose RGB or CMYK. At this point, the final size of the file is indicated next to Size.

7. Click on Build to build the output right away. Click on Batch to build the output later (for more information on batch building, see "Using the Batch command" later in this chapter).

If your composite contains an EPS file inserted using an EPS Insertion layer, choose the EPS command or the DCS command in the Export To pop-down menu. This will maintain maximum quality when you output your image: the image layers and other "FITS" layers will be output at the resolution selected in the Build dialog box, and the EPS Insertion layers will be output at the resolution of the PostScript output device used (an imagesetter, for example).

If you use any other output formats, the EPS files inserted in your composite are output using the 72-dpi preview and lose their resolution-independence.

Selecting the other build options

This section describes the other build options available in the Build dialog box.

Color Matching

Color Matching allows you to use the ColorSync 2.0 profiles. Activate Use ColorSync. Two options are available:

- Output To allows you to choose the profile of the final output device. It calibrates the output image to match the monitor colors as closely as possible. If the output device requires CMYK files, ColorSync will perform the separation instead of the Live Picture separator.

- Emulate On allows you to simulate the final output on a printer which is not the final output device.

For more information, see Chapter 29, "Quality Color Separations in Less than One Minute."

NOISE

Noise adds grain to an image. Use it to make color fills or gradients look less flat (see figures 28.3 and 28.4, where the blue sky is a paint gradient). It can also be used to simulate a photograph shot with high-speed film.

Noise cannot be applied selectively—it affects the entire composite.

To determine the amount of noise to add, use the Noise option in the General Preferences dialog box. This affects only the display. When the image on your screen looks good, deselect the Noise option, but remember the percentage used (leaving the Noise option selected slows down screen regeneration). When you build your output, enter the noise percentage in the Build dialog box.

USE COMPRESSED FILES

Use Compressed Files allows you to work with compressed and non-compressed IVUEs. For more information, see Chapter 30, "Compression, CD-ROMs, and Networking."

Figure 28.3 Image without noise

Figure 28.4 3% noise added

ANTIALIASING

Antialiasing is designed to avoid jagged lines, called "jaggies," which may occur along the edges of masks, stencils or any other hard edges. When you select antialiasing, it is applied to the entire image, but the difference is most noticeable along edges. Antialiasing does not decrease the quality of an image. On the contrary, antialiasing is recommended to obtain the best overall quality.

In figure 28.5, the small computer was silhouetted, and the edge of the mask is somewhat jagged. The oblique lines around the screen of the large computer, and the charts on the computer screen, are also jagged. Figure 28.6 shows how antialiasing smoothes these lines without any marked effect on the rest of the image.

Antialiasing is not required if all the following conditions are met:

- The images were scaled to roughly the same percentage in the FITS file. (The scale percentage of each image is indicated in the control bar in positioning mode, and in the Get Info dialog box.)

- No images were scaled to more than 100%.

- No rotation, skew or perspective was applied to any image.

- No brush distortion was used.

- No images were silhouetted.

- No hard-edged masks or stencils were created using the path tools (extra precision, hard edge, or low feather values).

Figure 28.5   Image without antialiasing   **Figure 28.6**   Image with antialiasing

- None of the original images contain any straight oblique lines, such as the slant of a roof.

A typical case where antialiasing is not required is a FITS file containing an image scaled to 100%, retouched using cloning and color-corrected.

NOTE: The Antialiasing option in the General Preferences dialog box only affects your monitor display.

SERVER

Select the Server option if your Macintosh is connected to a FITServer. The FITServer is a third-party FITS RIP developed by Torque which allows you to build your output files on a Silicon Graphics workstation. Before building, select the FITServer in the Chooser.

For more information, see Chapter 30, "Compression, CD-ROMs, and Networking." Also see any documentation supplied with your FITServer.

INCLUDE CLIPPING PATH

Use Include Clipping Path to export an image with its clipping path. The Path->Clipping Path command in the Mask menu allows you to convert a path to a clipping path.

Clipping paths are generally used to import images into page layout programs, such as PageMaker or QuarkXpress. If you select Include Clipping Path, all areas outside the clipping path will be transparent in the page layout program.

NOTE: When a clipping path is previewed in a page layout program, it may not appear to be "clipped." However, when printed, any text created in the program should flow around the image.

Include Clipping Path is available only if the image includes a clipping path, and if EPS, DCS or Photoshop 3.0 is selected in the Export To menu.

INCLUDE ALPHA CHANNEL

Include Alpha Channel allows you to export alpha channels. There are two ways to obtain alpha channels in a FITS file. They can be imported into Live Picture from another imaging application. You can also choose the Use As Alpha Channel in the Mask menu. When you choose this command, the visible area of the layer selected, in other words the mask and stencil combined, is transformed into an alpha channel during the build.

Alpha channels can be included when you build a TIFF, Photoshop 3.0 and IVUE file.

Things that affect build times

A number of factors affect the time it takes to build an output image.

- The size of the final output. The larger the output size, the longer it takes to build. The correct size appears after selecting the view, output file type, and color mode (RGB or CMYK).

- Number of layers used. The more layers, the longer it takes to build.

- Types of layers used. Not all layers affect build times equally. Image layers take the longest to build. This is particularly true of Image Distortion layers. Artwork layers also take longer. An Image Clone layer which uses just a small part of the image is quick to build.

- Complexity of masks and stencils. Images with complex silhouetted masks, and any layer with long paths, such as text, increase build times. Hard-edged masks and stencils take longer to build than edges with large feathers.

- Use of Antialiasing or Noise. Both of these options increase build times.

- Use of compressed images. If you are building an output with compressed IVUE images, the build will take longer than with non-compressed IVUEs.

- Use of export plug-ins. It takes longer to build a file using the export plug-ins. Photoshop 3.0 and Scitex CT files require the use of export plug-ins.

- Building in RGB or CMYK. It takes longer to build in CMYK than in RGB. This is not just because CMYK files are larger than RGB files. To output a CMYK file, the RGB data is separated into CMYK data. It is this separation that takes the extra time.

- Amount of RAM allocated to Live Picture. This becomes an important factor for complex composites containing many layers.

- Hard drive speed. Because Live Picture reads the IVUE files as it builds, a faster hard drive can improve build times. Also, if several hard drives are connected to your Macintosh, you'll improve performance if you store all the IVUE files used in a composite on the same drive. And optimize your drive periodically using a utility such as HDT, Public Utilities, or Norton.

Things that do not affect build times

The size of the IVUE files used in a composite does not affect build times.

Using the Batch command

The Batch command allows you to launch a series of builds. It is especially useful if you create several composites in a day. To avoid immobilizing your Macintosh for each build, launch all the builds together during a lunch break, at night, or any other time when your computer is not being used.

To use the Batch command, follow these steps:

1. Set the build parameters just as you would for an immediate build, but click on Batch instead of Build. The Batch Build of .... dialog box appears (see figure 28.7).

2. Enter a name for your output file.

3. If you did not save your FITS file, click on Save....

4. Click on OK.

5. Repeat steps 1-4 for each FITS file you create.

6. To launch the builds, close any open FITS files and choose Monitor from the Batch menu. The Batch Monitor dialog box appears (see figure 28.8).

    To begin batch processing, click on Start. You can remove files from the queue, modify the build parameters, or preview an output file by selecting the file in the queue and clicking on the appropriate button. You can also add files to the queue. To change queue order, drag a file to another position. Batch processing can be interrupted or canceled.

PRINTING IMAGES

You can print images to any printer using a Photoshop-compatible plug-in. In practice, this basically means dye sublimation printers such as the Kodak XLS 8600. To use the export plug-in, copy it to the Live Picture Plug-ins folder.

To print on any other output device, you need to open the image in a page layout program such as QuarkXpress or PageMaker, a graphics program such as Freehand or Illustrator, or Photoshop.

Figure 28.7 Batch Build of ....
dialog box

Figure 28.8 Batch Monitor dialog box

To print an output file using a printer export plug-in, proceed as if you were building the output, but select the printer export plug-in in the Export To menu. A resolution of 200 dpi is generally sufficient for a dye sublimation printer, so build a 200-dpi file. If you then require a higher resolution file for offset printing or a transparency, build the output file at the required resolution after proofing.

When you print an image using an export plug-in, you are actually building a TIFF file, which is then exported to the printer. The process is seamless, so you don't see the TIFF file. However, the time it takes to print is equal to the time it takes to build the TIFF plus the time required to print.

You can print an existing IVUE, TIFF, or Photo CD file directly using the Export command in the Converter menu. In this case, open the file first using the Open command. Then print the file using the Export command.

CHAPTER 29

QUALITY COLOR SEPARATIONS IN LESS THAN ONE MINUTE

This chapter describes color management in Live Picture. It begins with a description of the Live Picture color space. It then describes how to build CMYK output files, and how CMYK colors are handled in general. You'll learn how to separate RGB images using the separation table provided with Live Picture, as well as how to create your own separation tables and modify them. For files scanned in CMYK, the patented "adaptive separation" technology is described. A procedure for reusing separation tables from other software is also included. A short section on support for ColorSync 2.0 is also included.

A 48-BIT RGB COLOR SPACE

Live Picture's native color space is RGB (red, green and blue). If you are outputting to a film recorder, or use your images for video or multimedia, build an RGB output file.

However, if you output to an imagesetter, if your client wants a separated file, or if you simply want to control the separation process yourself, create a CMYK output file.

Live Picture's 48-bit color space allows you to create high quality separations. In other imaging applications, RGB color is defined by 8 bits per channel, meaning a total of 24 bits ($3 \times 8 = 24$). In Live Picture, each channel is described by 16 bits for paint layers, and 12 bits for image masks. So you are working with a total of 36 to 48 bits per channel.

When you build a CMYK output, Live Picture first builds a 36-bit RGB output file, and then separates it in CMYK. Since CMYK files contain 32 bits ($4 \times 8 = 32$), the RGB file contains more information than is needed for the CMYK file. Instead of separating 24 bits *up* to 32, 36 bits are separated *down* to 24. This enables a finer calculation of the CMYK file. The result: in a few extreme cases, minor banding, and in most cases no banding at all! Such results cannot be obtained in applications which work directly in CMYK.

Since paint layers are calculated in 48 bits, fills and gradients created in Live Picture are smooth, whether in RGB or CMYK. For some users, the ability to create a perfectly smooth 90 MB gradient in a few seconds is reason enough to buy Live Picture.

Also, if you create fluorescent-type colors such as bright greens and blues, the separated output will stay closer to the RGB colors than if you were working in a 24- or 32-bit application. You can "push your colors" to the limit.

....

NOTE: In Live Picture, you don't need to be a color wizard to create professional-quality separations. **All the images in this book are separated using the original, standard table supplied with Live Picture. No adjustments or modifications were made.**

....

COLOR MANAGEMENT IN LIVE PICTURE

Two color management systems are available for separating RGB files to CMYK: the table-driven Live Picture separator, and the ColorSync™ 2.0 output profiles. This chapter deals mainly with the Live Picture separator, with a small section on support for Colorsync 2.0.

Using the Live Picture separation tables

Live Picture is supplied with a standard separation table for building CMYK output files. You can also create separation tables using "Adaptive Separation," or "import" a separation table from another application. In addition, the Separation Control dialog box offers a full range of tools for modifying or fine tuning any separation table.

The procedure is different, depending on whether you scan in RGB or CMYK. This section begins with a description of the two procedures. Next, the procedure for using separation tables from other applications is provided. This is followed by a brief description of the Separation Control dialog box.

Click here ⌐

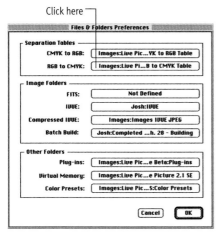

Figure 29.1 Selecting the separation table

IMPORTING IN RGB AND OUTPUTTING IN CMYK

If you scan directly into the IVUE format, or if you use other RGB image formats, you can separate your composite using the standard separation table supplied with Live Picture.

To use the standard separation table:

1. In the Edit menu, choose Preferences/File & Folders.

2. In the Files & Folders dialog box, click on the RGB to CMYK field (see figure 29.1).

3. Locate the table called "RGB to CMYK Table" and click on the Select button (it may already be selected in the table field).

4. Click on OK. The dialog box closes.

5. When you are ready to build your output, choose Build from the File menu and set the build parameters.

6. In the Build dialog box, choose CMYK from the Color Model pop-down menu.

7. Click on OK. When the build is completed, you will have a CMYK output file.

IMPORTING AND OUTPUTTING IN CMYK

The Live Picture color space is RGB, and IVUE is an RGB format. Therefore, if your images are scanned in CMYK, they are converted to RGB when you convert the file to the IVUE format. If you separate your final composite, the images are converted back to CMYK.

A special technology was developed to ensure that you maintain your original CMYK values through these conversions. This technology, called "Adaptive Separation," allows you to create a separation table for each CMYK image, or for multiple CMYK images if they were scanned using the same scanner or separation rule.

Adaptive Separation was tested and the results printed in Seybold's "Report on Desktop Publishing" (September 12, 1994). In this test, two CMYK scans were converted to RGB IVUE. Without making any further changes, they were built back out into CMYK. The idea was to see whether the CMYK values were maintained. The test results showed differences running from 0 to 3%. The tester points out that "...these differences are relatively minor, and will be seen only in close film comparisons...." They were not even visible on the Matchprint.

To maintain CMYK values, follow these steps:

1. Use the Converter menu to convert your image to IVUE. Use Open if it's a TIFF file. Use Acquire for Photoshop 3.0, Scitex CT and EPS/DCS (Photoshop-compatible) files.

2. When the Save As dialog box appears, select Adapt Separation Table (see figure 29.2).

3. The Table dialog box appears (see figure 29.3). Click on Create New Separation Table and click on OK.

4. After you save the file in IVUE format, the Table Name dialog box appears (see figure 29.4). Name the new table and save it in the Tables folder in the Live Picture folder.

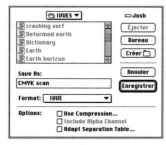

Figure 29.2   Using Adaptive Separation

Figure 29.3   Creating a new separation table

Figure 29.4   Naming the new table

5. Click on OK. The file is first converted to IVUE format, and then the new separation table is created.

6. In the Preferences/Files & Folders dialog box (Edit menu), select the new table in the RGB to CMYK field. This table will be used the next time you build a CMYK output.

   You can also select the separation table in the Separation Control dialog box (File menu).

If you scan your own images, begin by scanning a "reference" image. Reference images contain the full RGB spectrum, so the separation table created will account for the widest range of separated colors.

Reference images are often supplied with scanners. However, to create the most precise and complete separation table, it's better to use a reference *transparency*. Reference transparenies can be obtained on request directly from Live Picture Inc.

Scan the reference transparency on your scanner. Then follow the procedure "To maintain CMYK values" described above, using the scanned CMYK file in step 1. Then use the resulting separation table to output each image scanned using that scanner.

For a particular composite, you can make specific modifications to the CMYK curves using the Separation Control command (see "Fine-tuning the separation using Separation Control" later in this chapter).

If you have your images scanned by a service bureau or other facility, ask them to scan the reference transparency and give you the resulting CMYK file so that you can use it to create your separation table.

Many professional scanner operators slightly modify the scanning parameters for each image. You can use adaptive separation to create a table for each CMYK image. In this case, don't use the reference transparency. Use the image itself to create the separation table. Remember to load the appropriate separation table each time you create a new table.

You can also adapt an existing separation table. If you don't scan a reference image, the first time you create the table, it will be based on the colors of the CMYK scan. This scan will contain a more or less wide range of colors. Then, each time you scan a new image, you can adapt the *existing* table. This makes the separation table more accurate for a wider range of colors. To adapt an existing separation table, click on Adapt Separation Table (see figure 29.3). Then select the separation table you want to adapt.

....

NOTE: If several CMYK files used in a composite come from different scanners, or if different scanning parameters were used, they will all be separated with a single separation table. You can adapt the table for each image converted to IVUE. This will create an "average" separation table for all the images used. The resulting output file will be separated based on a single, consistent separation rule.

....

USING SEPARATION TABLES FROM OTHER SOFTWARE

To use a separation table from another program, you can create a separation table in Live Picture which duplicates those separation results.

To duplicate the separation results of another program, follow these steps:

1. Launch your favorite separation program.

2. Open the file called "LP RGB Target" located in the Tables folder.

3. Save it as a CMYK TIFF.

4. Launch LP TableMaker, the Live Picture separation application located in the Tables folder.

5. Choose Open from the File menu, and open the CMYK TIFF created in step 3. A new separation table is created.

6. Choose Save As from the File menu, and enter a name for the new separation table.

FINE-TUNING THE SEPARATION USING SEPARATION CONTROL

The Separation Control dialog box allows you to fine-tune a separation table. You can modify the composite CMYK curve, or each individual curve. There are also controls for UCR (Under Color Removal), GCR (Gray Component Replacement), UCA (Under Color Addition), black point, white point and dot gain.

To fine-tune a separation table, follow these steps:

1. In the File menu, choose Separation Control. The Separation Control dialog box appears (see figure 29.5). The Before preview shows what the composite will look like after being separated by the table currently loaded.

NOTE: If ColorSync is active, the Separation Control command is grayed out. See "Using the ColorSync profiles" later in this chapter.

2. If you use several separation tables, check that the correct separation table is loaded.

3. Fine-tune the separation table using the CMYK curves and other controls, as required. For more information, see the Live Picture User Guide supplied with the full version of Live Picture.

   The After preview shows what the composite will look like after the file is separated, using the current table and the modifications made.

4. If your printing house gives you specific dot gain requirements, click on Dot Gain. The Dot Gain dialog box appears (see figure 29.6).

5. Enter the dot gain values and click on OK.

6. Click on Save. The Save As dialog box appears.

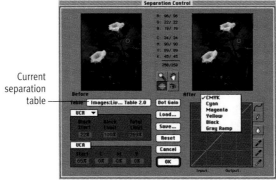

Current separation table —

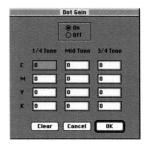

Figure 29.5 The Separation Control dialog box

Figure 29.6 The Dot Gain dialog box

7. Enter a name and save the modifications. The table itself is not modified. Rather, a separate file containing the modifications is created. For future separations, you can use the separation table with or without the modifications made.

8. Click on OK. The on-screen composite is not modified. The separation occurs when you build the output file.

SELECTING CMYK VALUES IN YOUR COMPOSITE

Live Picture works in the RGB color space. If you define a color using CMYK values, these values are interpreted in RGB, and then separated back to CMYK, based on the currently loaded separation table.

Two columns of values appear in the Live Picture color picker (see figure 29.7). The left-hand column shows the CMYK values entered. The right-hand column shows the values that will actually be output.

The values in the right-hand column depend on the RGB to CMYK table currently loaded in the Files & Folders Preferences dialog box. Therefore, if you select colors using CMYK values, or if you use the CMYK densitometers, it is important to load the table to be used for the separation as soon as you begin creating your composite.

CMYK values typed in —
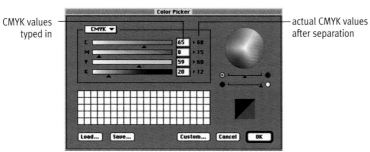
— actual CMYK values after separation

Figure 29.7 Right-hand column showing CMYK output values

TIP

If you use a CMYK mode in a Color Correction layer, to display the values you will actually obtain in your output, type the CMYK values in the value fields. Then click once on the After color field. The Live Picture color picker appears and displays the actual CMYK values. Click on OK. The color picker closes and the actual CMYK values replace the values entered.

NOTE: The values displayed by the CMYK densitometers are the actual separated values you will obtain in your output. To switch the densitometers from RGB to CMYK, choose Color Mode in the Edit menu, and select CMYK. All densitometers display CMYK values.

The Selective Color Correction dialog box available in a Color Correction layer allows you to modify colors selectively in CMYK mode (Shift CMYK or Converge CMYK). However, the value column in this dialog box functions like the left-hand CMYK column in the Live Picture color picker. So the values entered are usually somewhat different from the values you will actually obtain. Furthermore, if you modify a single channel (C, M, Y, or K), other channels will also probably be modified. This is due to the fact that Live Picture runs CMYK values through its own separation table.

A word on Colorsync

Live Picture supports ColorSync 2.0, Apple's open color management system. ColorSync is built around industry-standard profiles, which describe the color characteristics of a device or chain of devices. Many recent color devices (scanners, monitors, color printers) are supplied with their own profile, characterized by the manufacturer.

By having the proper profiles for your monitor, proofer and final output, ColorSync will help display accurate color on the screen, simulate the final output on your monitor or proofer, and print matching color in the final output. It will also warn you when a color will not be reproduced accurately on the final output due to limitations in the color range, or "gamut," of the output device.

If the output device prints in CMYK or generates separated films, the profile for that device and the Color Management Module (CMM) specified by that profile will be used to produce the separation (the default CMM is Apple/Linotype-Hell). In other words, ColorSync will manage the separation instead of the table-driven Live Picture separator.

NOTE: At the time of this writing, there are many devices for which no ICC profiles are available. If no ICC profile is available for your device, you can use a third-party device or application such as Colortron by Light Source, Color Synergy (version 1.1) by Candela or ColorBlind by Color Solutions to build a profile. These products also allow you to fine-tune existing profiles. For more information, see the documentation supplied with these products, or the Live Picture or Apple documentation.

CHAPTER 30

COMPRESSION, CD-ROMs, AND NETWORKING

This chapter explains the special relationship between Live Picture, the use of compression, CD-ROMs, and image handling over a network. The end of the chapter suggests new ways photographers, designers and production houses can work with and transmit images.

THE IVUE AND FITS TECHNOLOGIES: GATEWAY TO A NEW WORLD OF IMAGING

Live Picture introduces two new file formats: IVUE and FITS. These are more than simple formats—they bring with them a whole new imaging technology. An explanation of certain aspects of the IVUE and FITS technologies helps you understand when it can be advantageous to compress IVUE files.

The IVUE technology

When you open an IVUE image, only the amount of data needed to fill the screen is loaded into RAM. Therefore, if the IVUE is compressed, only the amount of data needed to fill the screen is decompressed.

The second important facet of IVUE with regard to compression is that IVUE is a read-only format. A new image is created when you build your output, but no writing is done to the IVUE. So no matter how many times you open an IVUE file, and no matter how complex the image manipulations you perform, the IVUE is only decompressed once—when you build the output file. This ensures minimum quality loss.

The FITS technology

The FITS technology works hand in hand with the IVUE technology. Image edits are stored as algorithms and not actually applied to the IVUE file. The masks and stencils you create are based on the IVUE file displayed on the screen, but you can replace that IVUE with another image. In fact, that is precisely what the Substitute command is for (see Chapter 5, "Handling Layers"). In the same vein, you can substitute a compressed image with a non-compressed image without any quality loss.

ADVANTAGES OF WORKING WITH COMPRESSED IMAGES

Why work with compressed images? What are the advantages? This section explores the different cases where using compressed IVUEs can actually accelerate image processing without compromising output quality.

Using CD-ROMs

For media which have slow access times, such as CD-ROMs, magneto-optical cartridges and Syquest cartridges, you can save time by using compressed IVUEs. Time is required to decompress each screenful of data. However, the compressed files are smaller, meaning faster access times.

Table 30.1 shows the times for opening the same IVUE in compressed and non-compressed form, from a CD-ROM, a 230 MB optical cartridge, and an 88 MB Syquest cartridge.

This test shows that for the 3 media, the time is faster when using compressed IVUE files. This time difference increases as the number of composited images increases. It also increases as you manipulate the images. For example, each time you zoom, the screen regenerates faster if compressed images are used.

To ensure that no quality is lost, you can use two versions of the IVUE, a compressed version and a non-compressed version. Use the compressed version to create your composite. Then, before you build the output file, use the Substitute command in the Get Info dialog box to replace the compressed version with the non-compressed version. With FITS, you don't actually modify the compressed file. By substituting the compressed file, the output quality is the same as if you had worked with the non-compressed file all along. But using the compressed file for display allows you to work faster.

TABLE 30.1	**TIMES FOR OPENING A COMPRESSED AND NON-COMPRESSED IVUE***		
		Non-Compressed	Compressed
	CD-ROM 4X	5 seconds	3.5 seconds
	230 MB optical	4.5 seconds	3.5 seconds
	88 MB Syquest	5 seconds	3.5 seconds

*Non-compressed file size: 76 MB. QuickTime compression: JPEG High quality.

Networking

If there are several Macs connected to a network, you can use compressed images to accelerate image processing. You can also download the build to a server equipped with Live Picture or a FITS RIP.

USING COMPRESSION

The same principle described for CD-ROMs, opticals and Syquests applies to networking. If your images are on a server, it generally takes longer to read them than if they were on your hard disk. By using compressed files, less information travels across the network, so you access the images faster.

Again, the idea is to have two versions of each IVUE file. Both versions are stored on the server, where any number of Macs can access the images. The compressed IVUE is used for display. Before you build the output, use the Substitute command in the Get Info dialog box to replace the compressed IVUE with the non-compressed IVUE. Image processing is faster, and no quality is lost in the final output.

If you have a FITServer, a dialog allows you to automatically substitute the compressed IVUEs with the non-compressed IVUEs. See the next section.

BUILDING THE OUTPUT ON A SERVER

If you have more than one version of Live Picture, you can make your production facility yet more efficient by building the output file on a server. The server can be either a Macintosh or a Silicon Graphics workstation.

If the server is a Mac, a copy of Live Picture must be installed. You can use a full version of Live Picture or Live Picture SE, a limited edition, but which contains all the build features. With the images on the server, copy the finished FITS file to the server and launch the build.

If the server is a Silicon Graphics workstation such as the Indy or Indigo, you can purchase a separate RIP developed by Torque, called the Torque FITServer. This is a dedicated FITS RIP. Coupled with the power of an SGI workstation, it allows you to build output files faster than on a Mac. The FITServer also offers interesting features such as the automatic substitution of compressed IVUEs with non-compressed IVUEs. For more information, see the documentation supplied with the FITServer.

Using a single Mac

If you work on a single Mac, you may not work faster using compressed IVUEs, unless the Mac has a decompression board. In fact, it may take slightly longer to open and manipulate compressed images, which seems normal. However, this really depends on your Macintosh—with the more powerful models, the time to decompress the image is often relatively insignificant. In some cases, you actually work faster using compressed IVUEs!

If opening and editing compressed images from your hard drive does not accelerate image manipulation, the only advantage is the decrease in hard disk space required. This brings us to the issue of storage.

Storing IVUE images

As you work with Live Picture, you may naturally be led to use large images. This is simply because there is no time penalty, and you gain in quality (better definition) and flexibility (you can enlarge the images at any time).

You can modify the FITS file at any time, but to do that, you must keep all the IVUE files used. So we're talking about storing several large images for each composite you create. There are two facets to storing large images: the medium used, and whether or not you compress the images.

USING COMPRESSION

You can save a great deal of space by compressing your IVUE files. As an example, an IVUE file compressed using JPEG with Most image quality (minimum compression) will result in a file roughly one eighth the size of the original non-compressed IVUE file.

Perhaps the best way to handle your images is to create the original composite using non-compressed IVUEs. When the job is finished, compress the IVUEs using Most image quality and store them. If a client asks for a modified version of the composite, build the new version with the compressed IVUEs. If you are concerned about quality loss resulting from compressed images, see figures 30.1 and 30.2 in "Compression and quality loss" later in this chapter.

CHOOSING A STORAGE MEDIUM

It is quicker to work with compressed images than non-compressed images if they are stored on a CD, optical cartridge, or Syquest cartridge. So these media are ideal for the storage of large IVUE files for two reasons: You can fit a lot of megabytes onto one CD or cartridge, and you can access the compressed files faster. In fact, some users work directly on CDs or opticals, using a compressed version of the IVUE to create the composite, and the non-compressed IVUE for the build.

Compression and quality loss

The different types of compression can be broken down into two categories: lossy, where some information is lost when you compress the image, and non-lossy, where you recover all the original information.

For photographic images, the most popular type of compression is JPEG, which is lossy. However, the loss is so small that, if you select Most image quality, the JPEG-compressed IVUE will be virtually indistinguishable from the non-compressed IVUE for most images and applications.

Figure 30.1 Non-compressed IVUE: 16 MB file   **Figure 30.2** JPEG-compressed IVUE: 2 MB file

Figures 30.1 and 30.2 show an IVUE file and the same file after JPEG compression with Most image quality. The non-compressed image is a 300 dpi, 16 MB file. After compression, it occupies 2 MB on the hard disk.

Virtually all the images created using Live Picture and printed in this book, including the cover, were built using JPEG-compressed IVUEs. Use your own judgment. To test compression on your own images, build an output using non-compressed IVUEs, substitute with the compressed IVUEs, build and compare.

Important: Compressed IVUEs are decompressed and recompressed when you use third-party filter plug-ins. Therefore, using the Filter Plug-ins command on a compressed IVUE may result in some quality loss.

Compressing images

Live Picture uses the QuickTime interface for compressing images. This section describes how to compress IVUE files using QuickTime.

To use a compressed IVUE for display, and a non-compressed version for the build, scan directly to IVUE, or convert another format to IVUE. Do not use compression. Then use the Save As Command in the Converter menu to create a compressed version.

To use compressed IVUEs for display *and* for building the output, scan or convert directly to a compressed IVUE.

NOTE: Only JPEG compression is dealt with in this chapter. The QuickTime interface supports other types of compression. They are described in the Live Picture User Guide shipped with the software.

Important: To compress IVUE files, QuickTime must be installed in the Extensions folder in your System folder.

Figure 30.3 Save As dialog box

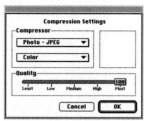

Figure 30.4 Compression Settings dialog box

To create a compressed IVUE file, follow these steps:

1. Choose the Open command in the Converter menu for TIFF, Photo CD, or IVUE. Choose the Acquire command for all other file formats.

2. If you chose the Open command, choose Save As in the Converter menu. If you chose the Acquire command, the Save As dialog box appears automatically (see figure 30.3).

3. In the format pop-down menu, check that IVUE is selected.

4. Click Use Compression. The QuickTime Compression Settings dialog box appears (see figure 30.4).

NOTE: You cannot compress an IVUE if it includes an alpha channel.

5. Select Photo-JPEG and choose a Quality level.

   Choose Most if you plan to build the output using the JPEG-compressed IVUE file. You can choose lower quality levels, such as Normal or Low, if you are using the JPEG-compressed IVUE for display only. This will improve access times if you are reading the IVUE across a network or on a CD-ROM. Image quality will still be sufficient for screen editing.

6. Click on OK. The Compression Settings dialog box closes.

7. Enter a name for the compressed IVUE.

8. Click on Save. The JPEG-compressed IVUE is created.

NEW PRODUCTION SCENARIOS

The new possibilities provided through the IVUE and FITS technologies can change the way you work and communicate with other players in the imaging chain. I've broken the scenarios down according to whether you work independently or for a larger facility such as a service bureau. However, all the scenarios may be of interest to both parties.

Independent photographers and designers

If you outsource your scanning, you can collaborate with a service bureau, for example, that has a copy of Live Picture.

1. When the service bureau scans your images, instruct them to create compressed versions of the IVUEs, along with the non-compressed versions.

2. Leave the non-compressed IVUEs with the service bureau.

3. Use the compressed versions to create your composite. The compressed versions are smaller, which means it's easier to transport them to your Mac, and they occupy less space on your disk. For screen viewing, the two versions are virtually indistinguishable.

4. When you complete your composite, compress the FITS file, which is only a few megabytes, and send it to the service bureau via modem.

5. The service bureau builds the output using the non-compressed images they kept, prints a proof, and makes color corrections if required. If additional changes are required, you can modify the FITS and send it back to build a new output. No time is wasted using couriers or other transportation services.

Larger facilities

For businesses with several Mac operators, there are several new and productive ways to work with images.

Firstly, to get the most out of Live Picture over a network, see "Advantages of working with compressed images" earlier in this chapter. Two other scenarios are described in this section: "Merging FITS files" and "Working simultaneously on one IVUE."

MERGING FITS FILES

The Merge command in the File menu allows you to create one composite from two FITS files (see figure 30.5). When you merge one FITS file into another, the layers of both files remain intact. With this feature, two or more operators can work on the same composite simultaneously.

Figure 30.6 shows a composite containing several objects which were silhouetted or cut out using the Path tools. Photographer Thierry Petillot did the job alone, but more than one operator could have been assigned to the job: one operator to isolate all the objects from their backgrounds, another to merge, position and color correct each object.

Figure 30.5
Merge command

By creating a FITS file for each isolated element, you can readily incorporate them into other composites. Figure 30.7 shows a FITS file with just the CD used in figure 30.6. This FITS file can then be merged into other FITS files. In figure 30.8, the isolated CD is merged into a new FITS file.

Figure 30.6 Final image

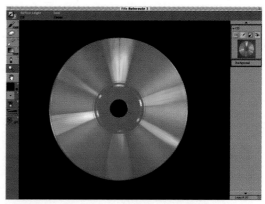

Figure 30.7 One-layer FITS file with isolated CD

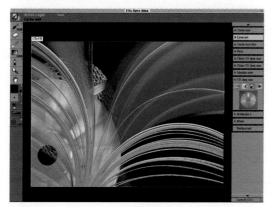

Figure 30.8 CD merged into new FITS file

Because you don't modify the actual image, you can have several FITS file describing the same image differently: a silhouetted version, a colorized version, a black-and-white version, and so forth. The IVUE file can be very large, but each version or FITS file is very small. In figure 30.6, the CD has perspective applied. In figure 30.8, no perspective was used.

To summarize, merging allows several operators to work simultaneously on a single composite. It also allows you to save multiple versions of edited elements (for example, silhouetted objects) for future use in other composites.

WORKING SIMULTANEOUSLY ON ONE IVUE

In "Merging FITS files" above, we saw how it is possible for several operators to work simultaneously on one composite. Several operators can also work simultaneously on the same IVUE file.

Because IVUE is a read-only format, the IVUE file is never modified. An IVUE on a server can be read by several Macs at the same time. For example, if you are bidding for a job and have 24 hours to put together a great image, several designers can create different composites simultaneously, using the same IVUE files. In addition, you can keep part of one designer's composite and part of another's—simply merge the layers containing the parts you like.

CHAPTER 31

RAM AND ACCELERATION TIPS

This chapter will give you an idea of how much RAM you need, depending on the type of images you create. It also provides tips on how to get the most speed out of Live Picture.

RAM

RAM (Random Access Memory) requirements in Live Picture are very different from RAM requirements in pixel-based imaging software such as Adobe Photoshop. Generally speaking, Live Picture requires much less RAM than pixel-based software to process large images. Even with large amounts of RAM, pixel-based applications often need additional memory, and therefore resort to using your valuable hard drive space as a virtual memory (scratch disk). Live Picture avoids this because of its efficient IVUE & FITS technologies—only a screen representation of each image is loaded into RAM.

RAM is expensive, so you don't want to buy more than you need. This section will give you an idea of how much RAM you need to run Live Picture.

Minimum/maximum RAM requirement

The minimum application RAM requirement is 18 MB. The maximum amount of application RAM is 68 MB for a Power PC and 64 MB for a 6800x processor. By maximum, I mean that there will be no noticeable speed increase if you allocate more than 68 MB of RAM to Live Picture.

In fact, tests show that operating speed increases up to 51 MB of application RAM (45 MB for a 6800x), and continues to increase, but at a diminishing rate, up to 68 MB. So you could say that 51 MB is the optimum choice in terms of speed/price. Now, let's move from the general to the specific.

Image size

One of the surprising yet logical things about Live Picture is that the RAM requirement is not affected by the size of the image files used. This is because no matter how large the image, only a screenful of data is loaded into RAM. Whether you open a 5 MB file or a 500 MB file, the same amount of data is loaded into RAM. So image size is not a factor.

Monitor size

Live Picture only loads into RAM the data needed to fill your screen. This means the larger your monitor, the more data is loaded, the more RAM you need. Monitor size is therefore a key factor with regard to RAM requirements. More RAM also speeds up screen regeneration.

Complexity of FITS files

What is actually loaded into RAM is the FITS file. The FITS file does not contain the images, it only contains a link to the images. However, it does contain the masks and stencils. The mathematical representation of these masks and stencils can be more or less complex. The more complex they are, the larger your FITS file becomes, and the more RAM it requires.

The basic RAM-greedy item is a sharp-edged mask or stencil. This generally means text, silhouetted images, and generally any masks or stencils created from paths, with small feathers or hard edges. The Extra Precision option in the Convert Path dialog box requires the most RAM.

Number and type of layers

The more layers you have, the more RAM is required. However, the type of layer is more important than the number of layers. Image Distortion layers and Artwork layers tend to require the most RAM, but this depends on how much distortion or how much artwork is used in a layer.

Working in CMYK

When you convert CMYK images to the IVUE format, when you build a CMYK output file, or when you select a color in CMYK, the RGB->CMYK and CMYK->RGB tables are loaded into RAM. Each of these tables is slightly more than 2 MB, so together they occupy close to 4.5 MB of RAM. This makes a difference if you are working with the 18 MB minimum RAM requirement.

There are two ways to select CMYK colors: You can enter CMYK values in the Live Picture color picker, or you can use the Shift CMYK or Converge CMYK modes in the Selective Color Correction dialog box. In both cases, the two color tables are loaded into RAM.

Using filter plug-ins

A third-party filter plug-in requires on average 2 to 4 MB of additional RAM (see the documentation supplied with the plug-in). If you have the minimum 18 MB or thereabouts, you probably won't have enough memory to use a filter plug-in.

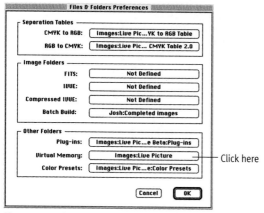

Figure 31.1   Files & Folders Preferences dialog box

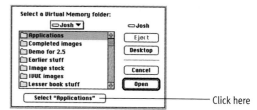

Figure 31.2   Select Folder dialog box

Virtual memory

When all the RAM available is used up, Live Picture uses your hard disk as virtual memory. You'll notice that screen regeneration takes significantly longer when this occurs. Generally, however, you'll only experience this if you work on a fairly complex FITS file with a minimum or close-to-minimum configuration.

The Files & Folders Preferences dialog box (Edit menu) allows you to select which disk will be used for virtual memory. To select a disk, click on the Virtual Memory field (see figure 31.1).

In the Select Folder dialog box, select the disk with the most space available, or select a folder in that disk. Then click on the Select "Applications" button (see figure 31.2) and click on OK.

How much RAM do you need?

Basically, the amount of RAM you should allocate to Live Picture depends on the type of images you create. It is difficult to provide precise figures for individual needs, but some ballpark estimates can be helpful.

If you do basic retouching, in other words insert a single image, correct contrast and color balance, remove spots and scratches, and do some selective color corrections in TSL or RGB, you can probably get by with the minimum 18 MB.

If you work with CMYK values, use third-party filter plug-ins, or if you use silhouetting and composite several images, you should be closer to the 36-45 MB range. And if you create complex composites with many images, hard edges, text and distortion, you'll be most comfortable with 51-68 MB allocated.

TIPS FOR SPEEDING UP LIVE PICTURE

This section contains tips to speed up Live Picture. They are especially helpful if you reach maximum RAM capacity and screen regeneration slows down.

Reducing document window size

You can accelerate screen refresh times by using a smaller document window. Drag the window to a smaller size and zoom to enlarge the image. Increase window size when necessary.

Hiding unused layers

Each time the screen is regenerated, all the layers are recalculated. By temporarily hiding layers you don't need to see, the screenful of data is recalculated faster.

Precise zooming and panning

Because the screenful of data is recalculated each time you zoom, it pays to zoom once, to the level you need. By learning to master the Zoom tool, you'll avoid waiting for unnecessary screen regenerations. The same holds true for the Pan tool.

Using views is an effective way to avoid wasteful zooming. Create a view for each area you want to zoom to, and use the Go To command in the View menu to jump to that view.

Not waiting for screen regeneration

You don't have to wait until the entire screen is regenerated to zoom, pan, reposition, and perform several other operations. Every few moments, the planet cursor stops turning. If your tool is already selected, you can seize these moments to zoom, pan or reposition.

Deselecting Quick Preview

The Quick Preview option in the General Preferences dialog box displays a low-resolution preview of your composite. The entire screen is regenerated at low resolution (see figure 31.3). The image is then updated, tile by tile, at screen resolution.

If you deselect Quick Preview, the image is regenerated directly at screen resolution, tile by tile (see figure 31.4).

Figure 31.3   Regeneration with Quick Preview

Figure 31.4   Regeneration with Quick Preview deselected

The advantage of Quick Preview is that it provides a quick overall view of your composite. However, the overall time to regenerate the entire image at screen resolution is faster without Quick Preview. Since you cannot use the creative tools until the entire image is regenerated at screen resolution, deselecting Quick Preview gives you quicker access to the creative tools.

To deselect Quick Preview, choose Preferences/General in the Edit menu. Then, in the General Preferences dialog box, deselect Quick Preview (see figure 31.5).

Using compressed images

If you are working directly from a CD, optical, or other slow-access medium, using compressed images for display will speed up screen regeneration. See Chapter 30, "Compression, CD-ROMs, and Networking."

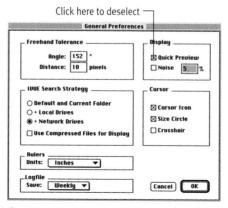

Figure 31.5   Quick Preview selected

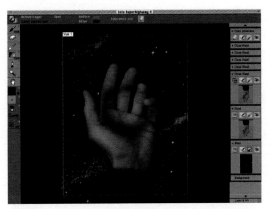

Figure 31.6   Original FITS file: 528 KB

Figure 31.7   File after intermediate build: 32 KB

Intermediate building

To reduce the number of layers in a FITS file, you can build an output file before the composite is finished. For example, if you insert an image, distort it, and perform IVUE Corrections, cloning, selective corrections and colorization on the image, you can build the composite to IVUE format and reinsert it as a single layer in a FITS file. What was once five or ten layers becomes one. This greatly reduces the size and complexity of the FITS file.

In figure 31.6, the starry sky image was inserted, the hand was silhouetted, five cloning layers were created, and a selective color correction was applied. The FITS file totals eight layers and 528 KB. By building the eight layers into a single IVUE image, a new FITS file was created (see figure 31.7). This FITS file contains just one image: no hard-edged silhouetting—no color correction, and so forth. The size of the new FITS file is 32 KB. New layers can be added, and image processing is much faster.

The disadvantage of intermediate building is that you can no longer modify the original layers. Therefore, this solution is appropriate when you are sure you won't change that part of the image. However, you can keep the original FITS file and original IVUEs. This allows you to go back and modify the individual layers if needed, and redo the intermediate build.

NOTE: If you tend to make intermediate builds, do not compress your IVUE files. Each time you build an output file, the compressed IVUEs are decompressed. If this occurs more than once, you may experience a loss in quality.

Season's Greetings, Bernard Rossi

Dark Days, Andreas Pfeiffer

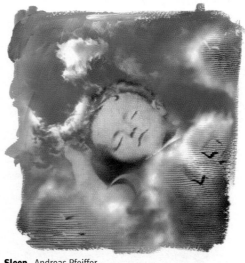

Sleep, Andreas Pfeiffer

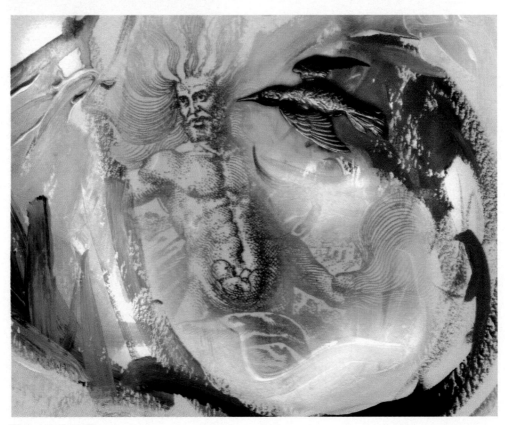

Wind, Andreas Pfeiffer

Meeting Jasiu, Jean-Luc Touillon

Eva in Prague, Jean-Luc Touillon

Letter to Nadja, Jean-Luc Touillon

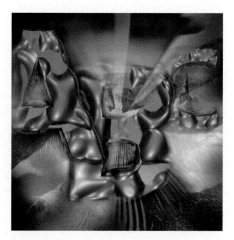

Freaky Type 1, Anders F. Rönnblom /Mariann Eklund, Studio Matchbox

Freaky Type 3, Anders F. Rönnblom /Mariann Eklund, Studio Matchbox

999 Poster, Anders F. Rönnblom /Mariann Eklund, Studio Matchbox

Stair to Heaven, Lee Varis, Varis Photomedia

Cybergirl Dance, Lee Varis, Varis Photomedia

No Box, Ich & Kar

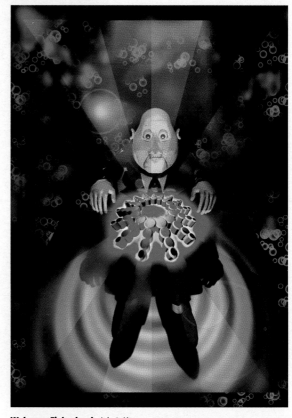

Welcome Fisherland, Ich & Kar

Millesia, Jean-Luc Michon

Sonia, Jean-Luc Michon

Optimistic?, Terri J. Wolf

Debbie Caught in Time, Terri J. Wolf

Rolex, Marc Harrold

Vodka, Marc Harrold

Poison, Marc Harrold

Clock, Didier Boutet

Pollution, Didier Boutet

Multimedia, Didier Boutet

New Beginnings, John Lund

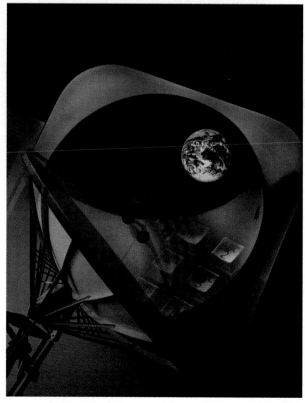

Radio Waves/TSI, John Lund

Car, Loïc Pénet, Studio Renaissance

Homage to Magritte, Loïc Pénet, Studio Renaissance

334

Retouched Building, Atelier Fournier Schneck

Taxi Girl, Bruno Juminer/Gérard Branchet, Hondo Associés

DIGITAL IMAGING – THE BASICS

For those of you who are new to digital imaging, this chapter describes the basic imaging production sequence, and explains such basic imaging terms as pixel and resolution. Also, it includes information specific to Live Picture when applicable.

THE DIGITAL IMAGING PRODUCTION SEQUENCE

There are three basic phases in digital imaging: acquiring images, retouching and compositing, and outputting.

Acquiring images

In computer language, to *acquire an image* means to put it into proper digital form. Images can be scanned, acquired using a digital camera, or purchased on a photo CD.

Today, the main means of acquiring images is by scanning them. Images taken with a conventional camera are analyzed by a scanner and converted into digital form. You can also acquire images with a digital camera. In this case, when the picture is shot, the image is created directly in digital form. Photo CDs are another popular source of digital images. You can buy a photo CD which already contains images in digital form, or you can have your own images put onto a Photo CD.

There are many different types of digital formats. You may have heard of formats such as TIFF, PICT, and DCS. Depending on the format, the data is arranged differently, but the image is basically the same. When you acquire an image, you acquire it in a particular format. The format generally depends on the acquisition or input device, and on what you plan to do with the image. Also, you can convert image files from one format to another.

In Live Picture, the format used is called IVUE. To composite an image in Live Picture, either scan directly into IVUE, or convert an existing file format into IVUE (for more information, see Chapter 7, "Inserting Images").

Retouching and compositing

Once you have your images in digital form (IVUE format for Live Picture), you can start retouching or compositing. Retouching includes such operations as modifying the contrast or brightness of an image, selectively changing certain colors, removing scratches, making an image sharper or more blurred, and so forth. Compositing means bringing together several different images to create a new image. It can include such operations as cutting out objects from their backgrounds and inserting or blending them into other images, adding creative effects, making text, or painting with digital tools.

Live Picture allows you to retouch and composite images. However, it is mainly known as a compositing application because of the unprecedented power and flexibility it offers. In this book, the term *compositing* encompasses both compositing and retouching. For our purposes, the difference is not crucial.

Outputting

Once you've finished your composite, you need to output the image. When you output an image, you generally retrieve it in non-digital form. For instance, you can output to a color printer if you want the image on paper. Film recorders output images on transparencies, usually $4" \times 5"$ or $8" \times 10"$. Imagesetters generate separated films which are used for printing.

Some imaging applications include a post-processing phase. This phase occurs before the image is actually output. Post-processing is generally used to save time during the image retouching and compositing phase. The actual calculations on the full image are not processed until the end. When post-processing is complete, the resulting file is ready to be output on an output device.

Live Picture uses a unique post-processing system, known as the "build," or "FITS RIP." The basic advantages of this post-processing technology are speed, flexibility and quality (see Chapters 2 and 27, "An Overview" and "The Most Flexible Software You've Ever Seen"). In this book, when I refer to building an output, or outputting an image, I am referring to this post-processing phase—the creation of a digital output file.

PIXELS AND RESOLUTION

This section describes a few basic words and concepts you'll need to understand.

Pixels

A pixel (picture element) is the basic building block of a digital image. When you scan a transparency, for example, you tell the scanner how many pixels you want it to create. All other things being equal, an image represented in digital form by a large number of pixels will be better defined than the same image represented by a small number of pixels.

So why not always work with a large number of pixels? There are several reasons:

- Each type of scanner has a maximum number of pixels it can create. Naturally, scanners able to create more pixels are generally more expensive to buy or use.

- On a given scanner, the more pixels you ask for, the longer it takes to scan the image. This makes sense, because you are asking the scanner for a finer analysis of the image.

- The more pixels contained in the digital image, the more space it takes up on your hard disk.

- The more pixels contained in the image, the longer it takes to manipulate the image, and the more memory is required—until Live Picture came along. This fourth point was in fact the greatest obstacle to the use of high-res images. If you use Live Picture, point four is no longer a concern. (See Chapter 2, "An Overview.")

In practice, the number of pixels or resolution you need depends on what you plan to do with the image. Will it be used as a quarter-page ad or a movie poster? Will it be output on a color printer, imagesetter or film recorder? If you don't scan in enough information, you won't have good quality in your output.

Size

The size of an image is a function of the number of pixels it contains. In computer language size is expressed in kilobytes (KB) or megabytes (MB). Do not confuse size and dimensions (see next section).

Resolution and Dimensions

Each digital image file is defined by a number of pixels. Resolution and dimensions basically describe the way those pixels are laid out. A resolution of 300 pixels per inch (ppi) or dots per inch (dpi) means that in one inch, there are 300 pixels.

Dimensions refer to the number of inches. If the resolution of the image is 300 dpi, and the image is 4"× 5", then the image can be described as follows:

1200 pixels (300 × 4) × 1500 pixels (300 × 5)

The higher the resolution, the more dots or pixels per inch. The more pixels per inch, the smaller the pixels. That's why, when you zoom into a low resolution image on your computer screen, you start to actually see the pixels—there are few pixels in each inch, so they need to be large to fill up the inch. With high-resolution images, this pixelization doesn't occur until you zoom in much further. There are many pixels per inch, so the pixels are smaller.

....

NOTE: Often, the term "size" is used when referring to either actual size (number of kilobytes or megabytes), or dimensions. Remember to take the context into account.

....

RESIZING IMAGES

When you acquire an image, you obtain a file with a specific number of pixels. Imaging applications allow you to increase or decrease the number of pixels. Interpolation and downsizing are the terms generally used to describe this change in the number of pixels.

Interpolation

If the size of the final image file is larger than that of the scanned image file, the computer has no option but to create new data. The means for creating this new data may be more or less sophisticated, but in any case, the data does not come from the original photo. It is calculated based on existing image data, that is, interpolated.

Data calculated based on existing data cannot be as close to an original photo as data created based on the photo itself, so there is generally some quality loss associated with interpolation. Small amounts of interpolation may be unnoticeable, so there is some leeway in increasing image size. This leeway depends on the image being interpolated, how the image will be used, and the interpolation technology used.

With Live Picture, tests show that you can generally interpolate up to twice the size of the original image without noticeable quality loss.

Downsizing

Downsizing is the opposite of interpolation. If the output image is smaller than the original image, then some pixels will be discarded.

Here too, there are more or less sophisticated methods for downsizing and recalculating the existing pixels. Most methods for downsizing generally produce a softer, more fuzzy image. However, with Live Picture you can downsize an image significantly and still retain the sharpness of the original.

NOTE: Unlike pixel-based software such as Adobe Photoshop, interpolation and downsizing in Live Picture do not affect the actual image file. These operations are part of the build (post-processing phase). This approach has many advantages. For more information, see Chapter 2, "An Overview."

TROUBLESHOOTING

This section is designed to give you quick answers to the most frequently encountered troubleshooting questions. It is organized in table form.

The first column describes the problem as you might experience it. The second column explains why it occurs. The third column offers a solution and a way to avoid the problem repeating itself.

Problem	Cause	Solution
I have created an Image Silhouette layer. I cannot zoom, pan, switch to the positioning tools, change the background color or use the layer stack.	These operations cannot be performed while you are in silhouetting mode.	Press Escape to quit silhouetting mode, or finish silhouetting the image. Next time, perform these operations before you toggle to the creative tools in an Image Silhouette layer.
I have opened an image. I can use the positioning tools, but I cannot create views, change background color or use the layer stack.	You are in Insertion mode (the Opacity tool appears at the bottom of the positioning toolbar).	Finish positioning the image, then click on the mode toggle to switch to Creative mode.
The Build command is grayed out.	The document does not contain a view, or you are in Positioning mode or View mode.	Create a view, or click the mode toggle to switch to Creative mode.
The Opacity tool does not appear in the toolbar.	The Opacity tool is only available in Insertion mode.	Toggle to the creative tools and use the Marquee to change image opacity.
The Crop tool is grayed out.	You selected an Image Silhouette layer.	To crop the image, use the Rectangle tool (Path tool) to create a stencil.
When I copy a mask or a stencil to a mask, nothing happens.	You must press the Option key before you drag the mask or stencil.	Press the Option key and hold it while you click and drag the mask or stencil.
When I copy a mask or a stencil to a mask, nothing happens in certain layers.	The masks or stencils of the two layer types are not compatible.	None.
When I reposition a path, one or several layers move with it.	The layers are selected.	Click the Background layer bar to deselect all layers before you reposition the path.
The Path–>Mask and Path–>Stencil commands are grayed out.	No path is selected, or no layer is selected.	Select the path you want to convert, and select the layer you want to create the mask or stencil in.
When I copy a mask or stencil, I duplicate the entire layer.	The layer was selected before you copied the mask or stencil.	Delete the duplicated layer. Deselect the layer you are copying the mask or stencil from, then copy.
When I try to reposition an image, the wrong things move.	The wrong layers or layer elements were selected in the layer stack.	Press Command-Z. Before repositioning, check to see what is selected. Note that layers or layer elements can be selected.

Problem	Cause	Solution
I'm using a tool, and nothing is happening.	The wrong layer is active.	Activate the correct layer.
I'm using a tool, and nothing is happening.	The layer has a stencil and you are brushing outside the stencil.	Deactivate the stencil to see what the layer looks like without it.
I'm using a tool, and nothing is happening.	The Direction control is active.	If the Direction control has a red line across it, drag the dial to OFF.
I'm using a tool, and nothing is happening.	One or more styles are selected, such as Pastel and/or Water, producing a very subdued effect.	If the Style control is colored red, deselect all selected styles.
The Image Clone command is grayed out in the Create menu.	No image layer is selected, or more than one layer is selected.	Select just the image layer you want to clone.
IVUE Correction is grayed out.	No image layer is selected	Select the image layer you want to color-correct.
The commands in the IVUE Correction submenu are grayed out.	More than one image layer is selected.	Select just one image layer.
I created an Image Insertion layer, but the image does not appear in the dialog box.	The image is not an IVUE file.	Convert the image file to IVUE.
The Acquire or Export plug-ins menu does not appear.	The Plug-ins folder has not been located.	Use the Preferences/Files & Folders dialog box to locate the Plug-ins folder. Then restart Live Picture.
The Presets do not appear.	The Presets folder has not been located.	Use the Preferences/Files & Folders dialog box to locate the Presets folder. Then restart Live Picture.
I've selected Auto View, but I cannot Go To that view.	The Auto View is not created till you leave Insertion mode.	Toggle to quite Insertion mode. The Automatic View is created.
I clicked on the Horizontal Flip tool, but the image does a vertical flip.	You rotated the image. The flip refers to the original IVUE before rotation.	Undo the horizontal flip. Then click on the Vertical Flip tool.
I'm double-clicking the layer bar, but the layer is not activating.	It takes some practice.	Select the layer, and choose Activate from the Layer menu.
The Eye icon indicates the layer is not hidden, but I don't see it.	It is above the active layer.	Activate the layer you want to see, or temporarily drag the layer below the currently active layer.
The Document Setup command is grayed out.	It is only available when the document is closed.	Close the open document.
The Batch command is grayed out.	It is only available when the document is closed.	Close the open document.
I'm adding files to the Batch queue, but they don't appear in the queue.	If you are building in CMYK, Live Picture may not be able to locate the separation table.	Locate the separation table using the Files & Folders Preferences dialog box. Then add the FITS file to the build.
I'm adding files to the Batch queue, but they don't appear in the queue.	The FITS file can't locate one or several IVUEs.	Open the FITS file. If a message prompts you to find an IVUE file, find it and save the FITS file. Then add it to the Batch queue.
When I use the Acquire command to open an EPS file, I get the message "Error finding image data in main file."	The EPS file is a PostScript file, in other words it is not a pixel image.	To convert the file to pixel form, use Photoshop or a plug-in such as Epilogue. To use the PostScript file, create an EPS Insertion layer and open the EPS file.

INDEX

D

E

M

T

PLUG YOURSELF INTO...

A VIACOM SERVICE
The Information SuperLibrary™

Bookstore · Search · What's New · Reference Desk · Software Library · Newsletter · Company Overviews

Yellow Pages · Internet Starter Kit · JK Lasser's Your Income Tax 1996 · Win a Free T-Shirt! · Macmillan Computer Publishing · Site Map · Talk to Us

THE MACMILLAN INFORMATION SUPERLIBRARY™

Free information and vast computer resources from the world's leading computer book publisher—online!

FIND THE BOOKS THAT ARE RIGHT FOR YOU!

A complete online catalog, plus sample chapters and tables of contents give you an in-depth look at *all* of our books, including hard-to-find titles. It's the best way to find the books you need!

- **STAY INFORMED** with the latest computer industry news through our online newsletter, press releases, and customized Information SuperLibrary Reports.

- **GET FAST ANSWERS** to your questions about MCP books and software.

- **VISIT** our online bookstore for the latest information and editions!

- **COMMUNICATE** with our expert authors through e-mail and conferences.

- **DOWNLOAD SOFTWARE** from the immense MCP library:
    - Source code and files from MCP books
    - The best shareware, freeware, and demos

- **DISCOVER HOT SPOTS** on other parts of the Internet.

- **WIN BOOKS** in ongoing contests and giveaways!

TO PLUG INTO MCP: ➤ WORLD WIDE WEB: **http://www.SuperLibrary.com**

FTP: ftp.mcp.com

Home Page · What's New · Bookstore · Reference Desk · Software Library · Macmillan Overview · Talk to Us

WELCOME TO LIVE PICTURE!

The CD-ROM that comes with this book contains five folders:

- **The Open First—LP 2.5 folder**. This folder contains a demo version of Live Picture 2.5

- **The Open Second—Instructions Folder.** This folder contains quick demo of Live Picture, created by Live Picture, Inc., and Adobe Acrobat 2.0, which is used to read the demo file.

- **The Copy me to Hard Drive folder.** This folder contains FITS files. Copy this folder to your hard drive to work faster.

- **The IVUE folder**. This folder contains IVUE images

- **The Oolor Easy Folder.** This folder contains an essay by photographer Joseph Holmes entitled "Editing Photographic Tone and Color in Live Picture."

For more information, see the READ ME FIRST file on the CD.

Important: All the images and composites contained on this CD-ROM can be used freely for the purpose of learning Live Picture. The images and composites cannot, under any circumstances, be redistributed, sold, or used for commerical purposes.